CHERRIES *on a* POMEGRANATE TREE

LI ER

Translated by
Dave Haysom

SINOIST

ACA Publishing Ltd
University House
11-13 Lower Grosvenor Place,
London SW1W 0EX, UK
Tel: +44 20 3289 3885
E-mail: info@alaincharlesasia.com
www.alaincharlesasia.com
www.sinoistbooks.com

Beijing Office
Tel: +86 (0)10 8472 1250

Author: Li Er
Translator: Dave Haysom

Published by Sinoist Books (an imprint of ACA Publishing Ltd) in association with China Translation and Publishing House

Original Chinese Text © 石榴树上结樱桃 *(Shi Liu Shu Shang Jie Ying Tao)* 2004, Jiangsu Phoenix Literature and Art Publishing, Ltd, Nanjing, China

English language translation copyright © Dave Haysom, 2023

Hardback ISBN: 978-1-83890-555-2
Paperback ISBN: 978-1-83890-554-5
eBook ISBN: 978-1-83890-556-9

A catalogue record for *Cherries on a Pomegranate Tree* is available from the National Bibliographic Service of the British Library.

CHERRIES ON A
POMEGRANATE TREE

LI ER

TRANSLATED BY
DAVE HAYSOM

SINOIST BOOKS

ONE

When Kong Fanhua had finished planting the wheat, the field looked like a newly shaved head. An exposed scalp, fresh, but raw. Fanhua's back felt raw too. Aching, mostly, with a hint of numbness, the way it felt when you'd spent that first month indoors after giving birth. But what can you do? Sure, she might be the village head, but someone still has to do the farm work.

Her husband Zhang Dianjun had moved here, to her home village, when they married. But now he'd left Guanzhuang for a shoe factory on the outskirts of Shenzhen, where he worked as a mechanic with a dozen or so underlings. He liked to say he was there "for the cause". Such a grand endeavour – how could planting crops at home possibly compare? Last year, he'd mixed up his dates and arrived home a day earlier than he meant to. Forced to do some actual work for once, he retreated to the house after a few hours claiming his piles were playing up again.

Fanhua received a phone call from him a few days ago. The fact that he'd taken the trouble to call at least showed he still knew he had a home here. Fanhua asked him when he was coming back. She wanted to tell him that the village elections were starting soon, and she needed him to help with drumming up votes and writing a speech. It was Dianjun who'd written the speech for her last time. He wrote the best compositions back when they were in high school. A bank of reddish clouds became a celestial palace under his pen. You had to make the

1

best use of your resources, just like you have to put your best steel into the blade of a knife, and right now she had need of his talents.

But he was going off on one about his piles again before she'd even had a chance to speak. He said the factory was rushing to get a shipment ready to send to Hong Kong and Taiwan, and they couldn't cut any corners. His comrades were busy, and he was busy, so busy his piles were getting worse, there was blood, he said. His voice skewed into a Guangdong accent when he said the word "comrades", but "Taiwan" came out clearly in Mandarin. He was doing his bit to help the unification of the motherland, he said, and he would feel joy in his heart no matter how tough the going might get.

"When they give me a medal for my outstanding service someday, half of it will belong to you," he added.

Fanhua lost her temper. "Forget my half, you can keep the whole damn thing."

Dianjun always kept his cool whenever Fanhua got mad at him. He started talking about cuckoos. Is that a cuckoo flying overhead, he said, am I dreaming the sound of that cuckoo cry? Dianjun, tch. The man sure could talk some nonsense. When are you most likely to hear the sound of a cuckoo? During harvest time, that's when.

Then he got on to Taiwanese separatists again, saying they could receive TV shows from across the straits where he was, and the sight of those splittists got him so mad his lungs could burst.

"Oh come on," said Fanhua, "it's just Lü Xiulian and her bunch of old biddies. A manly mechanic like you surely isn't going to let himself get worked up over something like that."

"Well, check you out," said Dianjun. "You've heard of Lü Xiulian, have you? But anyway, you can tell everyone not to worry. Those splittists have no chance."

"Listen up, Dianjun," said Fanhua, "you're best off not coming home at all. Wait until I've keeled over from exhaustion and then get yourself a new, younger version."

And a few days later, Dianjun came crawling back home. His face seemed to have been reskinned. There were more creases in the corner of his eyes, and the creases were full of dust. You expect someone to look refreshed when they return from the promised land in the south, but Dianjun's face looked like old sandpaper. He was wearing a peaked cap and sunglasses, the kind they called "toad specs" round these parts.

His daughter Beanie was playing with her rabbit in the middle of the yard on the afternoon he hauled his suitcase through the front gate. Beanie was singing a nursery rhyme that her grandma had taught her:

Upside-down, inside-out,
A pomegranate tree where cherries sprout,
Rabbit sleeps on doggy's leg,
Tabby cat sits in ratty's mouth.

"Come on now, dear," Beanie said. "Go to sleep on doggy's leg." The arm she extended towards the rabbit was as soft and tender as lotus root. Beanie had just turned five, and she hadn't seen her father for the best part of a year. She wasn't sure how to respond to him after so long, but she knew he was someone important. She didn't mistake him for a tabby cat, despite the patterned suit he was wearing.

Dianjun knelt down and rooted around in the pocket of his suit, eventually producing a rubber band, a bow and a sentence in Mandarin: "Daughter, oh Daughter, you're lovelier than a flower. Give your daddy a kiss."

As Beanie wailed, a clear bubble of snot expanded in her nostril. Dianjun hastily pulled a telescope out of his bag and hung it around her neck. Then he showed her a copy of the photograph they kept at home, in which he was sitting on the back of a camel.

"Look, this is me, your daddy." He pointed to the camel and asked Beanie to guess what it was.

Beanie tentatively suggested it might be a dinosaur.

Dianjun wagged his finger and mouthed the English word, "No, no."

Beanie suggested a donkey.

Dianjun repeated his "no".

Not understanding what a "no" was supposed to be, Beanie started crying again.

At this point, Dianjun's father-in-law stepped out of the house.

"Beanie," he said, coughing, "don't be afraid. This isn't a bad man, it's your father."

Dianjun quickly stood up and took off his sunglasses. The old man came over, stroking Beanie's head with one hand and moving to lift Dianjun's suitcase with the other. "You should have said you were coming," he said, spinning the suitcase wheels with his hand. "Fanhua could have come to pick you up at the station."

Dianjun asked after the old man's health.

"Still got a while left in me yet," he replied after coughing once or twice more. "Dianjun's back!" he yelled through the door. "Hurry up and roll him some noodles, woman!"

Dianjun leant down towards his daughter. "Beanie, where's your mother?" The girl had only just stopped crying, and her bleary eyes were still fixed on the sunglasses in his hand. Her grandfather replied for her, informing Dianjun that Fanhua had gone to a meeting at the county town.

Xiushui was the county town. Xiushui had originally been the name of the river, a river famous enough that it had been mentioned in the ancient *Commentary on the Water Classic*. A hundred years ago it had been a vast, steaming torrent, but only a trickle of sewage water was left. The town was built on either side of the river, and so the name of the town was Xiushui. Guanzhuang Village was ten *li* from Wangzhai Township, or about three miles, and it was another twenty *li* from there to Xiushui.

Fanhua still hadn't come back by seven o'clock that evening, and her phone was switched off. Dianjun was getting restless. He wanted to go and wait for her at the entrance to the village, but his grizzled father-in-law stopped him.

"Why would you want to go and wait for her? Sit down. It's not on you, you just got here."

Dianjun knew that the very sight of him made his father-in-law angry. The old man was well versed in his shortcomings. Most people would blame the wife when a male grandchild had failed to materialise, but this family was upside-down, inside-out – they blamed the man. Caught between standing and sitting, Dianjun glanced at his mother-in-law.

She glared at her husband and pushed the stool back towards him. "Dianjun, you can watch your television if you like. Or if you don't feel like it, maybe you could go out and buy me a bag of salt?"

This was her giving him an excuse to leave. Just as Dianjun was about to step outside, they heard a car horn, crisp like the sound of a flying telegram.

The old man raised his eyebrows. "She's back. They're in the car."

Sure enough, it was Fanhua, and she was sitting in a Beijing Hyundai. The driver got out and came around to the other side of the car to open the door for her, exchanging greetings with her father as she waved him goodbye. Dianjun chipped in with a breezy "bye-bye". Fanhua glanced around, looked him up and down, and then turned back to remind the driver to take care on the road.

When the car had moved off, she tossed her bag to Dianjun. "You have no idea how to behave. No idea. You'll be the death of me."

Inside the bag were gifts for her parents from Fanhua's younger sister Fanrong. Fanrong worked at a newspaper in Xiushui Town, and her husband was the deputy director of the county financial bureau. It was Fanrong's husband who had arranged the car to bring Fanhua home. Last year, one of the villagers of Guanzhuang had broken the law and secretly buried a parent instead of cremating them. When the authorities investigated the matter, they announced that Fanhua would be stripped of her position as village Party branch secretary. It was Township Head Bull who made the announcement. In the past, he'd always acted like the two of them were close – he called her "younger sister", she called him "older brother" – but he completely washed his hands of her at the first sign of trouble, the treacherous cur. They'd have dismissed her as village head, too, were it not for her brother-in-law.

As they were heading inside, Fanhua took the bag from Dianjun, though it was more of a "grabbed" than a "took". A provocative kind of grab. Dianjun stood in the yard. Not knowing what to do with his hands, he placed them in front of his crotch, still smiling fawningly.

Fanhua shook the bag in her father's direction. "Hat, scarf and a multipack of Mighty China cigarettes. My sister's husband certainly knows how to pay respect to his elders." Then she shoved the items back into Dianjun's hands. "You take these. You'll be the death of me, I swear." Dianjun cupped his hands to receive the gifts, then carried them over to give to his father-in-law. The old man tore open a packet of cigarettes and handed one to Dianjun.

"How's the unification of the motherland going?" Fanhua asked Dianjun. "I can't say I've seen anything about it on the news."

Dianjun bent slightly towards her. "My piles have stopped bleeding."

"Heard any cuckoos calling lately?"

Dianjun briefly looked up to the sky. "I can see a moon up there."

Their conversation was full of secret codes, like the argot of bandits. Neither of the old people could understand what they were saying.

"Cuckoos?" said Fanhua's father. "They all died out long ago. You'll not see so much as a cuckoo feather round here. And a moon? Are you sure your eyes are all right, Dianjun?"

It wasn't easy for a man to live with his in-laws. Dianjun had to stay on the leash when Fanhua's parents were around. Only when he and Fanhua were in bed could he let loose and remind himself what it felt like to be the man of the house. He tore off Fanhua's clothes, but Fanhua seemed to be holding back. She was reluctant to look him in the eye. When he mounted her, impatient like a monkey, she shoved him with her elbow and reminded him to put on one of those thingies. See that? Can't even bring herself to say the word "condom". But Dianjun had forgotten where the thingies lived. He told Fanhua to find him one, but she refused. That's the man's job, she said.

"Don't you have the ring?" he asked. "Oh, I see, you're worried I've picked up some nasty pox out there, is that it? Don't you worry, I'm not on the market, I'm clean as could be. See for yourself if you don't believe me."

Fanhua glanced at him out of the corner of her eye, then buried her head in his shoulder. She was going to bite him, but it ended up softening into a lick as soon as her teeth clamped down. She realised he was still wearing that peaked cap of his. What was this – trousers off, but a cap still on? She plucked the cap off his head, and underneath it, she discovered a complication – Dianjun's hair had completely disappeared.

"What happened to your hair?"

Dianjun played dumb. "What hair?"

"Since when have you been bald?" asked Fanhua.

"Are you talking to me? Oh! It's like this. It fell out all by itself. It's spot baldness, you know, 'the ghost barber'."

Fanhua reached out a hand to touch it. Ghost barber? Nonsense. The ghost barber leaves a completely smooth patch, but Dianjun's head retained a layer of stubble, hard and prickly. "Tell me the truth."

Dianjun eventually told her what had happened. He had taken a tumble while fixing one of the machines and ended up with a cut on the head that had needed two stitches. He rapped his head. "It's grown back now, though. Call me a cur if I'm lying." And then, as if to prove his canine affinity, he leapt onto Fanhua.

Fanhua was the equal of any man when it came to matters of the bedroom. She liked to ride as opposed to being ridden, which is to say, she preferred to go on top. She once heard from Xianyu, the village doctor, that women who took the lead in bed were bound to have a girl. You can't have it both ways, enjoy your fun *and* be blessed with a boy. Nothing's that easy in life, right? Can you lick a sugar-cane from both ends at once? So a woman ought to restrain herself. The key thing was to keep yourself tightly clamped. Oh, Dr Xianyu, it's so easy to be wise in hindsight. If you'd told me sooner I'd have made more of an effort to hold myself back, but it's a bit late for restraint when Beanie's already big enough to be starting school. These thoughts might have made her feel a twinge of emptiness, but they set her body free. No harm in smashing a jar that's already broken. She flipped over like a carp and pressed down on top of Dianjun. Liquid spilling out of her like fruit juice. She could smell the scent of incense creeping in through the crack of the door, which meant her mother was making offerings to Guanyin, the deliverer of sons. For an instant, Fanhua found herself in a kind of trance. So much liquid. How many potential offspring? But she could only let it go to waste.

She was brought out of the trance by the sound of a knock on the front door. Apparently Guanyin, the goddess of mercy, really had shown up to pay a visit. Though that seemed unlikely because Guanyin was supposed to fly ethereally through space, whereas this visitor was rattling the door against the chain and shouting, "It's me, hey, it's me!"

7

Fanhua recognised the voice. It was Meng Qingshu, the natural foe of Guanyin. Fanhua was annoyed, not so much because her moment with Dianjun had been ruined, but because she knew her mother would fret about having wasted her incense.

Dianjun poked his head out from the covers. "Who's that?" he croaked. "Who the fuck is that?"

"Who do you think?" said Fanhua. "It's Qingshu, Meng Qingshu." Meng Qingshu was an ex-army man, who had become a member of the Party while he was in the forces. Now he was both public security commissioner and the man in charge of family planning.

Dianjun chuckled when he realised who it was. "He sure knows how to pick his moment. I don't want to see him right now – I'll take him out for a drink another time and he can tell me all about the womanly work he's been doing."

This was one of the lines Dianjun used regularly to tease Qingshu. He called him Director of the Women's Federation, and Qingshu played along, claiming his hero was the comedian Zhao Benshan because Zhao Benshan had played a director of the Women's Federation in a skit on TV, which meant he understood the difficulties of Qingshu's line of work.

"He's been keeping himself busy lately, what with the elections coming up. He's already asking if he can 'shoulder a weightier load' when we put together the new committee."

"'Shoulder a weightier load'?" said Dianjun, laughing. "That's a nice way of putting it. Very refined. He's certainly been making progress."

"Well, that's because he's hitched his wagon to the right person. The speed of a fast train comes from the locomotive. Even a donkey could become a scholar after sticking with me for a few years." Fanhua drew herself up. "What's the matter?" she called out the window. "Has the sky fallen in? Or have we been struck by an earthquake? Can't it wait till tomorrow?"

"It's me," Qingshu continued to yell. "Hey, it's me."

Fanhua had no choice but to get dressed again. She patted Dianjun on the bottom like she was pacifying a child. "You be good and wait for me here. I'll show you a good time once we're rid of this meddlesome ghost."

Two

It was dark outside. The sky sealed everything like a saucepan lid. The moon was concealed by so much cloud that it may as well not have been there. The shadowy forms of two people took shape in the darkness. It was the perfume that Fanhua smelled first, a scent lighter than cold cream, with a hint of apricot flower and a hint of mint. It smelled like Pei Zhen. Fanhua led the two of them into the kitchen in the east wing of the house. Yes, it was Pei Zhen, the wife of the volunteer teacher Li Shangyi. She came from the same village as Pei Hongmei, Qingshu's second wife, and the two women were distantly related. Pei Zhen had once been a volunteer teacher at the local school too, and she considered herself something of an intellectual. She dressed the part, wearing a chequered skirt when the weather was warm, and a high-necked jumper when it was cold. Her knitting needles were currently zipping back and forth across the jumper she was making. Fanhua's first thought was that Qingshu must have had a row with Hongmei, and Pei Zhen – who thought of herself as a big sister to the younger woman – had frogmarched Qingshu over here for a tongue-lashing. She asked why Hongmei hadn't come herself, and Qingshu said she was already in bed, Hongmei being an early sleeper. Fanhua looked Qingshu over again. He would probably have a few scratches on his face if they'd been quarrelling. She picked up the big thermos flask and asked if they'd have anything to drink. They said they were fine, and Fanhua quickly put down the flask, as though they might change their minds if she moved too slow.

From outside came the sound of Fanhua's mother grumbling as she sprinkled water in the yard. "Making a kerfuffle in the middle of the night, yammering away like there's no tomorrow, I ask you." Fanhua quickly pushed the door to.

Presumably, Qingshu was here to find out what had happened at the meeting. Why such a hurry, Qingshu, hmm? You can't rush a plate of hot tofu, you need to let it cool. You'll find out everything in good time.

"So what's the matter?" Fanhua asked. "Pei Zhen, is Shangyi mistreating you? I wouldn't have thought so, a gentleman like him. Even his farts don't make a sound."

"Like he'd dare," said Pei Zhen, "knowing I have you to back me up."

"Not to mention Qingshu," said Fanhua. "He's a soldier and a scholar. He'd have no problem sorting out a mere teacher."

"Shangyi treats Pei Zhen right," said Qingshu.

"Not like the way Dianjun treats Fanhua, though," said Pei Zhen with a snort. "I remember how he'd peel an apple for her every day when she was pregnant with Beanie."

"Count your blessings," said Qingshu. "I've seen Shangyi shucking seeds just for you. Men of letters have fine feelings. Finer than the point of a needle. Finer than an awn of wheat."

But the two of them had not come over in the middle of the night to talk of peeled apples and hulled seeds, or needles or wheat for that matter. Fanhua asked Qingshu whether he had any urgent business.

"Let's start with the trivial stuff," he said. "Lingpei's been let out of jail. He's got a shaved head now."

Lingpei was the most notorious criminal in the village. He had served his apprenticeship in the backstreets of Xiushui Town, and the craft he had mastered was pickpocketing. His apprenticeship involved learning how to snatch a ping-pong ball out of hot lard. He was a veritable prodigy, and over the course of his career, he'd picked enough pockets to purchase a house of his own. The police had caught him six months ago, thanks to Qingshu. This gave Qingshu a pretext to brag about how he'd been "chasing down criminals", though the truth of the matter was that they'd come for Lingpei while he was lying in bed.

"Let's pay him a visit sometime soon," said Fanhua, "and give him a set of kitchenware. It would be a good idea for us to show him what kindness looks like."

"You can't expect a dog to get tired of eating shit," said Qingshu. "And he's hardly going to be wanting for food or clothes."

"We need to think about how to deal with this going forward. You can't solve everything with brute force. What else?"

Qingshu scratched his head and tugged on his earlobe. "There's a... situation. How to put it? It's tricky."

"If you've got a fart inside, you'd better hurry up and let it out."

"It's not really a big deal, but it's not exactly *not* a big deal. Why don't you listen to what Pei Zhen has to say?"

Pei Zhen didn't seem to have heard him; she carried on knitting without looking up. Her pinkies jutted in the air like the "orchid fingers" pose of an opera performer.

"Didn't we agree on the way here that you'd be the one to explain things, and I'd fill in the gaps?" said an impatient Qingshu. "The secretary needs to hear a first-hand account."

Fanhua interrupted to remind him not to call her "secretary". She'd rather they just use her name, or if not that, then "village head". "You can tell me," she said to Pei Zhen as she pushed the door shut. "No one else is going to hear."

Pei Zhen pressed her bamboo knitting needle to her chin and coughed. She told her story in a very roundabout way, with no sense of cohesion and numerous irrelevant digressions. Hard to believe she could ever have been a teacher. She started off with the family pig, then moved on to manure, and from there it was the toilet, and then toilet paper. She daintily covered her nose while she was talking about toilet paper. On his second cigarette by this point, Qingshu felt compelled to take over the narrative.

"Secretary, to cut to the chase, it's like this. Pei Zhen's house shares a latrine with Li Tiesuo's house. Why? Because Li Tiesuo's latrine caved in, and they couldn't afford to repair it. And that's where we get to... the trouble."

But as soon as he reached the word "trouble", Qingshu's voice got all quiet and mysterious, as though it was military secrets they were discussing. His voice was swallowed up in the sound of an animal's cry. Guanzhuang had water to the left and hills to the north, and most villagers did a sideline in rearing livestock. On the ground: donkeys, goats, rabbits. On water: ducks, geese. In the air: bees, pigeons, quails. Qingshu liked to joke that they had all three branches of the armed forces covered. His own speciality was budgerigars, but Qingshu raised them for pleasure, not profit. They kept him sane, he said. He claimed to have a budgie that could cheep the words to *Return from Target Practice*: "Red clouds in the western hills as the sun sets, the soldiers come back to camp from shooting at their targets." The sound they heard now was a donkey sneezing from afar. It belonged to Li Xinqiao's family, over on the east side of the village. She would be giving birth to a mule before too long, and the mixed breed she was bearing had agitated her.

This reminder of mixing breeds triggered an alarming thought in Fanhua's mind. Surely Li Tiesuo couldn't have caught sight of Pei Zhen while she was squatting on the toilet, could he? And what then? Or perhaps Li Shangyi had glimpsed Li Tiesuo's wife, Xue'e, when she was in there? That kind of unpleasantness could quickly turn nasty.

"And then Pei Zhen discovered something amiss, and it was something amiss in the neighbourhood of the knickers." Qingshu's voice had risen to a squeaky falsetto that made him sound more like a housewife than a military man. "A woman's knickers are periodically home to a rosy cloud, and yet Yao Xue'e's knickers have seen no rosy clouds for at least two months now."

Fanhua frowned. "Enough with the rosy clouds. You're talking about menstruation, yes? Sanitary pads?"

"Yes," said Qingshu, "that's the one. She hasn't had to use one of those for two months."

Fanhua leant forward and let out a deep breath, then leant back and inhaled. "So you're saying...?"

Qingshu lit a fresh cigarette and took a drag. "I can't claim to be wholly conversant with women's issues of this sort. But yes, I believe so."

"You mean...?"

"Secretary, I'm telling you what we can see on the surface. You'll have to do some investigating of your own if you want to find out the root cause. Anyway, it was Pei Zhen who was supposed to be telling you all this, not me. It all sounds rather unwholesome when a man talks about this sort of thing, and we Party members must always strive to oppose the unwholesome. Isn't that so, Pei Zhen?"

Pei Zhen gave no indication that she had heard him. She lifted up the jumper she was working on towards Fanhua. "Fanhua, what do you think, does this cuff need another row?"

"Whatever looks right to you," said Fanhua. She was past the point of exchanging pleasantries with Pei Zhen. What did they mean by all this talk of "investigating the root cause"? The obvious implication was that Xue'e was pregnant, simple as that. Fanhua could sympathise with Pei Zhen wanting to be circumspect, but Qingshu had an official governmental position – this was his job. Why did he have to hum and haw about it like this?

"Do you want to know what happened in today's meeting?" she asked him. "Yes, it was about arrangements for the village elections. But County Head Zhang made a big speech about family planning too. I was going to tell you all this tomorrow, but I may as well let you know now since it relates to your job. The Party give us all the threads, but we're the needle, and Zhang reminded us that the needle must stay sharp. Out-of-plan pregnancies must be dealt with decisively. One pregnancy, and the head of the village committee will be forbidden from standing for re-election. Two, and the entire group will be dismissed, with no chance of re-election for any of them."

Qingshu drew in a sharp breath. "Damn," he said, "that's harsh. They're sharpening their knives for us this time."

"That's not the worst of it. I'll tell you the rest later."

"The more power you have, the easier it is to get your way," said Qingshu with a sigh. "You lay your knife against one duck's neck and they all jump into line."

"Which is why I'm warning you," said Fanhua. "We all have a knife against our necks now. This isn't me trying to scare you. A lot of this falls on me, but you're responsible too. And Xue'e's had two children already."

"I had my suspicions they'd be coming down hard on family planning. That's why I came right over to tell you about this as soon as I heard."

"I'm not the one who's spreading the word around about this," said Pei Zhen. "Hongmei comes to me, her big sister, and tells me she's bleeding more heavily than normal, I'm hardly going to turn a deaf ear, am I? Well that's funny, I blurt out, I tell her she's the exact opposite of Xue'e, because Xue'e isn't bleeding at all. Not my fault if Qingshu overhears. I've nothing more to say. I don't know anything about it. Secretary, do you think I should cast off this sleeve here?"

Now Fanhua was starting to understand how things stood. Pei Zhen was poised and ready to enjoy the show. It just goes to show, you could never tell when it came to people; sometimes you might bite open a nice seed and find a nasty bug inside. Pei Zhen had motives of her own. She'd got pregnant a few months ago herself. She already had two boys, so she was surely due a girl this time. But Pei Zhen said that was all right by her, she wanted to complete the set. Besides, she said, it was just a fine, and her parents were hardly short of money. Fanhua had worn her lips thin explaining the politics of the matter to Pei Zhen and Shangyi. Pei Zhen said she understood. An oversized population undermines the economic foundations of the country, right? Well, don't worry about that, she said, we certainly wouldn't dream of doing anything to impede the progress of our nation. When our kids grow up, we're going to pack them off to America. If we're going to be adding our bit to the country's foreign currency reserves, surely that can't be against the law? Surely? But is it really going to be as simple as that, to send your children abroad? Fanhua asked. Do you know how much it costs? On Shangyi's salary of five hundred *kuai* a month? A handful of walnuts and jujubes, that's what five hundred *kuai* amounts to, as far as any American is concerned. Pei Zhen stormed off into the inner room. She kept ranting away as she sent objects crashing about. Five hundred *kuai*, she said, so what? At least their money was clean money, earned in worn-down stumps of chalk. This was a rank dog fart of an insinuation, implying that there were *some* people who had made their money by dipping into the public purse, even if she wasn't going to name names. I know I'm not going to get through to you, said Fanhua, which is why I came here to talk things over with Shangyi. Shangyi, she said, you're a Five-Good Family, and if you get rid of this child I'll pronounce you a Model of Family Planning. You get an annual three thousand *kuai* reward if you have both those titles. Would that, on top of your salary, be enough to pay for your sons' tuition fees? From the inner room, Pei Zhen called out: you think we're going to sell our daughter for three thousand *kuai*? Fanhua lost her temper and ran inside. "What makes you so sure it's a girl?" she yelled at Pei Zhen. "Have you seen it? Take a look at yourself in the mirror next time you go for a piss. Do you see a boy's future mother-in-law? Because I sure don't. Give it up already."

Having brought Pei Zhen to heel, Fanhua turned her attention to Shangyi. She revealed to him that the village had already banked the compensation they'd received from the state for the hundred *mu* – about sixteen acres – of village land that was going to become a new highway. Fanhua had decided that no one was going to touch that money. It would be used to give a little financial assistance to any family whose child went to university, a practical step in support of educational endeavours. Doesn't your eldest have the best scores in his grade? asked Fanhua. What do you think he's destined to do with his life? That boy was made to be a scholar, it's as obvious as lice on a bald man's head. So why don't you just keep your chin up and wait until you can get hold of your share of that money?

This was clearly making some kind of an impression on Shangyi. The official command's already come down the line, she added. If the quota's exceeded by one child, the person in charge will have to step down. And if I have to step down, then it won't be me deciding how that money gets spent. That's not what you want, is it, to be rid of me?

Eventually, after all this wheedling, Pei Zhen agreed to an abortion. Fanhua had let out a long sigh of relief at the time, thinking she could put it all behind her. But clearly, Pei Zhen was still holding a grudge. Maybe it would work out for the best though, Fanhua thought. What was the old saying? A watchful thief is worse than a thieving thief. Well, now she could count on Pei Zhen to watch over every swollen belly in the village. Not unlike the representatives of the United States Congress, who keep an eye on every level of the Chinese government, free of charge. If Pei Zhen was keeping an eye on all the potential pregnancies, then that was one less thing for Fanhua to worry about. Excellent.

Fanhua took the jumper from Pei Zhen. "You really have talent, Pei Zhen. Look at that, you've even stitched flowers on the top there.

Are these peonies or peach blossoms?" Or knotweeds, she barely managed to stop herself from adding.

Pei Zhen pouted. "They're roses. One white rose and one red rose."

"Well, no wonder I didn't recognise them," said Fanhua. "I've never seen anyone stitch roses on a jumper before. That's a new one on me."

"Peonies are tacky," said Pei Zhen, "and peach blossoms are tackier still. Roses are in vogue."

"And roses mean romance," Qingshu added. "They represent love."

Fanhua ignored him and continued to address Pei Zhen. "Shangyi's a very lucky man to have married you." She poured them each a cup of water. She'd barely sat down when she stood up again and clapped her hands. She'd forgotten, how stupid of her. Fanhua went over to the fridge and took out two golden oranges. These were also gifts from her brother-in-law, but she was suddenly in such a good mood that she told them it was Dianjun who had brought them back from a thousand *li* away.

"What, Dianjun's back?" said Qingshu.

"Oh yes," she said as she turned back towards them, "he's doing very well for himself, he has money to burn these days. You ought to grab him sometime soon and have him take you all out for drinks. Pei Zhen, you wouldn't object to Shangyi going out for a drink, would you?" She started slicing the oranges on the chopping board. "Pei Zhen, don't you think Qingshu here deserves a good slap around the face? He keeps on calling you by your name instead of showing you the proper respect and addressing you as 'elder sister'."

"This one's a government official," said Pei Zhen. "We can't expect him to follow the same rules as ordinary folk."

"It's nothing to do with my position," said Qingshu. "I'm older than you, that's all there is to it. I was old enough to piss standing up while you were still swimming around between your father's thighs."

"Take my advice," said Fanhua. "You call him 'elder brother', and you call her 'elder sister', and neither of you'll have cause to regret it." She handed the sliced orange to Pei Zhen. "Dianjun says that tangerines raise your internal heat, but oranges lower it, plus they're good for the digestion. Come on, you take the lot." Then Fanhua

16

addressed a question to Qingshu: "So, have you seen Yao Xue'e in the last couple of days? Has her belly grown at all? You pay such close attention to these things in your work, how did this one slip by you?"

"I've only got the two eyes," said Qingshu. "I can't keep track of everything. Besides, I'm a respectable comrade and a member of the Party – I can hardly go around staring at women's navels all day."

"Always the same," said Fanhua. "I believe I was talking about bellies, not navels."

THREE

The village had a cockerel for an alarm clock. Under normal circumstances, Fanhua woke up when the cock first crowed, but today it was on cry number three by the time she stirred. Dianjun was already awake, clipping his toenails as he leafed through a book.

"It's all your fault," Fanhua said, as she showed him the scratches his toenails had left along her calves during the night. "Rubbing against me this way and that."

Dianjun made a show of not hearing her and continued to stare at the book. It was called *300 Sentences of Conversational English*, and he turned the pages not with his hand, but with his chin. Fanhua had initially been concerned about how skinny he'd become, but she couldn't help laughing now she saw him making good use of his increasingly pointy chin.

"What do you think you're playing at?" she said. "Can you even remember all the twenty-six letters of the alphabet?"

"What," said Dianjun, "are you the only one who's allowed to read it? I don't see your name written on it."

Fanhua had in fact forgotten that she was the one who'd brought this book into the house. Now she remembered: it came from the county committee secretary, who had received a few of the more high-achieving village heads before the previous day's meeting. As usual, the secretary doled out some praise first, telling everyone how well they were doing and offering a few kind words for each of their villages before moving on to his requests. Chief among which was his request that they find a way to keep improving, to "take it to the next level". And just when they were about to leave, as though making polite chit-chat, the secretary mentioned "another little thing". He said he'd heard from one of his friends "upstairs" that a foreigner might be visiting Xiushui. Two possible reasons: he was either investigating their economic circumstances, in the search for a village-run enterprise with which to collaborate, or looking into the village elections. The friend upstairs was not in a position to reveal which of these was more likely. Nor did the secretary say who this friend might be, or whether he was at the municipal or provincial level. The whole thing was very mysterious. Also, he went on, apparently this was no ordinary foreigner. He was an American, which made him a more important variety of foreigner. The secretary said he had done some research online, and he had learned that the American who paid attention to China's village elections was a very impressive one indeed. The discovery was truly a startling one: it was Jimmy Carter, the former president. When they heard mention of a United States president, several of the village heads gasped, and some even bowed slightly. The secretary gave a light smile, like he was brushing away dirt with a feather duster. "Anyway, no need to get stage fright," he said. "Revolutionaries like us can hardly get stage fright, now can we? We used to say the American imperialists were a paper tiger, but now – in order to be polite, and to help them spend their money – we deign to grant them a little face. Nothing more than that." He started talking about Carter again, saying he was a tall man, tall like a mighty poplar. But compared with our basketball stars Mu Tiezhu, our Yao Ming, he was a mere Wu Dalang. And what was there to fear in a midget like Wu Dalang, hmm? A mere pedlar of sesame-seed buns. At this, all the bowing village heads straightened their backs. The secretary shifted his bottom and took the hand of the Xiuyang village head.

"If I am not mistaken," he said, "you are the one they call the Peanut King of Xiushui County. Last time I rewarded you with a certificate of merit, did I not?"

The Xiuyang village head had once been in the army. He immediately stood to attention, heel rapping against the ground, and snapped off a salute. "Reporting for duty, sir," he said. "On behalf of all my villagers, I offer you my thanks."

Still holding his hand, the secretary bade him sit down. "Carter used to be a peanut farmer too. The same line of work as you. You'd have something to talk about."

The Peanut King stiffened his neck as he grew excited. "If we manage to catch him, then I'll chat with him all day. I'll ask him whether he gets pests in his peanut crop, and–"

Startled, the secretary laughed loudly. But of course, he said when he'd finished laughing, it won't be Carter himself who's coming. And even if he did, he wouldn't make it as far as us. He'd be "carted off" by the provincial authorities along the way. So it'll probably be one of his underlings who comes. The village heads bent over again, but it was out of relief rather than anxiety this time. Somebody took a couple of puffs on a pipe. And as for when exactly this American would be coming, the secretary continued, it was hard to say. This remained an "unknown quantity". But they must be ready for battle. They would have to pay attention to strategy, and tactics too. The village heads should listen to those at the county level, and those at the county level should listen in turn to their superiors. But any work that needed to be done in advance should most definitely not be postponed. Don't wait until you're touching cloth before you decide to dig a latrine.

It was at this point that the secretary pulled a book from his suit pocket that was about the size of one of the Little Red Books back in the day. It was the *300 Sentences of Conversational English*. He waved it before them, just like he was waving the Little Red Book. His vigorous waving left him slightly red in the face. His tie was swinging back and forth under his head, a bit like the beard on a "flower-face" opera performer. He was attempting to dust off his own English, he said, to facilitate communication with the American when he did arrive. Then, to everyone's surprise, he produced a line of English. It was broken and shaky, like how the Xinjiangers selling mutton skewers sounded when they tried to speak Chinese, but Fanhua recognised the words "thank" and "you".

What the Peanut King heard, however, was not "thank you" but "fuck you". "Who's he talking to?" he muttered. "Why so aggressive all of a sudden?" County Head Zhang, who was sitting beside the secretary, led the applause, even rising to his feet to give him a standing ovation. And if the county head was standing up, then the village heads could hardly remain seated. The secretary first bade the county head sit down, then waved a hand towards all the village heads.

"Thank you, thank you everyone for your support. The village looks to the village, the family looks to the family, the masses look to the officials, and the officials? Well, they look to the more forward-thinking government officials, like the ones we have sitting in this room today. I merely desire to set a positive example." Then he informed County Head Zhang that their Xinhua bookstore had already ordered in several thousand copies of *300 Sentences of Conversational English* – which included a CD – and he'd had them deliver several crates here. Fanhua had picked up a copy at the time, and her brother-in-law gave her another one when he came to pick her up after the meeting. He told her that he and Fanrong had both been issued one from their work unit, and one copy was enough for their household. She could give the spare to Beanie. A second language at her age would be an impressive talent.

Fanhua's driver still hadn't shown up, and there were no other people around, but her brother-in-law kept his voice low all the same. "It won't be too long before the whole of Xiushui is caught up in a craze for English."

"Why? What's this all about?" asked Fanhua.

"This book was written by the secretary's nephew. It's been out for a year and it hasn't been selling. Now do you see?"

"The cheeky bastard. Fancy trying to pull a trick like that on us." Nevertheless, she decided that the village should invest in a load, and the school ought to buy their share too. Guessing what she was thinking, her brother-in-law told her that there'd be no harm in the village buying the book, but they definitely shouldn't allow the students to pay for their own copies. Confused, Fanhua asked him why.

"Because," her brother-in-law explained in an even quieter voice, "this secretary will have disappeared before too long, once he reaches the end of his term. And every new secretary likes to start things off with education. If the new regime comes in and decides you've been collecting money unnecessarily, you'll be out on your arse."

Damn, this was a tricksy business.

Now, as Dianjun flicked through the book, Fanhua asked him whether he understood it.

"Why don't you give me a test?" he replied. "Test me on some of the more obscure stuff, like camels, or donkeys." Fanhua couldn't believe Dianjun would know the English word "camel", so she asked him to spell it. Dianjun looked up at the ceiling and seemed to be wracking his brains. "I was only kidding around," he said. "Didn't think you'd actually try and test me. But I think I can do this one. It's 'c-a-m-e-l. Camel.' Is that right?" He pretended to be nibbling on a steamed bun: *ken-mo*. Close enough.

"And donkey?"

Dianjun eyed the ceiling again, but this time he failed to come up with an answer. How odd that he knew a strange creature like a camel, but was stumped by something as ordinary as a donkey. Fanhua grabbed the book from him and discovered the truth: he was on a page that featured a picture of a camel, with a donkey standing next to it. Fanhua attempted the word "donkey" a couple of times: "*dangkei, dangkei*". "*Dang*" meant "the Party", while in these parts, "*kei*" meant "rebuke". Thinking of her own situation, Fanhua couldn't help interpreting the word "donkey" as "the Party's rebuke". Now she'd be able to remember it. She explained to Dianjun what the secretary had told them, but she kept her brother-in-law's advice to herself. Telling him a secret was like tempting a dog with a dumpling outside its kennel. Turn your back for a second and everyone'll know.

"A foreigner's coming? Excellent news. Isn't Fanqi's son Xiangchao studying English? If the foreigner comes here, just bring Xiangchao back and tell the foreigner he's one of your underlings."

"OK. But I'd need to do right by Xiangchao. I'd have to pay for his train tickets, and give him a salary."

Dianjun closed the book and yawned. He said he hadn't had a good night's sleep, and now he felt like a nap.

"Really," said Fanhua, "you didn't have a good night's sleep, even though you managed to deafen me with the sound of your snoring?"

"Call me a cur if I'm lying. I kept hearing someone crying."

"Crying? Who was crying? How come I didn't hear anything?"

"It was creepy, really creepy. Like a wailing ghost, or a howling wolf."

Fanhua laughed. "That really was a howling wolf. They're raising one over at Qinglin's place." She slipped out of the covers and pounced on Dianjun with her hands raised into the shape of pointy ears. "A wolf! A big bad wolf!"

By the time the two of them had finished tussling, Fanhua's mother had made breakfast.

"Why don't you go out a bit later on," Fanhua said to Dianjun when they'd sat down to eat, "and see what kind of changes there have been around the village."

"I don't want to go anywhere. I want to stay in bed and sleep. I need to recuperate and build up my strength." Recuperate? Build up his strength? Fanhua was confused. Had something happened to him in Shenzhen? She looked him in the eye and asked him what the matter was. Was there something he was hiding from her? Had he got into trouble or something?

Dianjun snorted. "Are you kidding? Got into trouble, tch, I ask you. I'm on top of the world, I'm doing great, I might just wake up one day and discover I've become general manager overnight."

There he went again. Fanhua placed the back of her hand against his forehead and asked whether he was delirious with fever. He moved her hand away.

"When I see Qingshu and the others, they'll have to call me 'General Manager Zhang'."

The sound of his blustering coincided with Beanie outside practising the "upside-down song" her grandmother had taught her:

Back-to-front, inside-out,
Stones in the river roll right out.
Just one star in a sky of moons,
A million generals in one platoon.
You must never ever sing this song,
Else you'll hear a deaf man laughing along.

Beanie paused to ask her grandmother what a general was. Her grandmother replied that Beanie's mother was a general. Beanie asked, again, what a general was. Her grandmother said a general was someone who gave birth to a girl, a girl like you. Fanhua smiled to herself. Her parents were still hoping she'd manage to produce a son. Now *that* could be an upside-down song. The head of the village has to set the people a positive example. She couldn't have another baby even if she'd wanted to.

Dianjun cupped her breast and gave her nipple a tweak. "Just one star in a sky of moons. I shall suck on the moons and kiss the star."

Fanhua knocked his hand away. "Behave. The elections will be here soon. You need to start thinking about writing my speech."

"Very well. I, the mighty Chief Zhang, shall deign to be your ghostwriter."

What nonsense was this, Fanhua said, leave ghosts out of this.

Dianjun shook his head. "You have no idea what goes on out there in the world. A ghostwriter is someone who writes the speeches on behalf of the president. A very respectable position. They get to eat and drink whatever they like."

FOUR

Fanhua put down her bowl and headed out. She wanted to check on Xue'e's belly. Just thinking about it made her feel like the sun had risen in the west. A month earlier, the village family planning division had carried out a check, sending all the out-of-plan pregnancies off to the hospital for an abortion that very night. How had Xue'e managed to slip through the net? Could Pei Zhen have made a mistake? Her story about discovering something suspicious in the toilets was obviously bogus. It was the belly she had seen, that went without saying. But they were in trouble if Xue'e's bulge was already far enough along to be showing. It was a belly no longer, it had become a ticking time bomb. Just like the premier of the State Council, Fanhua had a brain that was forever occupied with a long string of digits, and the most firmly lodged in her memory were those to do with women. Guanzhuang had a population of one thousand, two hundred and forty-five, divided between five village clusters. One hundred and forty-three of those were women of child-bearing age, but seventy-eight of them'd had their tubes tied, and another four were barren. Which left sixty-one bellies that might start bulging at any moment. Thirty-seven of those were legally free to do so, but the remaining twenty-four? They were the time bombs. And if one of those bombs had been detonated, would the other twenty-three remain undisturbed? To borrow a phrase of Qingshu's:

it would be a nuclear disaster. The thought of it made Fanhua's scalp feel numb.

Xue'e's family lived opposite Qinglin. Fanhua heard the sound of quickly pattering footsteps as she approached. It was Qinglin's wolf. Qinglin had initially bragged about how he'd caught it himself, up in the hills. Only later, when he was informed that the capture of wild animals was illegal, did he admit he'd bought it from Hanzhou Zoo, and he had the certificate to prove it. He was allowed to keep it as a pet, but not to slaughter and eat it. Of course, Qinglin didn't want it as a mere pet; he planned to use it to breed wolfdogs. The first-generation offspring of a dog and a wolf was worth seven hundred *kuai*, which was the equivalent of two whole pigs. These days, Qinglin had given up on keeping dogs altogether and focused all his attention on the wolf. He hired it out for a stud fee and stayed out of the actual business of rearing wolfdogs. Son of a bitch, someone once joked, Qinglin's set himself up with a stud farm. "Not just sons of bitches," Qinglin had replied, in all seriousness. "Daughters of bitches too." Qinglin had named his wolf Grey. Funnily enough, he said, Grey had been born in the year of the dog. If man's fate was proscribed by the heavens, then so was a wolf's, and Grey's zodiac sign had destined him to a career among dogs.

Qinglin extended two fingers. "That's how much Grey earns me every time he hops onto a bitch's back."

"Twenty *kuai*?" Fanhua asked.

He gestured for her to multiply that by ten. Grey was a good boy all right, earning two hundred *kuai* just like that. Kong Fanqi, the committee mediator, had once said they would have to look into whether they should confer the title of Double-Civilised Household on Qinglin's family. Keeping a wolf was a form of ecological protection, which came under the remit of Spiritual Civilisation, on top of the Material Civilisation of their earnings. Times sure were changing. A dog in heat would usually end up costing you, but if it produced a crossbreed then you'd be in profit. What did you call that? A market economy, that's what. Oh Tiesuo, Fanhua thought, oh Xue'e. You'd be so much better off rearing mongrel dogs than producing children.

There was no sign of activity behind Tiesuo's door. On this side of the road, Qinglin was smashing bones with a hammer. He'd be grinding them up with a pestle next, to make a powder he could mix into food for the wolf.

"You treat that wolf better than your own wife," said Fanhua.

Tiesuo put down the hammer. "Oh, Village Head, it's you. Have you eaten?"

Fanhua said she had, and continued to squint at Tiesuo's front door. The sound of her voice brought Qinglin's wife outside. Qinglin had got his wife from Yangcheng County in Shanxi, for the price of a sack of rice and a jar of sesame oil, and after living here for over five years she still sometimes struggled with the local accent. She misheard what Fanhua had said, and remarked, "Aye, he do treat me well, my Qinglin."

"Never learns. Get lost," said Qinglin, without raising his head, like he was swatting away a fly. He tossed his hammer to the floor. "This cocking wife was a waste of a marriage," he said to Fanhua. "All she knows how to do is eat. We had someone bring their dogs over here from Baituogou the other day. He brought twenty *jin* of beef for the wolf. Soon's I turned my back, she'd gone and boiled up the lot. Grey was busting a nut all day, and he didn't get even a bite of meat to show for it."

Qinglin's wife smiled, apparently indifferent to her husband's words. "I give the wolf this big a piece," she said, indicating with her hands a size that grew and grew until it was half as big as a baby cow. She might not be a local, Fanhua thought, but she'd lived here long enough to understand the way things were done around these parts. She knew that if there was one thing more precious than oil, it was maintaining face. This was her way of showing off, of demonstrating that life was going well for her. Qinglin, however, did not appreciate his wife's efforts.

"Motherfucker," he said, his features contorted with rage, "how many times do I have to tell you, the wolf eats *raw* meat. It's science. If you don't listen to science, how's Grey going to have the energy to keep doing it all day long, hmm? You do my head in. You're lucky I don't chop your block off and feed it to the wolf."

It was then that Fanhua heard the sound of the knocker rattling against the opposite door. Teacher Shangyi was on his way out. He was walking along in a suit and had a book tucked under his arm, his neck stretched out as he struggled to tug his shirt collar into shape.

When he saw Fanhua standing outside Qinglin's place, he didn't greet her by asking whether she'd eaten, like normal country folk would, but instead extended a very polite "good day". When he'd walked a few paces away, he glanced back over his shoulder, with a lupine sort of nervousness. This nervousness told Fanhua that he knew Pei Zhen had reported the situation. Perhaps he'd even been the one who encouraged her to do it. She called out for him to stop, but regretted it as soon as the words left her lips. The street was not a suitable place to discuss the state of Xue'e's womb, obviously. But Shangyi had already turned around and was walking back towards her.

"Good morning," he said, before asking her what "instructions" she had.

"Teacher Shangyi," said Fanhua, "that sure is a fine-fitting suit you have there. Is it bought or home-made?"

"Fine fitting?" Shangyi replied. "Doesn't feel that way."

By now, Fanhua had had a chance to figure out what she wanted to say next. "There's something I'd like to talk to you about. I need you to help me come up with a few questions, and send them along when you're done."

"Not a problem," said Shangyi. "What exactly do they concern?"

"They're to do with family planning," said Fanhua, "and the elections. You'll have to make sure you keep them under wraps."

Shangyi wasn't stupid, and he immediately realised what Fanhua was driving at. "Is it for a quiz?" he asked quietly.

Fanhua's explanation was interrupted by a blare of sound from a loudspeaker. This happened at half past seven every morning. It was a custom that had been proposed by Qingshu and passed by the village committee following a lengthy discussion. It would be akin to a military reveille, Qingshu had argued. Fanhua had suggested that playing some kind of song might be more suitable than a military reveille, since this was the countryside, after all. Ideally, a song that would encourage progress while also fostering cohesion. Today's song was *Who Says My Village Ain't Lovely*:

Who says my village ain't lovely?
Yodel-ay, yodel-or!
A happy life for us – hey!

"The questions should be as practical as possible," said Fanhua when the music had died down. "No need to bring the likes of Marx into it this time." Fanhua had her reasons for this stipulation. Last year, when it was time for the military draft, Fanhua had also had Shangyi come up with some quiz questions in order to liven things up. His first question had been: what was the year, month and day of Marx's birth? Obviously, no one had managed to get the correct answer, so Shangyi had advised everyone that it was actually very easy to remember, if you simply used the mnemonic, "Eighteen eighteen was the year, clap your hands and stomp and cheer. May the fifth, fifth of May, capitalism runs away."

"Very well," said Shangyi. "No Marx this time."

"We want people to be able to enjoy themselves, right?"

"And yet," said Shangyi, "should we not ensure an appropriate balance between the intellectual, the amusing and the practical?"

Fanhua did not agree or disagree. "You'll figure it out," she said.

Shangyi tucked his book back under his arm. "Goodbye then."

Once Shangyi had gone, Fanhua heard a snort of laughter from Qinglin. He proudly informed Fanhua that there were only two people Shangyi said "good day" to: one was Fanhua, and the other was his boy Grey. The first time he ever came to see Grey, Shangyi said, "Good day, Mr Wolf."

At that moment, a throng of kids with backpacks emerged onto the street. They all poked their heads into Qinglin's yard on their way by, and a few of the more mischievous boys barked like a dog to send the wolf scampering this way and that. Fanhua caught sight of Meng Qingmao, the former village head, taking his granddaughter to school. Qingmao's granddaughter had a very special backpack, embroidered with a picture of Donald Duck as well as a stars and stripes. Clearly an American product. Even if it was a fake, at least it wasn't a fake Chinese product. The girl trotted proudly along, nose in the air like a little princess. The sight of Qingmao, in contrast, was enough to make your heart ache. The weather hadn't yet turned cold, but he had his hands tucked into his sleeves and his shoulders hunched. Truly old. When Fanhua called out to him – "Uncle!" – he stopped, pulled his hands from his sleeves, and rubbed his face.

"Ah, so you've come to inspect the work," he said.

"I just happened to be passing by. Might as well have a look while I'm here."

"It certainly deserves a look," said Qingmao. "That's not just a wolf – it's the most productive force in Qinglin's family."

"You're right there, Uncle," said Fanhua.

"I'm an old man," said Qingmao, swinging his hands. "No use to anyone any more. Just babbling. If I can come out with ten pieces of nonsense, then there's at least a chance I might strike lucky with one of them."

Fanhua's spirits briefly sagged. Qingmao had stepped down three years ago, but in such a short space of time, his hair had gone completely grey. There had been three of them competing in the last election: him, Fanhua and Xiangsheng. When it became obvious after the first round of voting that Fanhua was ahead of him, he announced there and then that he was withdrawing his candidacy, and urged everyone who had voted for him to choose her in the next round. It was a bit like the way these things happened in an American election. This had been a wise move on his part, as it allowed him to stand aside with his dignity intact. The village's Party secretary at the time was named Guo. Impressed by Qingmao's actions, Secretary Guo had commended him for his objectivity and the breadth of his vision.

"We follow in the footsteps of Confucius," said Qingmao, "and we must always strive to honour our ancestors through our respect for propriety. Respect for propriety is our village's most precious legacy. We're not like some of those other villages whose officials won't depart with bloodshed. Wasn't there a village in Nanyuan Township where someone was stabbed nine times? Deary me, just one shy of double figures. That's not a stabbing, that's chopping mincemeat for dumplings." Secretary Guo swiftly agreed. "I was born in the year of the horse," Qingmao continued, "and an old nag like me knows the lay of the land. Fanhua is a dragon, which means she was born to wear the dragon robes of office." This was a slightly unexpected tack, but Qingmao's heart was clearly in the right place. Secretary Guo nodded his approval.

Fanhua knew that Qingmao's words were partially meant for her ear. Propriety should be repaid in kind, as they say, and she would have to behave appropriately. She sent Meng Xiaohong, their secretary of the Communist Youth League, to buy a commemorative tablet in Xiushui Town to commemorate Qingmao's noble act. Xiaohong took the three hundred *kuai* she had been given, but when she got there she found the tablets only cost a hundred and thirty each, so she bought two. When they were adding the inscription, Qingmao suggested they write: "One harvest, one withering and flourishing, one flower across one world." Shangyi did the writing. He said that the "withering and flourishing" sounded a bit... you know. Qingmao said no, he didn't know, and Shangyi should try harder to speak sense.

"It sounds a bit... depressing," said Shangyi. "It's a bit too contrived, too rain-against-the-palm-leaves. It doesn't sound right."

Qingmao rapped his pipe against the tabletop. "Palm leaves shmalm leaves. I may not be your match when it comes to chewing on words, but I know what I like. *From* withering *to* flourishing – that means it's getting better every year." He relented in the end, but they left in the "one flower across one world". He had his own interpretation of that, too. The one flower – "hua" – was Fanhua, while the one world was Guanzhuang Village. Which meant this was his way of offering Fanhua his blessings.

Village officials had to be audited when they stepped down, and Fanhua's verdict on Qingmao was extremely complimentary. He deserved to be whisked straight to the seat of power in Beijing, she said, to Zhongnanhai itself, in a helicopter. He could skip the reserve list and go straight into the standing committee. There was a limekiln in the village that they used every time anyone needed to repair a road, or construct a house or build a bridge. Even a fool couldn't fail to turn a profit. After discussing it with the village committee, Fanhua put the limekiln under Qingmao's command

It was only six months later that Fanhua heard from Xiangsheng, the other candidate, that Qingmao's abdication had been decided by another Confucian saying: "A man ought not to be a slave, and a woman ought not to be a slave girl." Oh, so if you weren't number one, then you were a slave? Qingmao clearly still had some hard feelings. Annoyed, Fanhua increased his stipend in her second year.

FIVE

W hen Qingmao had passed by, Fanhua went back to look at the wolf. It was shut away in the west wing of the house. Being a nocturnal animal, it would lie down as soon as the sun came out and sink its snout into the sand. The wolf snored away, dreaming of its wives. You could easily have taken it for a dog, were it not for the jut of its ears, and a certain disdain for mankind in its eyes.

"He's a fussy one," said Qinglin. "If his sand isn't changed every day, he gets into such a strop that he won't even do his bridegroom's duties. Ech, he's got into bad habits."

"Well, he is an advanced force of production," said Fanhua. "You can hardly blame him for being a bit moody."

"Secretary, I've heard there's this medicine called 'viagra'. If men take it, they can keep at it all night long. Do you think it works on wolves too?" This question seemed to have come out of nowhere.

"Have you tried it?" asked Fanhua.

"I certainly wouldn't waste it on myself if I had any. Xiangmin was telling me about it. He said they look like slivers of mint, bright blue." Xiangmin liked to go on about how he'd brought advanced culture to Guanzhuang. Presumably, this wasn't what he meant. The reminder of Xiangmin was another headache for Fanhua. Such a nuisance. He'd been the first person in the village to strike it rich. A few years back, when Xiali brand cars were still a big deal, he liked to brag about how he had two cars: one was a Xiali, and the other was a Xiali too. There are many ways to kill a chicken, and some of those ways involve starting from the chicken's arse. Xiangmin's way of getting rich involved trafficking in livestock, and in people. He took animals from Xiushui to Shanxi, and brought women from Shanxi to Xiushui. It was through Xiangmin that Qinglin had acquired his wife. To the unmarried men of Xiushui County, Xiangmin was a god.

And then there was the fact that he'd gone and converted to Christianity. He once had a visit from one of the men he'd provided with a wife. He came over from Gongzhuang Village, this man, and he knelt outside Xiangmin's door and stared at him with desperation in his eyes.

"Please, I beseech you," he said. "Find me another one, I'll pay you whatever it costs."

"Fucking hell," said Xiangmin, "are you looking to start a harem now?"

"It's not like that," said the man. "My brother, he needs a wife too."

"Well now, you see, but it's been tricky lately," said Xiangmin, "tougher than usual." Keeping the man on tenterhooks. "The government has been calling for a fourfold economic increase, so they're doing their best to hang onto their workforce over there."

The man immediately saw how things stood. "We can work something out, I'm sure we can work something out. I can quadruple your fee, yes?" Yet he was apparently in no hurry to leave.

"What," said Xiangmin, "you think we squish women out of clay? You think I can whip one out just like that? Go home, get your money."

The man sucked on his gums and finally managed to stammer out his concern. "It's going to be a wife for my younger brother, so, I beseech you, please, when you're on the road with her, don't... don't do anything untoward."

"Fuck you. I'm a Christian, you know that? I belong to Jesus. I'm virtuous in all that I do, motherfucker. Go find someone else."

Not so long ago, Fanhua had heard a credible rumour that

Xiangmin was planning to donate some funds towards the construction of a church over in Wangzhai. A church could be a profitable endeavour, according to Qingshu. More cash donations than you could tally in an afternoon. It was a big step up from livestock trafficking, and no mistake.

Finally, some action. Tiesuo's daughters appeared, Manny and Laddy, and then Xue'e came chasing after them. When she caught up with Laddy, she stuffed a bundle of tissue paper into her pocket. "Wipe your snot on your sleeve again and I'll knock your lights out, you see if I don't."

Under normal circumstances, Fanhua wouldn't have noticed anything amiss, but it was unmistakable once you knew what you were looking for. There was a definite waddle to Xue'e's gait, a distinctively pregnant waddle. She was usually a graceful one, Xue'e, like a moth, but now she looked more like a penguin, the way she thrust out her chest and rear end. Fanhua waited until she was on her way back inside before calling out to her.

"Hey," she said, "what's Laddy done to make you want to knock her lights out? I'm not sure she could stand it, wispy little thing that she is."

Seeing Fanhua approach, Xue'e turned sideways to point at her younger daughter. "That one," she said, "she'll be the end of me. By the time she gets home, her sleeves are shiny like a barber's strop."

"Well, you can't blame Laddy for that. It's from her dad she gets it. Tiesuo was also a right little snotworm when he was younger. Worse than Laddy, even. At least she wipes it away – he used to just lick it into his mouth."

Fanhua remained alert. Her gaze was like a mine detector, scanning the surface of Xue'e's belly.

"I heard Dianjun's doing well for himself down in Shenzhen?"

"He's one of those men who always spends twice what he earns. No matter how much he makes, it won't ever be enough. Not like Qinglin here, quietly making a mint without so much as lifting a finger."

Qinglin looked affronted. "Who says I don't lift a finger? I spend all day looking after my wolf."

"Oh yes, and who's the one doing the actual work around here – you or the wolf?" Fanhua laughed at her own joke, and Xue'e joined in. Fanhua was able to make further deductions from the way Xue'e laughed, one hand placed against the small of her back and the other cupping her belly. Sore back, heavy belly. Second trimester by now, by the looks of it. So Pei Zhen's eyes hadn't mistaken her. Oh dear, Xue'e, it's the knife for you, whether you like it or not.

Qinglin's wife emerged from the latrine. She rolled up her sleeves and went over to help her husband mix up the feed for the wolf. Qinglin blocked her way with a raised arm and told her to clean her paws first. Qinglin might have a neck as black as axle grease, but he could be very particular about cleanliness when it mattered. If the Americans really did come to visit, Fanhua thought to herself, it'd definitely be worth bringing them here to see Qinglin's wolf. Show them how much the people of Guanzhuang cared about the environment. Aren't they always going on and on about human rights in China? Then see how well we treat a mere animal – feeding him meat and soup, providing him with all the wives he could want – and just imagine how well off the humans round here must be. She should get her sister Fanrong to put a picture of Qinglin in the newspaper. You could certainly fill an article about him. A reprobate in his youth, a philanderer who'd bought his wife for a sack of rice, Qinglin had pulled up his socks and – thanks to the supportive policies of the Party and encouragement from local officials – clawed his way to prosperity through animal husbandry. That was what you called cherries sprouting on a pomegranate tree, no mistake. Couldn't make it up.

Fanhua glanced again at Xue'e's belly. Once that had all been dealt with, she thought, maybe Xue'e could raise a dog. A bitch, obviously. Get Qinglin's wolf to knock her up and soon her belly would be swelling with cash, the Chairman's face smiling from stacks of hundred-*kuai* notes. Right now it was all bitches from other villages coupling with the wolf, which was like spraying your fertiliser across your neighbour's field. Obviously, regional protectionism was unacceptable in today's market economy, but surely there was no harm in putting your own bitches first. Qinglin's usual price was two hundred *kuai* a pop, right? Well, she might not be able to talk him down to half price, but she could surely manage at least a twenty per cent discount. And then her sister could write about how the village was united under one flag, maximising its resources and optimising efficiency thanks to the wise leadership of the village officials. If the human birth rate went down and the animal birth rate went up, then everyone would be better off. It'd be just like the song went: "Yodel-ay, yodel-or! A happy life for us – hey! For one thousand years, ten thousand, more!"

SIX

Guanzhuang's village committee was based in a large
courtyard. It had been a Confucian temple, once upon a
time. Not one of those big ones with a wall on each side,
but they did have the statues of Confucius and a copy of the family
tree from his birthplace in Shandong. During the days when Criticising Lin Biao and Criticising Confucius were official policy, the
residents of Guanzhuang had demonstrated their criticism of
feudalist hierarchies by burning the place down.

According to legend, it was Kong Zhaoyuan who'd lit the first
torch. Zhaoyuan, the head of the village revolutionary committee at
the time, had summoned the villagers to a meeting at the temple
where he criticised "Baldy Lin" and "Cockfucius". They were
scoundrels, he said, the pair of them, traitors and bastards who had
ganged up to undermine the cornerstone of socialism. He got
increasingly worked up as he went on with his criticism.

"The hell with it," he said as he turned to face the temple. "I
want to burn the whole damn temple to the ground." At heart he
was a good man, Zhaoyuan, all the old folk said so, and he'd frightened himself with his words. He shivered and he cowered. But even
good men have their flaws. He looked around the crowd, waiting for
someone to oppose him, but what he heard instead was a burst of
cheers and voices yelling, Burn! Burn! Burn!

A loosed arrow can't fly back to the bow. But at this crucial moment, Zhaoyuan dithered. He slapped his pockets, looking for matches. "Anyone got a light?" he said, when he'd checked every pocket twice. "Matches? Anyone?"

Someone did eventually step up and provide him with matches, and it was the boy who would one day grow up to become public security commissioner. Meng Qingshu was only four or five years old at the time, still wearing split pants. While his dad was distracted, he'd tugged out his matches. His hands were swifter than Lingpei's, the old folk said, because little Qingshu hadn't had to waste time looking out for the cops. Thinking Zhaoyuan was wanting a smoke, he tried to take his father's pipe, and when his father wouldn't give it to him, he started bawling and wailing. Suddenly, he was the centre of everyone's attention.

"Damn," said Zhaoyuan, "get on up here. Look at this kid, a true child of Chairman Mao. He's the one who'll be continuing the revolution when we're all gone. That's what you call revolutionary consciousness. Damn, you're not afraid of anything, are you? You might be small, but there's nothing small about your ambition."

Once he had the matches, Zhaoyuan asked if anyone could provide him with some dry hay for kindling. Plenty of people had brought hay along to make sitting on the ground more comfortable, but nobody volunteered to give him any. Eventually, someone shouted out: "There's hay under your wife's arse!" This left Zhaoyuan with no choice but to head into the crowd and retrieve the hay that his wife was sitting on. He tried to tug it out from under her, but his wife sat there holding their son and refused to budge. On his third attempt, he finally managed to pull out a handful of hay, only to discover that it had been soaked right through by his wife's piss, and was now frozen in the shape of an egg. Nevertheless, it would have to be lit, and so that's what a sweating Zhaoyuan attempted to do. But despite his best efforts, he couldn't get the fire to take.

The occasion would eventually come to be commemorated in an upside-down song:

Zhaoyuan, Zhaoyuan, let's talk about him,
Subjected Confucius to criticism.
Sunset in the east, sunrise in the west,

In the cold of winter, he was hot with sweat.
A hand growing out from the end of a leg,
His wife she laid a frozen egg.

Though this particular upside-down song wasn't altogether upside-down, since most of what it described was fairly accurate. The way the old folk told it, Qingmao, who was barely twenty back then, fancied himself a share of the limelight. He piped up with a Chairman Mao saying to egg Zhaoyuan on: "Be resolute! Fear no sacrifice! Surmount every difficulty to achieve victory!"

If you're fighting a tiger, as the saying goes, you'd best have your family at your back. At this crucial juncture, Zhaoyuan's father stood up.

"Oh come on," he said, "are you blind? Everyone here has straw under their arse." But Zhaoyuan couldn't even hear his father. He continued to struggle with the frozen lump of straw, causing his father to stamp his feet with frustration. "Deaf too are you? May as well lop off your ears and feed them to the dogs." Still, Zhaoyuan failed to respond. His father grew so enraged that he wiped his hand across his face, stomped over and lit a fire himself.

He was a sly old fox though, Zhaoyuan's father. Instead of handing the fire over to his son, he somehow ended up falling over and dropping it to the ground, at the feet of the revolutionary committee members in the front row. They had no choice then but to add to the fire. Like the proverb says, the fire blazes brighter when we all add fuel. In less time than it took to finish smoking a pipe, the fire had spread inside the temple. A swarm of rats came scurrying out, chittering like they'd lost their minds, sending cats fleeing in terror. The flames were so high they turned the sky red.

But Zhaoyuan was frequently seen walking around the ruins in the days that followed, his hands behind his back and a look of chagrin on his face. Round and round he went, like a donkey pulling a millstone. A few days later, he made an announcement. "This place is too empty," he said. "Doesn't feel right. Let's put up a stage here so we can perform revolutionary operas and disseminate Mao Zedong Thought." Ten thousand years is far too long to wait. Seize the day and get things done.

Zhaoyuan made his speech, and it was so. They completed the

stage during winter when there was no work to be done on the farms. For the roof ridgepole, they used the trunk of the one ginkgo tree in the village. It was older than the village itself, this tree, dating back to the days of the Emperor Kangxi, or so they said. For the purlin beams, they used a hundred-year-old scholar tree, hard like a rock. So hard it broke the blades of their carpentry planes.

But fortunes can rise as well as fall. Many years after they'd criticised the hell out of him, Confucius became popular again. Meng Qingmao, who'd once egged Zhaoyuan on with his Mao quotations, now became branch secretary. His first act on assuming office was to announce a prestigious new construction on the site of the old temple: a three-room wing on the east side of the stage, with white-washed earth walls and a tiled roof. All they were missing now was the statue of Confucius and the copy of his family tree. The statue could easily be replaced by slapping together a few handfuls of clay, but it would take a trip to Qufu to get a new family tree. And who did they decide to send? Zhaoyuan's son. Off he went, armed with public money, but a fortnight passed and there was still no sign of him. Eventually, it became apparent that he hadn't gone to Qufu at all. He stayed in Xiushui Town, at a house belonging to a relative of his, eating out at every opportunity so that he could use up the money and go home. Funnily enough, he did still manage to produce a Confucian family tree. It was Zhaoyuan's wife who finally gave the game away. Zhaoyuan, she revealed, had preserved a copy of the village original, back in the day, and he'd come home and consecrated it with incense the very night of the fire.

In any case, the main thing was that the temple had been restored to glory. Qingmao refurbished the stage while he was at it, strengthening the foundations and adding a layer of stone cladding to the exterior. He even had a picture carved above the stone. "Dragon and Phoenix, Harbingers of Prosperity" it was called. Brought in an artist from the provincial capital, and he did a splendid job of it. You had the dragon flying through the air, jaws parted, body twisted so it could look towards the phoenix, and the phoenix soaring on open wings, gazing up at the dragon. Clouds floating all around them. All suitably auspicious.

Some at the time suspected he was primarily laying down the foundations for a lengthy career of his own, but Qingmao decided against dedicating his life to officialdom. When he stepped down, this courtyard, this foundation, passed down to Fanhua. The year before last, she had added another extension on the west side, three rooms with glazed blue roof tiles, just like the west wing of a traditional hutong home. Now it was complete: a true courtyard, with a wall on each side. A courtyard was a good thing, according to Xiangchao, who'd been a teacher in Beijing. All the leaders in the Party Central Committee lived in courtyards, and you could plant a pomegranate tree in it and have glossy green leaves in spring, and glowing red flowers in summer, and a veritable bounty of fruit come autumn. Why a pomegranate tree? It signified a bounty of sons and a bounty of joy, Xiangchao explained. Some people were keen to plant one right away, but Fanhua resisted. No, she wasn't worried about the fruits getting snaffled – it was just that Xiangchao's spiel about a bounty of sons seemed a bit too... well. Wouldn't it contradict their line on family planning policy?

Rather than whitewashing the walls, Fanhua lined them with ceramic tiles, inside and out, not unlike the public toilets in a city. Ceramic tiles were a precious commodity at the time. The roads and alleys of Xiushui were covered in the things, apparently as a part of the urbanisation process that was supposed to bring the town closer into the orbit of the provincial capital. The county head back then was named Wang, and it was thus that he acquired his nickname of Tile King Wang. Thanks to all this "urbanising", Tile King Wang was swiftly promoted to the position of deputy mayor in Hanzhou. Fanhua had needed her brother-in-law's help just to get this one shipment of tiles delivered.

The east was draped in blazing clouds. Dawn clouds are like red silk, and dusk clouds are like glowing embers. The whole courtyard seemed to be lined in red silk when Fanhua arrived at the village committee headquarters. The few sparrows that had descended into the silk had been dyed red too, red like wild berries. The farmers have a saying: red sky at sunrise, don't you go outside; red sky at sunset, walk up a sweat. Which meant bad weather ahead.

Qingshu was on the phone in his office. He looked very serious, sitting there in his Mao suit buttoned up to the chin. His hair was combed back and so slick with pomade a fly would've struggled to

41

find a foothold. Startled by Fanhua's entrance, he hastily hung up the phone.

"What are you doing up so early?" he asked. "After Dianjun's gone to all that effort to be back here." He moistened his lips and gave her a sly grin.

"Behave," said Fanhua. "Any more crap like that from you and I'll tear your mouth to bits, you see if I don't."

Qingshu moved his face closer to her. "Go ahead. Tear away! Who's going to do your work for you when it's in bits?" He asked her whether she'd seen the early morning news, and she told him she never watched daytime TV. That's a shame, said Qingshu, a great shame, a truly great shame. Fanhua asked him what the hell he'd seen. Had one of the top leaders died? War in the Middle East again? Or had some terrorists blown up another subway?

"More interesting even than the Middle East," said Qingshu. "The provincial channel featured your meeting in a news report. There was even a shot of you."

"Bullshit," said Fanhua. "Why would they have showed me, out of all those people sitting down there?"

"Because you're the only woman village head in the whole county, and you're the county representative to the National People's Congress. Flower stuck in a cowpat, that's what you are. Who else would they want to show?"

"I didn't make Guanzhuang look bad, did I?" she asked more quietly.

"As if. You brought honour to Guanzhuang, and to the people of Xiushui County. Our ambassador, that's what you are."

Qingshu liked to hold onto his phone when he was out and about. He took it out of his pocket now, passing it back and forth between his hands. Fanhua asked him where he was headed, and he told her he had to pay the school a visit. The headmaster had made a call to inform him that the Township Education Bureau was going to be making a visit to Guanzhuang Elementary to sit in on a class. The headmaster was anxious about the condition of the desks, many of which were propped up with bricks because their legs were broken. The little pricks had broken a few windowpanes, too, and they needed fixing if the place was to look respectable.

"You can find the right hole for any radish, and you can find the right man for any job. Why don't you send Xiangsheng?"

Xiangsheng was the committee member for culture, education and public health, as well as the village bookkeeper. In the last few years, however, he'd been increasingly busy doing business in Xiushui Town, where he sold cold noodles. Generational hierarchy meant he called Fanhua "aunt" and Qingshu "uncle", even though he was going on fifty – older than both of them.

"I tried calling, but I couldn't get hold of you. So I gave Xiangsheng a try, and he told me to do it for him."

"Is he still off in Xiushui selling cold noodles?"

"You know what they say – you maintain your army for a thousand days, all so it's ready for that one day when you need it. But when we need him, he's never around. When he gets back here, I'm going to march him down to Qinglin's place."

Fanhua was confused. What did Qinglin have to do with any of this?

Another dirty grin appeared on Qingshu's face. "Because if he doesn't care about our village any more, then that makes him a little bitch. And where do we send all the bitches around here?"

Fanhua was responsible for handing out money for official village use when Xiangsheng wasn't around. She gave Qingshu two hundred *kuai*. "Fix up any tables that need fixing, and sort out the windows. Figure something out yourself if that's not enough."

Qingshu was apparently deeply moved that Fanhua was giving him this money. There was a look of something in his eye that might have been respect.

"Don't rush off just yet," she continued. "I need you to find out how Xue'e managed to slip through the net."

Qingshu scritch-scratched his head. It had been bothering him too, he said. Xue'e must be approaching the end of her first trimester by now, so how had they not spotted it a month ago? Could she conceivably have installed some kind of radar-resisting technology in her belly? There you go again, Qingshu, always finding a way to bring the military into things. Fanhua was getting impatient, and it was her impatience that made her bring Xue'e's expected date forward.

"First trimester? More like the second. And it'll be the third

43

before we know it if we're not careful, and that sprog will be out of her in a flash."

Family planning was the most crucial issue in the village. As the old saying goes, all the trouble in the world adds up to less than you'll find in one belly. Which used to refer to hunger, but was more applicable to pregnancies nowadays. Another swollen belly, another one up the duff. When Qingshu had mentioned that he was ready to shoulder a weightier load, Fanhua had pointed out that his load was plenty weighty already. The most important appointment in America was secretary of state; the most important appointment in Guanzhuang was the director of the Women's Federation. She'd given him his own office as a way of highlighting his importance. And now here he was, swinging the key on its chain as he led her inside.

The first thing you saw on stepping through the door were the two posters on the wall. One showed the acupuncture points on the male and female body, from the front, the rear and either side – every individual point carefully plotted and labelled, right down to the ones on the ear. He'd got this poster from Dr Xianyu. The other was a table listing all the women of childbearing age in the village. The detailing on this poster was even more precise. Each name was placed in one of four categories – Recently Married, Currently Pregnant, With the Ring, Sterilised – and each of these categories was divided into sub-categories, and sub-sub-categories to form a kind of pyramid shape. The Recently Married, for example, were divided between those who had made the application for their birth alloca-tion and those who had not. The former was divided between those who had been approved and those who had not. There were also various little pictures across the paper. Underneath the name of every woman who had remained within her quota was a little ear of wheat icon, to symbolise harvest – though the only person who actually reaped any reward from this "harvest" was Qingshu himself. The women who'd only had the one child got a red flag and star to indi-cate that they were "vanguard troops". Anyone who had the ring got a full moon. Anyone who'd been sterilised got a crescent moon, which was actually a sickle, according to Qingshu.

Qingshu opened a drawer and took out a retractable television aerial, which he carefully wiped with a handkerchief. Then he stepped towards his poster, puffing out his chest and thrusting his legs apart like he was a military general standing before his scale model of the battlefield.

"Quit standing there like an idiot. Hurry up and check," said Fanhua.

Qingshu's antenna roved between the ears of wheat, stars, moons and sickles, until it arrived on the name "Yao Xue'e". Then it followed the direction indicated by a red arrow towards a box marked "Regular Check-Ups". The tip of the antenna tapped against the paper, sometimes resembling a soldier marching on the spot, sometimes looking more like a dragonfly skimming across water.

Qingshu eventually made his report. "No doubt about it. There was no seed in that belly."

"She's already showing," said Fanhua. "How can there have been no seed?"

Qingshu stepped on a chair so that he could lean closer to the top half of the form. "Nope," he finally concluded, "definitely no seed. It's weird. Cherries on a pomegranate tree weird." He jumped down in a special way that involved vaulting over the back of the chair, like a gymnast on a pommel horse. After landing, he looked back up towards the rafters in thought for a while. Then he suddenly pulled open another drawer and took out a copy of the *People's Liberation Army Illustrated News*. Pasted within its pages were various receipts issued by Wangzhai Hospital. Qingshu licked his finger and flicked through them until he found what he was looking for: the receipt for Xue'e's check-up. In the space marked "pregnant", the machine had quite clearly printed the word "no".

"Nope," said Fanhua, "not falling for that one."

"Fucksake, must be a mechanical fault. Hey, you heard about that laser-guided bomb the Americans have now? Controlled by a computer it is, the most advanced in the world, and still they can't eliminate every mechanical problem. And that, as Chairman Mao taught us, is why American Imperialism is a paper tiger."

Fanhua lost her patience completely. "Enough of this crap. Quit twiddling your cock and get yourself over to the hospital. Sort. This. Out."

But then she laughed. There *was* something fishy going on, and she had figured out what. She whistled, in a manly sort of way. The name on the slip was Xue'e's, but the age was wrong. How old was Xue'e? Thirty-five at least, but the age on here said thirty. And, more pertinently, it also noted her "underdeveloped ovaries".

"Make sure you hold onto this," she said to Qingshu. "It may well come in handy."

"Don't worry, Secretary," said Qingshu. "I'll look after it like I would my own eye."

Fanhua again told him not to call her that.

"Well, hurry up and get your job back," he said, "so I won't have to worry about making that mistake."

Fanhua wasn't sure whether Qingshu was playing dumb, or if he genuinely didn't understand that it was her superiors who would decide whether she'd have a chance of being reappointed secretary, not her.

SEVEN

Qingshu didn't want to go to Wangzhai Hospital. He was acting more like a newly-wed bride than a military man, the way he kept finding excuses. He grumbled about how they always laughed at him at the hospital, asking him whether he was the one responsible for this or that pregnancy. It was infuriating. "Better we send a woman," he said. "What about Xiaohong?"

What a suggestion! How could an unmarried maiden like Xiaohong be expected to involve herself in these affairs of the nether regions?

In the end, it was Fanhua who went. First, she looked for Dr Xianyu. Xianyu frequently went to collect medicine from Wangzhai Hospital, so he knew the people there. But when he realised she was asking about Xue'e, he waved her away and spat several times on the floor. Fanhua remembered that Xue'e had history with Xianyu's wife, Cuixian. One of Xue'e's hens had once managed to hop the wall of her yard and had gone and laid an egg in Xianyu's straw pile. Cuixian had taken the egg and boiled it up in a pot. This was the cause of the quarrel, and it was a quarrel that had involved hair-pulling and also biting. Xue'e had turned her sights on Dr Xianyu when he attempted to intervene. He was a rotten one too, she said, you could tell from the look that came into his eyes every time he gave a woman an injection. Not to mention those hands of his, always fondling your arse. A woman could count herself lucky she had only the two arse cheeks because if there was a third available you can be sure he'd try to fondle that one too. Then she turned back on Cuixian. Oh yes, Cuixian might claim she was helping her husband with the injections, but all she really cared about was separating every man in the village from his pants.

Now, as Dr Xianyu looked over the check-up slip, a mysterious smile appeared on his face. "I'm not having anything to do with that insufferable woman."

Fanhua laughed. "Just imagine it's your wife instead of Xue'e. I'm afraid the people in the hospital are going to pull the wool over my eyes, and that's why I need an expert like you."

"If that woman was my wife, I'd have put her to sleep a long time ago. And anyway, there's bugger all I can do if they do try to trick you."

"Don't you know them all pretty well?" asked Fanhua. "I just need to get the result verified and see some actual evidence."

Xianyu's mouth suddenly gaped open. His eyes bulged and his face went blank. Fanhua had no idea what he was playing at. It turned out he was preparing to sneeze. Around these parts, a sneeze was heavy with potential symbolism. It could mean that someone out there was missing you, but it could also mean that someone was badmouthing you. Fanhua worried that Xianyu would apply the latter interpretation to this sneeze. The more afraid of ghosts you are, the more likely they are to come knocking on your door. Sure enough, Xianyu decided someone must have been badmouthing him, exactly as Fanhua had feared he would.

"Has someone been feeding Tiesuo rumours or something? He must be slagging me off behind my back."

"He doesn't know shit," Fanhua hurried to assure him. "Upon the spirit of the Party and my own integrity, I swear your secret's safe. There's nothing to be afraid of. Relax."

Xianyu laughed. He was calm, almost indifferent. He slapped himself across the chest. "I've no need to worry if my rice comes out runny, and if my rice comes out thick, then I'll fuck up that prick. What do I care if he's badmouthing me? What's he going to do about it? Besides, it wasn't like I was doing it for myself. I was carrying out a key national policy. Fuck, I could hardly have done anything more."

The hospital was the vanity project of Wangzhai Township, and a vanity project needed to be reported in the newspaper – or else how would anyone's vanity be satisfied? They had just finished the expansion of the yard, which had been planted with varieties of trees Fanhua had never seen before. The tallest among them was a ginkgo, which was a tree Fanhua *had* seen because there was one in Guanzhuang until it became the ridgepole of the stage roof. This ginkgo in Wangzhai Hospital had been brought in from further afield. It was a bare trunk, shorn of all branches, with several bottles hooked onto it like an intravenous drip. The building to the left of the ginkgo had been newly roofed in glazed tiles, and the building to the right had been topped with a tapering spire above a tin-clad globe, not unlike the Oriental Pearl Television Tower that frequently showed up on the Shanghai satellite TV channel. The fact that this project had been overseen by Township Head Bull had caused some people to remark on how much this construction looked like a bull's pizzle, complete with testicle. This was the first time Fanhua had seen the expansion since it was finished, and she had to admit the resemblance. The gynaecology department was in that building, Xianyu informed her.

"That's weird," said Fanhua. "Why would they make all the pregnant women who come here climb all those stairs?"

"Maybe it's to put them off ever getting pregnant again," Xianyu joked. "Anyway, they do have a lift."

They went to the lift. It smelled of urine, which was appropriate, Fanhua thought, if this elevator shaft was the urethra to the pizzle.

On reaching the right floor, Xianyu looked around for the doctor he knew. When she saw who it was, Fanhua couldn't help feeling a little uneasy. It was the same doctor who'd delivered Beanie. Dianjun had gone to give him a red envelope stuffed with five hundred *kuai* before the birth. The man was named Wang, and he was a native of Wangzhai. And a total wanker, according to Dianjun, who told her they'd been wasting their money. The doctor showed no signs of having recognised her, however. Xianyu offered him a cigarette and then produced the slip of paper.

"The text looks quite clear to me," said Dr Wang.

"This is a woman who's given birth to a child," said Fanhua, "but it says here she has a problem with her ovaries."

"Who says it's not possible for problems to emerge after childbirth?"

"But it says her ovaries are underdeveloped."

"Well, doesn't that just show you the power of science," said Dr Wang. "Number one productive force, that's science. Underdeveloped ovaries isn't necessarily an unsurmountable problem. There are ways of encouraging their development."

"But doesn't underdeveloped ovaries indicate an illness? And besides–"

"Even if it does, it isn't such a big problem. Just a case of slicing off a few ounces of flesh."

"What she's trying to say, Dr Wang," said Xianyu, "is that there's a mistake on this slip. The ovaries of this woman are in excellent condition, but here it says they're underdeveloped. Furthermore, there's an error regarding the woman's age."

"Fuck," said Dr Wang. "Asking a woman her true age? You may as well try to grope a tiger's arse. Who can say when it comes to that sort of thing?"

"Has there been a problem with the machine?" Fanhua asked.

"There can potentially be a problem with anything in life. And that certainly includes machines."

"Look," said Fanhua, running out of patience, "we know this woman is pregnant, but this slip says she wasn't. This is not an insignificant mistake."

"Well, it would be worse off for this comrade of yours if it was the other way round, wouldn't it? How heartbreaking if the form were to tell her she was pregnant when she wasn't." Dr Wang handed the slip back to Xianyu and headed back into his consulting room.

Fanhua lost her temper. "What a total wanker," she muttered. "Is he really that stupid or just pretending?"

"He's pretending, of course," replied Xianyu. "No one wants to go asking for trouble."

Fanhua looked at the signature on the slip. It resembled the wrigglings of a worm, or possibly something a spider had woven, but definitely not the work of any human hand. She pushed Xianyu in the direction of Dr Wang's door. "Ask him whose signature this is."

Xianyu reluctantly did as he was told. Though it was myopia Dr Wang usually struggled with, he now seemed to be having a problem with seeing things up close. He held the slip out a long way in front of him and shook his head. From out in the corridor, Fanhua gave Xianyu a look that told him to show it to the doctor opposite.

But the doctor opposite shook his head too. "This is a highly flamboyant hand," he said. "A cursive script, very quick and refined. So much so that I can't even read the characters. Can you?" he asked Xianyu. Xianyu admitted he could not. "Well then, there you go," said the doctor. "How do you expect me to decipher it if you can't?"

Fanhua wondered whether they ought to go and find Township Head Bull but quickly decided against it. The winter before last she had crossed swords with him over the use of township funds. And the Bull was still nursing a resentment over the closure of the paper plant. Everyone knew he and the factory boss were pals. When the Bull had gone travelling around Southeast Asia to investigate duck husbandry and rice cultivation techniques, it was the boss of the paper plant who'd paid for the trip. It was only thanks to the influence of Fanhua's brother-in-law that the Bull had magnanimously decided not to turn his back on her completely. There'd be trouble if he found out about Xue'e. Might even mean Guanzhuang being made into an example for other villages to learn how not to behave. But fuck it, a mistake was a mistake. Perhaps it might end up being a good thing if the fault really did lie with the machine. That would mean all the villages around here would be left with a few out-of-plan births. Guanzhuang wouldn't be the only one. Besides, she knew she could deal with Xue'e, and there were plenty of other village heads out there who lacked her capability.

Fanhua and Xianyu took the lift back down and emerged from the base of the pizzle. They went out to hail a ride in the street. Fanhua was about to stop a minibus, but Xianyu stopped her. "Let's at least take a proper car," he said.

"What, afraid of losing face?"

Xianyu looked embarrassed. "I already lost all the face I might have once had." Then he suddenly slapped himself on the head. "I just thought of something. I know someone who could help us."

Fanhua realised at once who he meant. There was a woman named Fan, an educated youth who had been sent down to the countryside. She was a barefoot doctor when she was younger. Back in those days, there were two people Dr Fan had idolised: one was the eponymous barefoot doctor of the film *Spring Beansprout*, and the other was Li Xiuming, the actor who'd played the part. In a way, she was one of the very first fangirls. She even changed her own name from Fan Kangmei, borrowing one syllable each from the character and the actor to form the name Fan Miaoxiu. She and Xianyu had been an item when they were studying together at Xiushui medical college. These days, she was the head of the inpatient section.

Dr Fan was just stepping out of the ward when Xianyu and Fanhua found their way to her part of the hospital. From a distance, her freshly dyed hair made her look young, but the effect was ruined when you saw her up close. Looked like black wood-ear fungus growing out of rotten wood. But you could still see a certain youthful jealousy in the way she regarded Xianyu, blended with bitterness and a hint of mockery. And a trace of something rancid.

Fanhua told her how young she was looking. Younger than ever.

Dr Fan gave a tight smile. "So, who's ill in your family?" she asked Xianyu. "Not your better half, I take it?"

"Hey, am I only allowed to come and see you when disaster strikes?" said Xianyu.

She led them into her office and sat them down. "I won't offer you any water," she said. "We've run out of disposable cups. So come on then, what is it?"

Xianyu waffled on for a while, then had Fanhua bring out the slip as he explained the situation.

"Don't bother," said Dr Fan when she'd taken a glance at the slip. "Give up now."

Fanhua was startled. She pressed Dr Fan for an explanation.

Dr Fan glanced outside and then closed the door behind her. "This can't be a mechanical fault. It's just a urine test, very simple indeed. Mistakes are rare."

Xianyu gave Fanhua a look that said: Finally, we've found the right person.

"No matter what I might say to you now," Dr Fan continued, "I'll deny everything once you step out of that door."

"Understood," said Xianyu.

"We were never here," added Fanhua.

"This person has already been transferred elsewhere," said Dr Fan. "She has... ascended."

"You mean... she's dead?" said Xianyu.

"Well, she's certainly heading in the direction of the heavens," said Dr Fan. "You might know her, actually. The name's Zhang Shiying. Quartz Zhang. She has an older sister living in your village."

"Who's that?" asked Fanhua. "First I've heard."

"She's very beautiful, Quartz's sister. Her name's Zhang Shiliu, Pomegranate Zhang."

"Pomegranate Zhang?" said Xianyu. "She's good-looking all right, but no use to anyone. There are only four barren women in the village, and she's one of them."

"I don't know for sure whether that's true of her younger sister as well," said Dr Fan, "but I suspect it might be. Do you know the Korean actress, Kim Hee-sun? No? Xianyu, I thought you were a man of letters, don't you ever take time out of your books to glance across a newspaper? This Kim Hee-sun is the most beautiful woman in Korea. And this woman I'm talking about? People call her the Chinese Kim Hee-sun. Times have changed. These days, you can count on your looks to earn you a living. Or indeed a promotion."

"So she's been promoted?" asked Fanhua. "To the Xiushui gynaecology department?"

"Higher."

"Director of Xiushui hospital?" tried Xianyu.

"Come on, you can do better than that. Higher."

"Any higher than that would be the moon," said Xianyu. "She can hardly have turned into a moon goddess like Chang'e."

"Chang'e remained a widow forever, remember. This one wouldn't last a day as a single widow. She married the son of the county head. Cherries sprouting on the pomegranate tree, eh? Now she's the number two at the bureau of hygiene."

Fanhua was confused. Why would such a person be inclined to help Tiesuo?

"There are two possibilities," said Dr Fan, who certainly wasn't one to mince her words. "Either she made a genuine mistake because she's an embroidered pillowcase – nice to look at, but empty inside. Or she did it on purpose because it costs money to embroider a pillowcase, after all."

Fanhua was stunned. For a while, she didn't know what to say. If it weren't for Xianyu's reminder, she would have forgotten why they were here.

"Could you do another check," he asked, "to prove that the last one was definitely a mistake?"

"Not a problem," said Dr Fan. "We do the tests once a month. Just bring her along when the time comes."

That would be splendid, said Xianyu, wonderful. Also, he asked, would it be possible for her to check the result personally this time, to make sure there was no room for error? For the sake of his own reputation.

Dr Fan glanced at him. "This sprog in her belly," she said. "It's not yours, is it?"

Xianyu hastened to explain, vowing this and swearing that and clutching at Fanhua's arm so that she'd corroborate his story. Dr Fan's gaze moved along Fanhua's arm and up to her face. Almost as if she thought Fanhua was the woman whose name was written on that medical report slip. What a dreary woman, Fanhua thought to herself. I was going to thank her for all her help, but now I don't think I'll bother.

EIGHT

Qingmao had a catchphrase when he first assumed office, a quotation of Chairman Mao's concerning the importance of ideological work: "The dust won't sweep itself up if no broom comes along." He gave this catchphrase another airing when he reached the end of his term, reminding the new officials not to forget this most precious legacy. When Fanhua went to see Xue'e the next day, she was planning to use the broom of ideology to sweep the dust off the pregnant woman's belly. She took Qingshu along with her.

"You're the one who should be dealing with this in the first place," she said. "This is your domain."

But Qingshu was in no mood for gratitude. He said that County Head Zhang had announced on TV that every village needed to have one leader who was ultimately responsible for everything. Which meant Qingshu was basically no more than an errand boy. Qingshu, Qingshu, when the going gets tough, he's more likely to retreat into his shell like a tortoise than to go charging off towards enemy lines.

"Well, you do as you see fit," she said, frowning.

Qingshu continued to mutter his complaints, but he fell in line behind her.

Tiesuo had gone off to work on the new Xiushui Town highway, leaving Xue'e alone at home. He wouldn't have been given this job in the first place were it not for the village's recommendation. Thanks to her brother-in-law, Fanhua had managed to arrange positions for ten men from Guanzhuang Village who were lacking decent prospects after suffering losses in the livestock business. All Xue'e had to look after were a dozen or so hens, and one pig. The cluck of hens, a baby's cry, one fat hog in the pigsty. Twelve years ago this would have meant a prosperous family, but not any more. It had been twenty years of reforming and opening up already, and only the most hopeless basket cases were still living off hens' arses. The black pig was currently scratching itself against a scholar tree, its skinny little tail wiggling in the air to whisk the flies away. It looked to be quite content with its lot. Fanhua gazed at the pig and tried to figure out what she was going to do with Xue'e. The remaining leaves on the branches cast shadows the size of old copper coins against the wall. Every time the hog scraped against the trunk, the shadows were thrown into chaos.

Xue'e came outside, cooing to her hens as she brought them a broken bowl brimming with maize.

"Quiet down," she told them, "Auntie's here."

Fanhua was forced to improvise. "We're here to check out that big colour TV of yours," she said. She'd lost count of how many times she'd heard the story of how Tiesuo won the Hitachi television in a raffle, but she acted like it was news to her. "So Tiesuo picked the raffle ticket to win this TV," she continued. "How did he get such lucky hands? Was it scented oil he rubbed into them on the day of the draw, or soap?"

A wistful expression came across Xue'e's features. Her eyes closed halfway as she luxuriated in the memory, like she was savouring some delicious dessert. When Tiesuo went out that day, with his shovel across his shoulder, he'd run into a monk. When was the last time anyone'd seen a monk in Guanzhuang? Must have been a hundred years at least. And he was no ordinary mortal, this monk; he had reached the point of transcending mortality and achieving enlightenment. What were the chances? A monk, here, and for Tiesuo to be the one who ran into him? (Fanhua didn't bother pointing out that there were several monks living at the Temple of Universal Salvation just round the corner from Guanzhuang, and she'd encountered them on the road herself.) That day, Xue'e continued, it just so happened that they'd built the road as far as the entrance to the new

Xiushui Town supermarket. Tiesuo remembered how Manny and Laddy had been squabbling about buying a pencil case, so he went into the supermarket on his lunchtime break. They were cheap though, the pencil cases, just four *kuai* each, so he bought two of them for eight *kuai*. He wasn't in the habit of getting a receipt with his purchases – no one bothered with that in the countryside – but he asked for one when he realised that was what everyone else was doing. The lady working in the shop told him he'd have a chance of winning a prize if he bought something else to bring the total to ten *kuai*. Because he was a sensitive soul, more delicate than an eggshell, Tiesuo found it hard to turn down a lady. So he bought a rollerball pen too, and then went along with the others to pick a raffle ticket. The Buddha was smiling on him that day. The person in front of him won nothing, and the person after him won nothing, but Tiesuo, yes, Tiesuo, he got lucky.

"You should thank Manny and Laddy as well then," said Fanhua. "Tiesuo wouldn't have won anything if they hadn't wanted those pencil cases, no matter how gifted he might be."

"Gifted my arse," Qingshu butted in. "Talent had nothing to do with it."

"Well anyway, you have a good pair of girls there, no matter which way you look at it. Linghui's out there working on the road too, right? He had an equal chance, and he didn't win anything."

"That's right," said Xue'e, "Linghui spent more than seventy *kuai* that day, and he still came back empty-handed."

"That's why you're lucky to have those two," said Fanhua. "When they grow up, you and Tiesuo can sit back and wait for the riches to roll in."

Then Fanhua asked how much Tiesuo earned in a day working on the new road. Xue'e didn't reply. She stood up and went into the inner room, shifting things around until she found the plastic bag she was looking for. She turned it upside down, and several pairs of leather shoes tumbled out.

"That fucking cunt," she said, "this is all he sends me. Last month it was five pairs. Worth seventy *kuai* each he says, a famous brand name. I used to wear good brand-name stuff, you know, back before I got married. To hell with it, I thought, let's act like I bought these for myself. I tried on one pair, but my toe went right through

57

them before the week was out. Eventually, I find out that they were made by the sister-in-law of the traffic bureau chief. That's right, made in Xiushui!"

"Well now," said Fanhua, "you ought to return them, but you've already worn them. You've clearly been had. You need to be more careful about this sort of thing. Why didn't you look them over more carefully before you started wearing them?"

"Is that Bureau Chief White you mean?" Qingshu interrupted. "He was in the army with me."

Xue'e pointed at Qingshu. "White, right, that's the one. A white-faced crook, that's who he is."

Qingshu evaded her wagging finger. "He might be White in name, but there's nothing white about his skin. He's as black as they come. Back in our army days, he was a paragon of Learning From Lei Feng. He learned from the model soldier Lei Feng, we learned from him, and the new recruits learned from us. We'd do anything he told us to do."

Eventually, they got onto the check-up slip. "You see Xue'e, you're just too careless, that's your problem. It's no big deal when we're talking about mixing up mung beans and sesame seeds, or dealing with those shoes. But you can't be careless when it comes to something like a medical check-up, now can you? Did you realise there was a mistake on your form when you last went to the hospital? No, I didn't think so. Qingshu, could you please take out that slip and show it to Xue'e? Have a good look. There's the mistake, see?"

Something strange came over Xue'e's expression, something like a smile but not a smile. Though she continued to sit there, motionless, her hair somehow flopped down to cover half of her face.

"Lucky it was just a family planning test," said Fanhua, "because that's something we can correct easily enough. If it was something involving an actual illness, and we hadn't spotted it, well, that could have been serious."

Xue'e looked at the slip. The sound of her breath grew louder, and she pressed her tongue against the inside of her cheek like she was suffering from toothache.

Fanhua's criticism of her continued. "If you're careless when you oughtn't to be careless, you can end up getting into trouble. Obviously it's not your fault – the responsibility lies with the hospital. But you must be sure to look over the slip carefully when they give it to you. I'm guessing they somehow got you mixed up with someone else. It might be that this other woman has a problem but doesn't know about it. She might be forever urging her man to knock her up, not realising that it'll do no good. Cherries can't sprout on a pomegranate tree, now can they?" She was smiling as she neared the end of her speech. "Qingshu, what do you say?"

"Sprout my arse," he said. "They sure as hell can't."

When you've built your bridge, it's time to cross the river. When you've tied up your donkey, it's time to turn the millstone. Fanhua was now in a position to ease Qingshu into the conversation. "Now Xue'e, there's no need to thank me. Qingshu's the one you should be thanking. It was his sharp eyes that spotted the problem."

Qingshu was momentarily flustered. "Who, what, me?" It was like he'd been scalded. "I'm not looking to take any credit," he said, shaking his head.

"Well yes, I was the one who asked Qingshu to double check, of course. And it was when we did the double check that we discovered the mistake. So there's no time to waste! Let's get you back to the hospital for another check-up. And you'd better make sure you're not so careless this time. Pay closer attention. Don't worry about the cost, the village will pay for everything."

Xue'e tucked her hair behind her ear. She repeated this gesture several times. The same unnatural smile remained on her face. Well, thought Fanhua, you can't say I haven't given you an exit. Now all you have to do is walk through it.

But Xue'e's reply astonished her.

"Looks fine to me," she said, handing the slip back to Qingshu. "Can't see anything wrong with it."

Now it was Fanhua's turn to smile unnaturally. Then she was laughing out loud, so hard she bent over double. "Seriously?" she said. "You can't see anything wrong with it? How about the damn ovaries?"

Xue'e was calm now. "What are these things you call 'ovaries'?" she said, crossing one leg over the other. "Where do they grow? Can you show me?"

"Where exactly did Manny come from?" asked Fanhua when she

had brought her laughter under control. "And Laddy, where did she come from? Did they spring from a crack in a stone, hmm?"

"The same place as your Beanie, that's where," said Xue'e.

"The ovaries are where ovulation occurs," said Qingshu.

"And what might 'ovulation' be? You're not going to fool me, I've been to high school too you know. You're talking about eggs, hens. Director Meng, have you seen a woman lay an egg?"

"No," Qingshu admitted, "I have not. Secretary, have you ever seen such a thing?"

"Xue'e, don't play dumb," said Fanhua. Her tone was hardening. "Do as you're told. Go have another check-up. This is for your own good."

"How do you expect me to check my ovaries when I've no idea what an ovary even is? What am I supposed to get checked?"

"Or would you like to step into the inner room," asked Fanhua, "where you can take off your clothes and I'll point them out for you."

Xue'e's tongue was pressed against the inside of her cheek again. For a long time, she said nothing. It was so quiet you could hear the hog snuffling outside. Through the bamboo screen, Fanhua saw a cockerel gliding down in cheerful pursuit of a hen, his wings spread wide. The wall of the yard was covered in soapwort flowers, and a leopard cat was sauntering across it, arching his back and meowing. He appeared perfectly at ease. The atmosphere inside, by contrast, was so tense it felt like being inside a pressure cooker. Fanhua pointed outside, in an attempt to lighten the mood.

"Look, Xue'e, everyone's keeping busy in your house, even the chickens."

This evoked no response from Xue'e, who was gnawing on her knuckles and staring at the ceiling, acting like there was no one else present.

"What, do you really not understand?" asked Fanhua. "Take off your trousers then, and I'll explain."

Xue'e lifted her arse out of her seat, as though she really was going to pull off her trousers, but when Fanhua stood up she sat right back down again. "If you were Cuixian, I'd take them off," she said, "but you're not. Cuixian pulls trousers off women as well as men. Even little Manny knows the word for that. A *homosexual*."

60

Ugh, Xue'e, so spiteful. Incapable of missing any opportunity to have another go at Xianyu's wife. She was trying desperately to stall them because she was too stupid to see a good deal when it was staring her in the face. Xue'e was the kind of person who'd refuse to squeeze out a tear until the coffin was actually in front of her.

Fanhua wasn't laughing any more. "Xue'e, let's speak frankly. Are you pregnant again? It looks to me like you are. Do my eyes deceive me? No? Then this is an out-of-plan pregnancy, which is no laughing matter. There'll be a fine to pay, and it'll cost you more than ten of those television sets."

Xue'e suddenly stood up, drew aside the bamboo screen and stepped outside. Neither Fanhua nor Qingshu had any idea what she was playing at. They peered through the screen as she waddled outside into the middle of the yard, before springing explosively off the ground, sending the feeding hens scattering.

"Motherfucking cunt!" she yelled to the four walls. "Think you can come in here and walk all over me? Go ahead and take a leak so you can have a good hard look at yourself, reflected in a puddle of piss. Think I'm a pushover? Fuck you, and fuck all your ancestors too!" She yelled another expletive to the west, and then another to the east, and then she leapt three feet high in the air again. "Fed your conscience to the dogs, have you? A dog who thinks he can catch mice, that's what you are. Fuck. This. Cunt. And all. Her. Ancestors."

Qingshu was smiling. "She does have a way with words."

Fanhua had lost her temper, along with any inclination to indulge this sort of talk. "Watch it."

"Look at her though," he said, pointing at Xue'e. "She was fine a minute ago, and then just like that she turns into a vicious little shrew."

"There's no reasoning with a woman like this," said Fanhua. "Get yourself over to the work site and bring Tiesuo back here. And let me know as soon as he arrives."

A crowd of women and children had gathered outside the front gate to see what all the fuss was about. One of them was Pei Zhen, still knitting her jumper.

"Is there a fight going on?" she asked when she saw Qingshu. "How can Tiesuo treat her that way? It's not easy for Xue'e, looking after the kids at home on her own." She turned to the woman standing next to her, Gawp's wife. "No matter how we stiffen our spines," she said, "the fists of our husbands will always be harder."

Gawp's wife came from the same village as Xue'e, so she was naturally going to take her side. Gawp and his wife were cut from the same cloth: he was dumb and she was dumber. A pair of morons they were. Gawp's wife spat the phlegm from her mouth before speaking. "Hey," she said, hands on her hips, "look who it is, the director of the women's association. You'd better make sure you stand up for the women around here." She grabbed hold of Qing-shu's sleeve when she saw that he was attempting to leave. "A runaway cock! Our uncle from the PLA's attempting to desert. You're going nowhere."

Naturally, the sharper members of the crowd had figured out that this had something to do with a pregnancy. Qingmao, the former committee secretary, was one of them. His wife was carrying their six-month-old grandson, Merry, and she carried on feeding him milk from a bottle as she spoke: "That Tiesuo is a piece of work. What has Xue'e ever done wrong, apart from failing to produce a son? And what's so good about a son? They're good for nothing except driving you crazy." She spoke in a solemn voice, but there was kindness in her solemnity. These were the qualities that came from having been the wife of a high official. She tucked the milk bottle under her arm so that her hand was free to tickle Merry's little willy. "Merry! Am I right, or am I right? All you know how to do is eat, and all you know how to do when you've finished eating is how to drive people crazy." And then she sang a song about the benefits of daughters:

> *A daughter is a gift divine,*
> *She'll make a coat from melon rind,*
> *With pumpkin peel a sleeve she'll hem,*
> *She'll carve a button from gourd stem,*
> *And when she's finished her costume,*
> *She'll find a squash to be her groom.*

She handed Merry over to Qingshu, and went off to try to mediate the dispute before he had a chance to react. Qingshu clutched this squidgy object like it was a plate of tofu he didn't know what to do with. His palms suddenly became hot, an alarming sensation that almost made him lift the baby over his head. Merry had pissed himself. Qingshu hurriedly passed him onto Pei Zhen. She tried to duck out of it, but Qingshu knew how to handle her. He leant in close and whispered something in her ear. Stunned, she meekly took the baby from him. "You have the sharpest of eyes," he said quietly, "and the committee thanks you."

Once Qingshu had left, all the onlookers rushed into the yard. Gawp's blustering wife took the lead.

"Tiesuo, you get out here," she yelled. "When has Xue'e ever put a foot wrong? She spends all day working on your behalf, and then she climbs into bed with you at night. Does she have it easy? Come on, get out here."

The bamboo screen was drawn aside, and out stepped Fanhua, carrying a pair of leather shoes.

Gawp's wife was dumbfounded. "Well I'll be damned." She took a step back as Fanhua moved in her direction, and when her feet bumped into the tree she crouched down on the floor and covered her face with her hands.

Laughing, Fanhua pulled her back to her feet, addressing her respectfully as "sister-in-law".

"Take a look everyone," said Fanhua, standing in front of them all with the shoes in her hand. "These shoes were issued by the authorities, and as you can see, they've split at the toes after just a couple of days of wear. Who wouldn't lose their temper over such a thing? How are ordinary folk supposed to get by? I'm sure you'd respond with strong language if it happened to you." By this point, Xue'e had already ducked back inside. "Don't worry Xue'e," Fanhua called after her, "I'll take care of this for you." She went over to the door and pulled back the screen. "When all's said and done, it's just a pair of shoes. Nothing worth getting worked up over. It's bad for your health, anger like that. If you're not careful, we'll have to get Tiesuo back here to look after you." Fanhua was an impressive performer, and the neighbours eventually drifted away, convinced that Xue'e had lost her temper over a pair of shoes and there was nothing more to see here.

All the amicability disappeared from Fanhua's face when she and

Xue'e were the only ones left. "Made enough of a scene for one day, have you? If you haven't, then by all means carry on. And then, when you've got it all out of your system, you can take yourself down to Wangzhai Hospital. Have Tiesuo go with you. Don't worry, Xue'e, the village'll reimburse him for lost earnings. Does that seem generous enough to you? We're solid, you and me, right? The bones might break but the tendons still hold us together." She stuffed the shoes into the plastic bag. "You can't leave the Buddha halfway to heaven, and you can't leave a good deed half finished. Dianjun's back in town. I'll take these and get him to fix them for you. And if he doesn't do a good job, you have my permission to beat the crap out of him."

NINE

It was a big lunch. Fanhua's mother had made a selection of dishes, both meat and vegetable. There was one dish that was especially meaty: pizzle and potato stew. The bull's member came from a jar. Every now and again, Fanhua's brother-in-law passed on a selection of the food jars he'd been given as gifts. Every time Fanhua's father dredged the dish with his chopsticks, he somehow managed to end up with a chunk of potato. Dianjun's face reddened as he chewed on a length of pizzle. Fanhua didn't dare allow herself to laugh. There's a poignancy in the love parents show their children. She knew how much it would mean to them to have a grandson to hold, and this pizzle was their way of encouraging Dianjun, of giving him an extra boost.

And then there were the potatoes. The potatoes had significance too, of course. A fortnight ago, Fanhua's mother had told her that she'd heard you were supposed to eat more potatoes if you wanted a boy. When Fanhua asked who'd told her this, her mother replied that it was an intellectual, and intellectuals were the kind of people who knew what they were talking about. Fanhua suspected she meant Pei Zhen, and her suspicions were soon confirmed. Pei Zhen told me it's not enough to eat potato, her mother continued. You have to eat a *lot* of potato. At least two. Because what do two potatoes look like when you put them together? A boy's balls, that's what. Fanhua's mother

65

blamed herself, she said, all her decades of life had been a waste when she'd failed to learn such basic principles.

What was Pei Zhen thinking? Was she making fun of an old lady? Sure was lucky she's a teacher. Was that what she was hoping for, for Fanhua to make the mistake of getting pregnant? Some days later, when Fanhua was out doing maintenance on the ridges in the field, she had the opportunity to ask Pei Zhen what potatoes were supposed to have to do with producing a boy. She said nothing about potatoes looking like balls this time, instead coming up with some sciency speak about how potatoes increased the alkalinity in the womb, which made the conception of a male more probable. Obviously, Fanhua's mother would have struggled to understand any such talk of alkalinity, but the resemblance between balls and potatoes was a notion she could get her head around. As a result, however, she didn't realise that Fanhua was the one who was supposed to be eating the potatoes, and now she was placing another of them in Dianjun's bowl.

"Dianjun," said Fanhua's father, gazing at the potato, "it's not new year, or a festival. Why have you come home?"

Dianjun's reply was a glib one. "Mainly so as to show the appropriate filial respect to my in-laws."

"Oh, well, aren't we blessed," said Fanhua's father.

Conscious that her father wasn't impressed, Fanhua hastened to explain: "I was the one who asked him to come home because I need his help." Her father didn't respond. "I needed him to come home and help me write my speech." Her voice turned girlish. "I'll need my two men to lead the applause when the time comes, OK?"

Her father's immediately assumed a serious expression. "Everyone must applaud," he said, rapping his bowl against the table. "We can't be having any awkward silences," he said to his wife.

"That's right," said Dianjun. "You know what they say, when one dog barks, a hundred more join in."

"Dog, what dog? Who are you calling a dog?" asked Fanhua's father.

"It's only an expression," Dianjun hurriedly explained. "I just mean that once one person leads the applause, everyone else will follow."

Fanhua was still waiting for Qingshu to get back with Tiesuo.

Dinner was over, the dishes were washed, and still there was no sign of them. Getting nervous, she decided to take Beanie out for a walk with Dianjun. As well as wanting to relax, she was also keen to show Dianjun what had been going on around the village, and – more importantly – to draw his attention to her achievements, so he knew what to put into the speech when the time came. She had other plans for him too, of course. She was hoping he'd meet up with some of his less reputable friends and learn which way they were leaning. Call it canvassing on her behalf. There was no shortage of reasons why she ought to retain her post and reclaim her Party secretary title, but still, better safe than sorry. How does that saying go? Human hearts are clad in skin, and canine hearts are clad in fur. You can never be sure what people are thinking. If anyone was planning to cause her trouble, she'd like to know about it in advance. Heck, her blueprint for success was only half done, and she could hardly leave it unfinished.

Dianjun picked up a packet of Mighty Chinas and put on his shades.

"Take those toad specs off!" Fanhua said, grabbing them from him and passing them to Beanie to play with. Dianjun pulled out his toy telescope again so that he would be able to fully appreciate the mountains of home, he said, and the rivers of home, and the passing clouds of home, just like in that Fei Xiang song.

Fanhua gave his nose a tweak. "Never mind the passing clouds," she said, "it's the result of our reforming and opening up you need to be concentrating on."

When they arrived at the entrance to the village, she stamped her foot on the asphalt road. "See this?" she said to Dianjun. "I got it resurfaced. Remember the year you married me? This is where your car got stuck in the mud when it drove into the village. But now, as you can see, it's smoother than a threshing floor."

"But don't forget, it was you who married me, not the other way round."

Fanhua gave him a shove. "Enough of that. Haven't I promised already? Once my parents aren't around, Beanie's going to take your surname, Zhang. So you tell me who married who."

To the west of the village was a river, which the villagers referred to as "the west river". On the far side of the west river, there had once been a paper plant. The plant belonged to Wangzhai Township, which'd paid twenty thousand *kuai* to Guanzhuang each year for the use of village land. Twenty years ago, that would have been a considerable sum, enough to buy two hundred pigs, or pay the entire village's electricity bill, or build two whole stages. But nowadays it would barely pay for half a stage. Even more infuriating was the sewage from the plant. It was like baby cack, yellow, thick and putrid. Contaminated the whole river.

When Qingmao was in office, he'd promised the villagers he'd renegotiate the deal with the paper plant, and force them to clean up the sewage themselves, and if they didn't comply, then the village would have no choice but to block the gates to the plant. But several years passed, and the sewage continued to spill into the river. They did prettify the entrance to the mill, however. The limestone sentry lions were replaced with white marble lions. One of the village idiots claimed these were foreign lions, because when he was a soldier in Beijing – back when he still had his wits about him – he had encountered several foreigners, and the skin of these foreigners was white. It stood to reason then, he argued, that white-skinned foreigners would produce white statues. His absurd logic somehow caught on, and many villagers became genuinely convinced that these lions were foreign imports.

Two foreign lions sprawled outside the village. You couldn't ask for a better symbol. What did they symbolise? The fact that the paper plant was in the ascendancy, and Qingmao was losing. He almost slapped himself in the face during one village meeting, but he insisted he wasn't entirely to blame. His reasoning was simple: you might walk to the ends of the Earth, or even fly to the moon in a spaceship, but an arm could never triumph over a thigh. Guanzhuang Village was the arm in this analogy, and Wangzhai Township was the thigh. And this was why Qingmao could not be held responsible.

Fanhua pointed towards the west river and asked Dianjun if he remembered how she had dealt with it. I wasn't having any of that, she said. Township Head Bull was the problem, and despite his inflated sense of self-importance, he was still only a township head, at the end of the day. The thigh might be strong, but the thigh of the state was stronger still. If he was chairman of the whole country, well, then I might have had to admit defeat. But he's not.

Fanhua wasn't lying. She started renegotiating the deal with the paper plant immediately after assuming office. A female general in the field is truly the equal of two men. She persuaded them to install streetlights for the village and managed to get them to "sponsor" the school's purchase of desks, projectors and a computer. And she had them build a brand-new stone arch bridge across the river, under the pretext of consolidating the bond between village and paper plant – as well as making it easier for the children of the plant workers to get to school. They grumbled about it at first, but they coughed up in the end without too much complaining. Of course, Meng Xiaohong deserved some credit for that, because she was the one who came up with the plan. She said she'd heard about some rule changes regarding education. In order to lighten the burden on primary school students, it would no longer be permitted to assign them homework. But the school could get around it by having them do their homework in the classroom; add an extra hour onto the school day, and make the students stay until they'd finished all their assignments. In which case, Xiaohong said, she was sure they wouldn't have to wait longer than six months before one of the plant workers' children fell into the river on their way home from school. Which would simplify the negotiations considerably. Under normal circumstances, no one would have paid much attention to an inexperienced girl like Xiaohong, but Fanhua had a lot of respect for her. She took her advice, and sure enough, before too long there was an incident involving not one but two children falling into the river, a boy and a girl, both from important families. Splendid, said Xiaohong, it's a dragon and a phoenix bringing us prosperity all right. Good things come in twos. Soon enough, the new bridge had risen over the river. Finally, they managed to get the plant to make a one-off payment of five hundred thousand yuan as a pollution penalty. Once the money had arrived, Fanhua used her sister Fanrong's connections to get a bunch of reporters over from the provincial capital to do an exposé on the sewage disposal. And soon enough, the decree came down from the provincial authorities announcing that the plant would be shut down. Fanhua knew that her next step was going to involve taking control of the paper plant. She had already examined the original documents and discovered that the lease on the land to the township lasted for a period of twenty years. That period would come to an end on the fifteenth day of the next lunar year. This was a big deal.

The return of the paper plant to Guanzhuang would be comparable to the return of Hong Kong to China, as far as the villagers were concerned. It would go down in the annals of history.

"It's my proudest achievement. But you can't mention my name in connection with the plant, or Fanrong's. Those fuckers'd try to find some way of getting revenge. Find some way to mention it, but leave it at that. Say the village committee respects the will of the people and has succeeded in its endeavours to bring the sewage problem under control. And if I get re-elected, then I'm going to raise the funds to take control of the plant and make a fresh start. You can emphasise that."

"What kind of factory are you going to turn it into?" asked Dianjun.

Fanhua laughed. "Don't you have your telescope? Have a look and tell me what you think."

"A shoe factory, maybe," said Dianjun, "but you don't have enough skilled workers like me. And as for a wholesale shoe market, well, we're too far away from any of the big cities."

Fanhua lifted up her daughter and pointed towards the wall of the factory. "Beanie, tell me, what do you see?"

"A zoo," Beanie exclaimed. "Where are the dinosaurs?"

"You see, Beanie gets it. I want to set up an animal-breeding farm. You'll have to help me figure out what animals to breed. It was Qinglin and his wolf who gave me the idea. Make the whole village rich, that's the dream. You won't need to go off to Shenzhen. It's just a temporary job, after all. You can find another one any place. You can stay here and help me keep an eye on this place."

"I understand. Milady's dream is to mate and to breed, and to breed and to mate, in order to bring everyone prosperity."

"Behave," said Fanhua.

They encountered various other people as they were walking along. There was nothing unusual in the greeting they offered Fanhua – "Have you eaten?" – but there was deference, and a hint of reserve, in the way they said it. Dianjun might have been a head taller than Fanhua, but their eyes always went to her first. They weren't so reserved when they spoke to Dianjun. It was all "damn this" and "fuck that", and it wasn't long before he'd given away almost all of his cigarettes.

"Where did you get them from?" Fanhua asked him every time he handed one out. "They're not fakes, are they?"

This was Dianjun's cue. "Fakes?" he swiftly replied. "Fuck no! With other brands, I can't always tell real from fake, but I sure as hell know what a real Mighty China tastes like!"

TEN

Behind Guanzhuang was a range of hills, spread across an area of three hundred *mu*. There was once a time when they were covered with fruit trees. Pear trees, apricot trees and peach trees on the lower slopes, and walnut trees higher up. But the imperative to overtake Britain and America during the Great Leap Forward, to produce vast quantities of iron and steel, led to them disappearing overnight. Later, they were replanted, but the campaign to "Learn from Dazhai in agriculture" was introduced before they had a chance to bear fruit. Which meant what? Cutting them down again, that's what. A few years ago, they'd planted trees there yet again. Poplars and elms, this time, rather than fruit trees. A wise decision, the villagers believed, because these were fast-growing trees, and if circumstances did require them to be chopped down once more, then at least they could be used for timber, and no one would have any great cause for grief. But no matter how fast the trees grew, they were still too slow to keep up with the times. The poplars had barely reached the diameter of a man's arm when a real estate tycoon from Xiushui Town showed up, accompanied by a county-level official, and announced his desire to build villas on this land. Qingmao did the maths: if one *mu* sold for a hundred thousand, then three hundred *mu* would make thirty million. The village would struggle to amass such a sum even if everyone stopped eating and drinking for a decade. This was a shortcut to prosperity. Qingmao would have to be the stupidest moron in all the land to turn down such an excellent opportunity. It was a no-brainer. The trees were soon chopped down again. But the real estate tycoon never came back, and when they made inquiries they learned that the fucker was in jail.

Fanhua had come here for two reasons: to relax, yes, but also to get Dianjun to help her figure out what to do with this land.

Mantled by sky, the undulating hills stretched out as far as the eye could see. The white mirror in the distance was a body of water. There was still the occasional poplar, a strut between earth and sky that looked like a lonely orphan from this distance. Not too far off from the village was a hollow in the ground where the weeds grew to waist height. This was the spot where the two of them had once rolled about together in the days before their marriage. They might have ended up covered in burrs, arses criss-crossed with red and black scratches, but they were happy. Their hearts felt like they were brimming with honey. The sight of the place now brought a faint smile to each of their faces. Without saying anything, they started walking in that direction.

"You could raise camels here," said Dianjun. "They'll eat anything, camels."

On their way, they ran into Li Hao and his flock of sheep. The three of them had all been school classmates. Li Hao had two nicknames back in Xiushui Number One Middle School: one was "Chemistry Brain" and the other was "Decimal Point". Chemistry Brain was because his mind was quicker than any ordinary human brain, and Decimal Point was due to his ability to recite a long string of the digits of pi. He did have one other nickname, but no one dared say it to his face: "Iron Crutch Li". Crippled by congenital polio, Li Hao had always refused to use crutches. His greatest nemesis was the comedian Meng Qingshu most adored: Zhao Benshan. This was because Zhao Benshan had once performed a skit entitled "Selling Crutches", and for a long time afterwards some kids used to shout "Zhao Benshan!" at Li Hao whenever they saw him. It wouldn't be entirely accurate to say he *never* used crutches when he was at school. There was at least one occasion each year when he did, and that was the end-of-year prize-giving ceremony. Being disabled, all he had to do was whisk a broom around and he'd be hailed as a model worker; hence he was invariably selected as one of the best students in the grade. So he had to make sure he looked the part when he made his way onto the stage to receive his commendation before all those staring eyes. Had they only been a little less stringent in the physical check-up section of his university entrance exam, he would have easily soared to the heights of officialdom, where there are mistresses aplenty. But instead, it was only sheep he had jurisdiction over now, and he'd failed to even find a wife. Fanhua had considered getting him made treasurer of the village committee, but he'd been absent during the last round of elections. Off in search of a prospective match. Li Hao had said to Xiangsheng that "problems of the cock" were the primary problem of revolution, and the rest would follow once they were resolved. But Li Hao failed to resolve his "problems of the cock", and missed out on the chance to be elected. There were reports he'd taken out his anger on his sheep, beating several of them so badly they were crippled as a result. You can buy a remedy for any sickness in the world, but there's no medicine for regret. Mistakes can't be undone. Fortunately, there's always a next time. Fanhua was once again planning to bring him into the administration. There were a dozen or so handicapped people in the village, and – a couple of idiots aside – they all had their wits about them, to a certain degree. Li Hao was basically their leader, and if Fanhua had his support then she could count on all of their votes too. It would be to their advantage if she did eventually manage to get this breeding farm going. The sharper among them could take on management jobs, and the less sharp could sweep floors, answer telephones, handle mail. And the two idiots? Well, since they were incapable of distinguishing a foul smell from a fragrant one, they may as well take charge of dealing with the manure.

A dozen or so sheep were dotted across the hills like little white clouds. Beanie wriggled around in Dianjun's arms when she saw them and demanded to be let down so she could go and play with the nice sheepies. One of the sheep came trotting towards them. A burr glittered in its wool, sharp like an awn of wheat. Fanhua quickly plucked it away, concerned it might scratch Beanie. Beanie started hollering about how she wanted to ride on the back of the sheep. Li Hao turned towards them. He uttered one word before turning away again: "Fucksake."

Fanhua smiled. Dignity was a big deal for disabled people, most of whom had a strong sense of self-respect. Li Hao would never offer you a greeting unless you greeted him first. He lay down on the ground, leaning against a mound of earth, and even pulled his smock over his face as though he were asleep. It was covered with long grass, this mound, and topped with a bare elm that might have been alive or dead. Fanhua had almost forgotten that this mound of earth was actually a tomb, and there was a solitary old woman buried underneath it. This woman's son, Kong Qinggang, had valiantly set off across the Yalu River to take part in the Korean War, which made her the mother of a hero. She used to go thumping about with her mulberry walking stick, her cheeks bulging with the rock candy she was forever sucking. Hers was always the first house in the village to put out a red flag on National Day. But Qinggang didn't come home when the fighting was over. When asked, the old woman thumped her mulberry stick against the ground and said he'd died, the bastard, but he died to bring honour to Chairman Mao and that made it a good death, a great death. Years later, during the Cultural Revolution, the truth emerged. It turned out that Qinggang had been captured by the Americans, not killed, and had eventually escaped to Taiwan. That day, the old woman was publicly denounced, and that night, she hanged herself.

Fanhua's mother had just moved to Guanzhuang that year, and she told Fanhua how she'd gone over to see what all the fuss was about. The old woman's tongue was so long it looked like a dog's tongue on a hot summer's day, lolling out onto her chin. There were ants crawling across it. Why? Because at the time of her death she'd still been sucking on her very last piece of rock candy. She was born in the neighbouring village of Gongzhuang, and Zhaoyuan had made the trip personally to tell her relatives and invite them to come to collect her body. But they were far too busy revolutionising, they said, and when he persisted, they told him to just throw her to the dogs and be done with it, she was just an old bag of bones. Zhaoyuan lost his temper, and left after a parting shot: "Our Guanzhuang dogs are dogs of the proletariat, and they'd rather eat proletariat shit than the bones of the bourgeoisie." What was to be done? They couldn't just leave her to the maggots, so they wrapped her up in a tatty old mat and buried her. The Kong family wouldn't allow her to be buried in their ancestral plot, so it had to be out here, in the wilderness. This place was even farther away from the edge of this village in those days, and even wild dogs couldn't be bothered to come round here. The tomb had already disappeared by the time Fanhua and Dianjun were rolling about in the nearby grass. But her family had sent someone more recently to restore the shape of the mound. Two years ago, Fanhua remembered, when Xiushui County was making cremation mandatory, the authorities had announced that the dead must make way for the living in order to increase tillable land, and the tombs in every village would have to be flattened, without exception. Any secretary who left behind even a single tomb would be stripped of their post. Heck, how had she managed to forget this one? But she couldn't have been the only one. The whole village must have forgotten, and everyone in Gongzhuang too.

Li Hao had clearly forgotten, or else he wouldn't have been snuggling down against it. Just when she was about to call out to him, Fanhua heard the plummy voice of the news anchor Zhao Zhongxiang echoing across the hills.

"Who shall wake first from the great dream? How obvious the answer seems!"

His voice was imbued with an almost nauseating degree of emotion. Obviously, Zhao Zhongxiang hadn't actually come here, to Guanzhuang, in person, and he certainly wouldn't be out here in the hills with the sheep if he had.

"I look out from this hut of mine, and see the dawn taking its sweet time."

It was Li Hao reciting poetry in the voice of Zhao Zhongxiang. It was funny. You couldn't ask for a better example of "taking your sweet time" than a bachelor approaching forty. This was surely his roundabout way of informing them of his woes. Hardly an insurmountable problem, Fanhua thought. Join me, become my treasurer, and with your new wealth and status, you'll have women flinging themselves at your feet.

She shared her thoughts with Dianjun.

"Don't get the wrong idea," said Dianjun. "It's a Zhu Geliang poem he's quoting. Tch, Iron Crutch Li – get him in a good mood and he fancies himself as the Crouching Dragon himself."

"Yes, yes," said Fanhua, "you're the bookish one, fine." Then she called out, "Hey, Decimal Point! Your wicked chums are here to see you."

Li Hao rolled over. "Who's that, who's there?" he called out from beneath his smock. "Who's so desperate to ruin my sleep?"

Dianjun whipped down his smock and yelled: "Iron Crutch Li!"

Now Hao Li rolled away like a donkey, spinning across the grass to sit upright. He inspected the brand of the cigarette Dianjun handed him, and spat out the grass stalk he'd been using as a toothpick.

"Fuck me," he said, "you're certainly doing *well*." He stressed this last word, lengthening the vowel until it turned from a compliment into something altogether stranger.

"Fat lot of good it does him," said Fanhua. "An idle life's better by far. When does he ever get a chance to be idle? You live the life of a god. From now on, I'm going to stop calling you Decimal Point. I hereby dub you Living Immortal instead."

Li Hao picked up his shovel and dug out a clod of dirt to fling at his sheep. "You got that right. Keep an eye on the sheep, enjoy the scenery, and there's a skyful of stars above you any time you lift your head. Only one mouth in need of feeding, and that's mine." Li Hao might have a mind full of learning, but in some ways he was very much like a dog; toss a chunk of brick in his direction, and he'd assume it was a tasty spare rib. That comparison to an immortal had him flapping his smock like a fan and singing a song called *Strategy of the Empty City* – another reference to Zhu Geliang:

Up there on the ramparts, admiring the view,
I hear the sound of tumult from beyond. I see
The shadows of the army banners swaying back and forth.
These are the soldiers sent by Sima Yi.

His voice seemed melancholy at first, but then you became aware of a hidden note of joy. Somehow it seemed to evoke a happy encounter over a glass of wine. Except that if you carried on listening, you sensed a deeper element of sorrow, a kind of bitterness that never seemed to end. The clouds slid slowly above them, the largest of which turned from grey to pink to crimson. Li Hao remained deep in the story even after he'd finished singing, his eyebrows slightly raised, his gaze distant, a handful of smock still fluttering in his grasp. A grasshopper flew between them, fluttered around in a circle, and then settled down in the grass beside Li Hao's foot. Once it had been green, but now the insect was dark red, like it was covered in rust.

"You may be the Crouching Tiger," said Dianjun eventually, "but I'm no Sima Yi. I am a mere cobbler."

Li Hao didn't answer at first. "Of course you're not Sima Yi," he said at last. "The son of Sima Yi became emperor. You, on the other hand, are the husband of an empress."

"Don't try to put a hat like that on me," said Fanhua. "We do democracy round here, which means we take it in turns to be emperor. Might be my turn tomorrow, might be yours the day after."

Again, there was a pause before Li Hao responded. He finally seemed to have returned to reality, and his face had resumed its usual crafty expression. A crafty look was usually chilling – frightening, even. But there was a quiet kind of warmth to Li Hao's craftiness. His gaze drifted down from the clouds.

"There was this one time when I was tending my sheep," he said, "and a few of my old classmates came along. It was the ones who'd been to university. Now *they* are doing *so* damn well. They'd become fed up with city life so they'd brought their beer and tins of food out here to spend a weekend in the wilderness. I killed one of my sheep for them, put it on a barbecue with some wild garlic. They ate until their mouths were smeared with oil, until they were even farting grease. What about Kong Fanhua? they said. I said Fanhua's off somewhere with the committee doing an inspection of some sort. I didn't tell them you were empress – no, I said you were queen. Dianjun, can you guess what they said to that? Well, they said, that makes Zhang Dianjun Prince Philip. So no, I don't think you're Sima Yi. I think you're Prince Philip."

"But he doesn't have it anywhere near as cushy as Prince Philip," said Fanhua. "It's the hard life for him. He has to do it all himself because I can't help him with anything. He's the provider for me and Beanie." Then she asked him casually who these old classmates he mentioned might be. When she heard that their number included Ace Liu, the head of Nanyuan Township, Fanhua was indignant. "Ace Liu? He was supposed to be there on the inspection with the rest of us, but he said he was too busy with work. Not too busy for a nice jaunt over to Guanzhuang, clearly. I'm going to give him a piece of my mind when I see him next."

"Has Ace bought a place in the county town?" asked Dianjun.

"Of course," Li Hao replied more quietly, a colder look appearing in his eyes. "If he has his own place then he can play the host, which means he can learn his enemies' schemes, which means he can thwart those schemes, which means he can get promoted and make his fortune. It's the first link in the chain."

"Never mind that guy," said Dianjun, "we need to get together for a drink some time, Li Hao. We'll drown all our sorrows. My treat."

"You know full well that I can't stomach my drink," said Li Hao. "It's not my fate to ever be an immortal of liquor."

"We won't force you to drink too much," said Fanhua. "There are a few matters I'd like to hear your thoughts on."

Naturally, a man as smart as Li Hao knew straight away what she was implying. You see? He was already bowing his head in contemplation. "It's a matter of the red beans and the black beans, no?" he said at last. "You don't necessarily need to count them all out to know you have more red beans than black."

This talk of beans was an allusion to an old film called *Guerrillas of the Plains* in which one of the guerrilla fighters says the masses hold two beans in their hands, one red and one black. If someone does something good for the people, they will place a red bean behind his arse. If someone does something to oppress the people, they will place a black bean behind his arse. And it's tomorrow's reckoning they should be concerned with, not today's revelry. When the time comes to count the red beans and the black beans, there'll be no problem telling the good men from the rotten scoundrels. Remembering this detail when he was running for office, Qingmao decided to make use of it. A month before the election, he said he had a relative in the tofu production business who had received several sacks of soybeans from the northeast. Alas, when he opened up the sacks he found that the soybeans had somehow become black and red beans! It was like waking up to find your hen had turned into a duck. In all the years since the primordial being Pangu clove earth from sky, since the Three August Ones and the Five Lords roamed the earth, when had anyone ever heard of tofu made from red or black beans? Seeing how the stress of it all had turned his relative's hair white overnight, he was moved to take these sacks of beans off his hands. But what was he to do with them, now that he had paid for them? If he put them aside, they'd end up as food for the worms, but there were far more beans than he was capable of eating by himself. Qingmao said he had made some inquiries and discovered that red and black beans were good for the health of the elderly, an aid to digestion, so he made a point of inviting all the old men and women in the village to come and have a taste. When the election arrived, Qingmao offered the village committee a suggestion: since many of the villagers were illiterate, why not have them cast beans instead of ballots? A red bean should be placed in the box of the candidate they wanted for village head, and a black bean in the boxes of the candidates they didn't. Kong Jisheng, the most senior of all the villagers, had fled here during Shanxi's famine years, and he said he remembered the elections held by the warlord Yan Xishan. Bean votes, he said, that's what this is called, and it's exactly the way Yan Xishan did it. They'd even come up with a catchy little ditty: "A bean must not be tossed at whim; beans are silver, beans are gold. Choose the right man, do the right thing; throw your bean into the right bowl."

Qingmao came up with his own version:

A bean must not be tossed at whim,
Beans are black and beans are red.
Choose the right person, do the right thing,
Cast your red bean, go ahead.

It was only after the election that people realised the majority of the old people Qingmao had fed with beans were illiterate. And so there were some villagers who said it was thanks to those red beans that he came to power, and without them, he would never have amounted to anything more substantial than a fart in the wind.

So Fanhua smiled at Li Hao's mention of red beans and black beans. "Nothing gets past you, hmm? I need your advice."

"What choice do I have but to do as my empress decrees? And yet, there are some deeds that cannot be accomplished with too many people, or with too few."

This seemed like the kind of oracular proclamation that lay folk couldn't hope to fathom, and it left Fanhua stumped. Li Hao explained that it was something General Wu Yong said in *Outlaws of the Marsh*, and it meant that it was impossible to get things done when there were too many people involved. There would be no one else involved, Fanhua quickly assured him. Just three old classmates enjoying their time together.

ELEVEN

F anhua decided to call in at the school on their way back from the hills. The headmaster, Xu, was new here. He had previously worked in the township education bureau, and there were rumours it was his ungentlemanly conduct that had resulted in his demotion to a rural primary school. Fanhua hadn't had very much to do with Headmaster Xu, not because she was concerned about the gossip, but because the school fell under Xiangsheng's jurisdiction. She knew there was invariably going to be some money getting skimmed off the annual purchases of furniture and teaching materials, and she had no desire to get involved. Xu happened to be pacing the playground when they arrived, hands clasped behind his back, legs akimbo, like he was strutting across a stage. When Fanhua called out to him he stopped at once, then spun swiftly around, extended his arms and came trotting over towards them.

Fanhua introduced him to Dianjun. Xu said he had long been thinking of inviting Mr Zhang here to come and teach a class at the school.

"What could *he* possibly teach?" asked Fanhua.

"He could talk about the wondrous progress of the reform and opening up. Who, in all our village, has a greater abundance of experience than Mr Zhang?"

"I might know some things," said Dianjun, "but my knowledge isn't very well organised. I'm just an ordinary engineer."

Fanhua shot Dianjun a look. "Teacher Xu, don't listen to his bragging."

Xu's face stiffened. "Secretary Kong, seeing as I am several years your senior, I feel qualified to offer a criticism of you. Mr Zhang's accomplishments are undeniable. He is a man of great success, surfing the tide of the future. Where does Mr Zhang work? Why, in Shenzhen! And what sort of a place is Shenzhen? The very vanguard of reform and opening up! If Mr Zhang does not speak of his achievements, then who in Xiushui County will ever be brave enough to mention the words 'reform and opening up'? A sense of perspective, *that* is what counts. If time is money, then perspective is profit. When it comes to education, in particular, a sense of perspective means success. And therefore, Secretary Kong, I'm afraid I cannot allow you to keep him all to yourself."

Fanhua wondered how the authorities had been able to part with a man so proficient in the art of arse-kissing. It must have been something more serious than ungentlemanly conduct. "Headmaster Xu, we can discuss this some other time. I've heard that the authorities will be coming here to sit in on a class. Why, out of all the villages they had to choose from, did they settle on Guanzhuang? Are we an easy target, the softest persimmon on the tree?"

Xu sniffed. "Soft persimmons? What persimmon could be harder than we are? You are the county representative at the National People's Congress. There are no weak soldiers under the command of a mighty general. With you at the helm of the village, our school can hardly go too far wrong. It's our turn for a visit, that's all. Don't worry about us. Our teaching is on a par with the best in the county, and now we have a chance to prove it."

Fanhua asked whether it would be a good idea to take their visitors out for a meal. That depended on who was leading the group, Xu replied. If it was the director of education then a meal would be unavoidable, but it might not prove necessary if it was his deputy.

"You mean the deputy keeps his nose relatively clean?"

Xu laughed. "Clean? I suppose you could say that. In reality, he's keeping a low profile, waiting for his moment. Which is why he's sticking to the straight and narrow for now."

"Then you should definitely take him out to dinner," said Dianjun. "If you wait until he's moved up in the world, you'll be too late."

He slapped his hand against the telescope hanging around his neck and widened his stance into a pose more befitting a man of his success and initiative. "If the mountains will not move to the water, then the water must move to the mountains. We should think about these things in the long term. Anyway, Fanhua, it's not like the village will be worried about such a trifling sum."

"There you go," said Xu, pointing a finger at Dianjun. "Perspective. Nothing's more important when you're in the education business. The sun can be discerned in even the tiniest drop of water. Mr Zhang's every utterance distinguishes him from the common herd."

Fanhua inwardly groaned. Bringing Dianjun along had been a mistake. He was an expert in giving advice but had no idea what it was like to get his hands dirty. It was always necessary to grease the wheel with these guys, but you couldn't overdo it. They were slick operators. It would cost several hundred *kuai* to take them out to dinner – a sum that amounted to the annual earnings of an ordinary farmer – and there would be no getting that money back once it was spent.

"Let's wait until Xiangsheng is back," she said, staring off into the distance. "We'll look into it then. Has it been decided whose class they'll be attending?"

Xu said that they'd requested to hear a volunteer teacher. There was talk that they were planning to select two or three exceptional volunteer teachers from around the county and offer them official positions. He was already thinking of Li Shangyi, when Shangyi put his own name forward. He could always be relied upon to roll up his sleeves and dig in.

"Splendid," said Fanhua, "a meat pie fallen out of the sky. How's Shangyi's Mandarin?"

Xu whistled. "Superb. He's up there with the likes of Zhao Zhongxiang."

When they got home, Fanhua was staring at Dianjun. He brushed his hands against his face, thinking he must have something stuck there, and went to look in the mirror. Fanhua continued to stare at him.

"Well," she said. "Well, well, well."

Dianjun was alarmed. "What? If you've something to say, then say it. Why do you keep staring at me like that?"

84

"All right then. When exactly did you wake up and find you'd become a master of engineering?"

Dianjun looked embarrassed. A film of sweat sprang to his forehead. Eventually, he cleared his throat. "A man must have spirit like a tree must have bark," he replied, ambiguously.

"What does tree bark have to do with anything? I can't speak for any of your other skills, but you sure are an expert at blowing your own trumpet. I don't even know when you're telling the truth any more. Dianjun, be honest. There's not something you're keeping from me, is there?"

"Don't be silly. I'm completely devoted to you And anyway, it's not like I actually *said* anything. Your dream is to lead the village of Guanzhuang to prosperity. Mine is to become an engineer, and a capitalist. What of it?"

Fanhua wasn't going to waste any more words on him. Instead, she picked up Xue'e's shoes and plonked them down in front of him.

"All right then, Mister Engineer. Mend these shoes, if you'd be so kind."

TWELVE

The sun buried itself in the clouds to the west, as though it was entering the bridal chamber with no intention of ever coming out again. Only a narrow slit of light remained, a bloodied knife in the sky. As the knife sank, the blood darkened. This was a quiet moment in the village, quiet enough to hear the sound of a donkey sneezing and rolling around. Soon enough, Xinqiao's donkey would quiet down, and the village would start to come alive. What was that English word for "donkey"? For a moment Fanhua was stumped, before she remembered: the Party's rebuke, *dangkei*. The noise of the *dangkei* stomping around was soon drowned out by the other sunset sounds of the village: adults calling out to children, and the neighing and lowing of livestock returning home. A crowd of ducks went quacking past, the drakes sounding slightly huskier than their mates. Behind them came the geese, like clouds skimming across the ground. They belonged to Lingwen, and Lingwen's wife was driving them on their way with a stick. Fanhua was now like someone who still jumps at the sight of a rope having been bitten by a snake years ago. She shivered when she saw a faint bulge in the belly of Lingwen's wife. She soon realised her mistake, however. Lingwen's wife only looked that way because of her posture, having spent so much of her time with the geese that she'd started to resemble them. Right down to her headgear: her fake plastic cornelian hairband was the same persimmon red as the knob on a goose's bill.

It was then that the fancy car came past. Fanhua assumed it was her brother-in-law since it looked like the Beijing Xiandai model he drove. No matter how the driver honked his horn, the geese refused to let him pass. Oh, so you think you're the only one around here who can honk? Allow us to demonstrate. The white goose leading the flock extended his neck: *Ger-gaw! Ger-gaw!*

But the driver who stepped out of the car was not Fanhua's brother-in-law. It was a middle-aged man whose hair was thinning on top. The passenger sitting inside cranked down the window to stick his head out and take a look around. He was wearing a Mao suit, in contrast to the Western-style suit of his driver, and it was buttoned all the way up to the chin. He wore a pair of sunglasses, too, the kind of aviators Dianjun liked to wear. The enraged driver aimed a kick at the white goose. But this goose was a lot more nimble than he looked. He immediately set upon the driver's foot with his beak. Consistently leading by example, this goose was surely destined to be reincarnated as a Party member someday. He had led his flock in their march across the road, and now he led them in the assault on the driver. Still pecking away, he raised one of his wings as though he were issuing a battle cry. The other geese soon came flapping to his side. They levelled their necks at the driver like gun barrels and joined together in a chorus of honking. Trembling, the driver sank to his haunches, shielding his head with his arms. Fanhua yelled at him to get back in his vehicle.

He almost managed to do it. His head was inside the car, but his arse was not. The squeal he produced when the leading goose pecked at his arse did not sound altogether natural. The other occupant of the vehicle was still sitting there in his shades, head jutting out of the window, elbow leaning on the car door, watching this battle between goose and car.

"Are you trying to get yourself killed?" Fanhua shouted to him. "Hurry up and get that window shut."

A goose had now appeared on top of the car, and it started attacking the roof with its wings, beak, feet and carnelian coxcomb in turn. The strain of its exertions made it pop out an egg, which rolled down from the top of the car like a grenade. Then, just to add to the confusion, a leopard cat came along – the same one Fanhua had seen on the wall of Xue'e's house. It leapt onto the roof of the car and assumed a pose of profound contemplation, picking at its ears with its front claws.

Fanhua was struggling to contain her laughter. "Come on, time to get going," she called to Lingwen's wife.

"OK, I'm going," Lingwen's wife replied, setting off on her own and leaving the geese behind, which was not at all what Fanhua intended.

A large crowd of onlookers had gathered by now, and they were shouting their approval as they revelled in the carnage before them. Too afraid to sound his horn again, the driver could only quietly reverse his car. The goose on top of the car swooped down like a hawk, while the goose that had been mauling the windscreen wiper went off after Lingwen's wife, honking like he was expecting some acknowledgement of a job well done.

Fanhua had been waiting for Qingshu, but what she had got instead was the sight of a goose-versus-car showdown. When the crowd had dispersed and there was still no sign of Qingshu, Fanhua tried to give him a call. But his phone was switched off, which was strange because Qingshu never switched his phone off. Whenever they submitted their mobile phone bills for expenses, his was always the highest. His wife Hongmei said that Qingshu never had time to talk to her because he spent all day speaking to his phone and his parrots. On one occasion, their house phone had rung while she was out feeding the pigs. It rang for a long time, but Qingshu didn't bother to get out of bed and answer it. When she finally picked up, she discovered that the dialler was Qingshu himself, calling on his mobile from his bed, just a few footsteps away, to remind her to feed his budgies. But now this man who never switched his phone off had apparently done just that.

When it was almost dark, Fanhua made a call to Meng Xiaohong, the secretary of the Communist Youth League branch, to tell her to inform the officials that they would be having a meeting after dinner. Fanhua couldn't exactly say why, but she had always been fond of Meng Xiaohong. Sometimes you just get along well with someone. And she had gone further up in Fanhua's estimation since she had offered that piece of advice about the paper plant bridge. Xiaohong had once had an older brother, but he had drowned in the year of the great flood. He was diving in the river for firewood when a piece of timber drifting past knocked him out. His body was so bloated it was round like a rice-husking roller by the time it floated back to the surface. Which meant Xiaohong would follow in Fanhua's footsteps someday, and find herself a man to come and live with her family. Maybe it was her destiny. Her mother said she was facing the ground when she came out of the womb, which meant – according to the local tradition – that she would die in her mother's home. Fanhua's mother told her she was born the same way. Word had reached Fanhua's ear that Lingpei was keen on Xiaohong. But they were a generation apart, and besides, how could a pickpocket like Lingpei hope to marry a girl like Xiaohong? Xiaohong was a golden phoenix, and a golden phoenix could only alight on a phoenix tree. Lingpei was certainly no phoenix tree. He was a stooped, stumpy willow, trailing twigs across the ground. And Xiaohong was obviously a bright girl. Back when they were rerouting roads within the village, they decided they would have to knock down some of the old houses and allocate new homes. Xiaohong's father was one of the many people who applied to have his family home relocated to the east side of the village, where the feng shui was supposedly better. The hassle of dealing with all the applicants who were determined to move east had left Fanhua with a sore throat.

"When they build the new highway," she told Xiaohong, "it'll be on the west side of the village. It's being funded as part of a national project, so you can count on the government paying out. Your situation is different from other girls – you won't always be able to rely on a husband."

Xiaohong took the hint and changed the application. And sure enough, when the time came, they received a sizeable sum in compensation from the government. The rules stipulated that the village had to accommodate the families whose homes were to make way for the new road. After a meeting to consider the issue, the village committee decided to assign them a new plot of land in the east. Xiaohong had killed two birds with one stone: she had behaved like a model Party member, and she still managed to get that house on the east side her father had wanted. Plus, she made a tidy profit.

And there was one other thing that had brought home to Fanhua how sharp Xiaohong was. Fanhua had suggested to her that she might want to change her name. How about "Meng Zhaohong" instead?

Can you guess what Xiaohong replied?

"All the characters in old plays named Little Red are dutiful servant girls," Xiaohong replied, "and I play the part of a dutiful servant girl too. My job in the committee is to do your bidding."

Who could fail to be pleased by a remark like that? And it wasn't just empty flattery. Xiaohong's words were borne out by her behaviour. She was a cut above all the other silly girls her age who knew only how to flirt and flaunt their looks.

"We're fated to work together," Fanhua had told Xiaohong. "Fanhua and Xiaohong – Flower and Red. Red flower. Only a red flower truly deserves to be called a flower. You're still young, still such a brilliant red. You have so much ahead of you. Keep working hard, and I'll be giving you a weightier load to shoulder before too long."

"There are plenty of other capable people in the village," Xiaohong replied modestly. "They're the ones you should be offering responsibilities to, not a foolish young girl like me. I'm not up to the job." This was a fitting reply, proving she knew her place and didn't have an overblown sense of her own importance. Unlike Qingshu, who only ever thought of himself, clutching shamelessly at power with no notion of biding his time and waiting for the right moment.

When the elections were over, Fanhua thought, it wouldn't be such a bad idea to go ahead and hand family planning over to Xiaohong. It would be a weight off Fanhua's mind. Xiaohong had the courage the job required, as well as the talent. Fanhua was reminded of another way in which Xiaohong had earned her respect. It concerned Guo Linna, the wife of a villager named Fanchuan. Despite her vaguely foreign-sounding name, Linna was an utter moron who would struggle to count the fingers on one hand. Linna had already given birth to one girl and one boy, but she still wanted another baby. So Qingshu went to work. He started with Fanchuan, then moved on to his idiot wife. Attempting ideological reasoning with a halfwit was like wasting oil on a lamp for a blind man. Linna was gnawing on a cob of sweetcorn, and when she finished it she started gnawing on a second. She paid no attention to Qingshu whatsoever. When Qingshu eventually lost patience with her, he threatened to have her carted off to Wangzhai to be sterilised. Guo Linna may not have been a woman of many talents, but she did have one noteworthy ability, and that was biting. She clamped down her jaws and nearly took a chunk out of Qingshu's hand.

In the end, it was Xiaohong who dealt with this idiot wife. "Linna, my dear," she said, "they're not going to take anything *out* of you, no, they're going to put something *in* you."

The idiot wife asked what sort of a something this might be.

"Your son likes to play at rolling his metal hoop, doesn't he? Well, it's just like that, a hoop. Though you'd best not give it to him to play with."

The idiot wife asked how they'd manage to fit a hoop of that size inside her.

"Oh, it's much smaller than that one," said Xiaohong. "Smaller and *better*."

Stupid she might be, but this wife was no idiot when it came to wheeling and dealing. When she heard how small this hoop was, she decided she wasn't interested and plopped down on the floor, legs splayed, refusing to move.

"But think of a wristwatch," said Xiaohong. "A wristwatch is smaller than a clock, but more expensive. And there are lots of different kinds. They have plastic ones, steel ones, gold ones, silver ones. Which would you like?"

Guo Linna said she wanted a gold one.

"Then gold it is," said Xiaohong. "And after a couple of years, you can take it out and turn it into a ring to wear on your finger. Who wants silver anyway? We've got plenty of silver bracelets already."

Guo Linna asked what a ring for your finger might be. Xiaohong told her it was no different from the thimble you used for sewing insoles. The idiot wife said she wanted a thimble *and* a silver bracelet, and she wouldn't settle for anything less.

"Very well," said Xiaohong. "Then we'll give you a thimble, and we'll give you a bracelet." And then she led Guo Linna away. Fanhua followed behind, lost in admiration.

When they got to the hospital, Xiaohong made a show of asking the doctor, "Could you do me a favour? Give her two, one silver and one gold."

This story inspired the following upside-down song:

91

Sunrise in the west, sunset in the east,
A pomegranate tree where cherries grow.
A clap of thunder makes no sound,
Linna's snatch is a treasure trove.
Ever since Fanchuan crossed the threshold,
His prick's been bound in precious gold.

"Shall we just have the doctor neuter her and be done with it?" Xiaohong asked Fanhua once the nurse had taken Linna inside.

"It would certainly make things easier," Fanhua replied. "But I don't know how Fanchuan would take it."

Xiaohong would have been prepared to go ahead and sterilise Linna right there and then if Fanhua hadn't said anything. Young people are certainly bold, Fanhua thought. She praised Xiaohong for going about her work in the correct manner. Xiaohong understood that plates, saucers, cups and bowls all had to be handled differently. There was an individual solution to every individual problem, and this was the fundamental essence of Marxism.

Xiaohong squirmed and fiddled with her hair braids. "No more, please, I beg you. I don't know the fundamental essence of anything. I'm just a simple idiot, barely more intelligent than Fanchuan's wife. That's why I can sometimes come up with ideas that wouldn't occur to smart folk. Just my stupid little strategies."

Now would you look at that, *that's* what you call awareness. Oh Qingshu, you and Xiaohong are as far apart as mud from clouds. It was at that moment that Fanhua decided she wanted Xiaohong to take over family planning after the elections. Just in part, initially, and then she could take charge of the whole thing in a few years' time, once she'd established her reputation. Fanhua had already decided to step down after a couple more sessions, and when the time came she'd make sure Xiaohong was able to inherit her position. Xiaohong was her shadow, after all. The two of them came as a package, so it shouldn't matter too much to people which one of them was in charge.

"I won't make an announcement over the loudspeaker, then," said Xiaohong upon hearing that the meeting would concern family planning. "I've just finished eating, so I felt like going out for a stroll anyway. I'll call in on each of them individually and let them know. I take it there's no need to inform the village cluster group leaders?"

You see? Smart people are just smart. No need to waste time explaining things to them. Making an announcement on the loudspeaker would definitely have been a bad idea. It was like Li Hao had said: the fewer people involved, the better. They definitely didn't need to let everyone know, and there was no reason for the five village cluster leaders to attend. This wasn't going to be some official gathering of congress where everyone would have a chance to air their views.

Xiaohong also made a point of letting slip another piece of news, or "intel" as Qingshu would put it. She said she'd seen Qingshu and Xiangsheng in Gongzhuang Village that afternoon. Qingshu had parked a car outside the entrance of Gongzhuang School. His chin was resting on his arm, his arm was leaning on the car window, and he was chatting with the village secretary of Gongzhuang.

"And Xiangsheng?" asked Fanhua. "Isn't he supposed to be in Xiushui Town? What's he doing back in the village?"

"Who knows. But they all certainly seemed to be getting along. Xiangsheng gave him a cigarette, and then another one after that. Very chummy." Xiaohong said she'd waved at them, but they acted like they hadn't seen her.

Gongzhuang was the neighbouring village, and pretty much everyone in Guanzhuang knew pretty much everyone in Gongzhuang. The secretary of Gongzhuang was named Gong Weihong. His childhood nickname was Scrawny Dog, but these days he'd turned into a Paunchy Dog with a big beer belly. He and Qingshu had been in the army together, though Qingshu had enlisted a year later than him. Scrawny Dog had all the luck, Qingshu once said. There'd been a flood during his first year, and serving in the disaster-relief forces meant he'd been fast-tracked into the Party. For his part, Qingshu had only managed to get into the Party when he was about to delist, even after doing all kinds of shitty work and distributing gifts to all the right people.

"As for Qingshu," said Xiaohong, "looking right at me and acting like he didn't see me, a co-worker of his. What a humiliation."

"Is he back yet?" asked Fanhua.

93

"His car arrived right after I got back. It glides along, that car of his."

Fanhua quickly turned to ask her parents whether Qingshu had been to visit.

"So young, and such a poor memory already," said her father. "He was here last night, don't you remember? He ate those oranges from the fridge?"

"Hey, do you use laundry powder or soap?" Xiaohong suddenly asked.

"Sometimes laundry powder and sometimes soap," Fanhua replied. "What of it?"

It was nothing, Xiaohong said, she was just curious.

Fanhua was angry. When Qingshu showed up, he'd be getting a criticising from her, and no mistake. Tch, Qingshu, have you been nibbling on leopard gall bladder, to suddenly turn so gutsy? He hadn't shown up to make his report, even though he knew she was waiting for him.

Inside, Dianjun was rummaging around in search of the kit he used to use to fix shoes. It didn't sound like he was in a very good mood, the way he was crashing around the place. Fanhua sat down to watch TV while she waited. She took out her anger on the TV remote. Channel One was showing *Topics in Focus*: there had been another gas explosion in some Shanxi coal mine, and they were putting the bodies in the cages they usually used to transport coal, winching them up to the surface, like sweet potatoes from a cellar. The sweet potatoes kept on coming. It was a chilling sight. *Topics in Focus* was usually Fanhua's favourite show. As the head of the village, she had to pay attention to national goings-on, to domestic goings-on, to goings-on of every variety. She also had to be attuned to all manner of rumours, wherever they might come from.

But today, she clicked past and onto Song Zuying's song *Today Is A Good Day* on the Shanghai channel. She'd heard that Song Zuying was popular with all the leading officials, but she didn't know if that was true. Fanhua liked her, in any case. For her eyebrows, as well as her voice. She had a sweet voice, so sweet it made your teeth feel like they were sinking into sugar, even if you'd been chewing on the bitterest goldthread. And those high eyebrows, especially when she tilted her head at a forty-five-degree angle – the way they jiggled around under that fringe of hers, well, Fanhua could easily imagine the old ladies itching to adopt her as their daughter, never mind the men. And her eyes, needless to say, were like fireflies illuminating the night. Fanhua usually enjoyed listening to her singing *Today is a Good Day*. *Little Back Basket*, that was another good one of hers, and *Fiery Girl*. "Fiery girl is peppery, fiery girl looks fine." Fanhua was something of a fiery girl herself. How could she ever hope to keep all these old men in line otherwise? Looking fine? Not so much as she used to, naturally, but probably still the finest of all the village-level officials in Xiushui County, seeing as how she was the only woman among them. The flower of Xiushui, that was what County Head Zhang had called her. But Fanhua clicked Song Zuying away too. A good day? What was so good about it? She kicked at the pile of shoes at her feet, and one of them narrowly avoided flying into Dianjun.

"Beanie, come and look," said Dianjun, "your mother's turned into Princess Bright Pearl from the TV."

Her parents looked on critically. "She's gone crazy."

Fanhua flung the remote against the sofa. "You go ahead and enjoy watching TV," she said. "I've got a meeting to go to."

She always took her black leather notebook to these meetings. It was real leather, Dianjun said, and would make a fine shoe. It had been a present from her sister Fanrong, brought back from a provincial-level meeting by her brother-in-law. The cover was embossed with the words "Provincial Finance Department". But now she couldn't find it anywhere. She asked Dianjun whether he'd seen it. Dianjun was chuckling over Xue'e's leather shoes.

"I wasn't laughing at you," he explained, waving his hands when she grabbed him by the collar. "I was laughing at the shoes. Fuck, you call those things shoes? More like a pair of carrier bags."

Fanhua asked her mother. It took a long time, and much gesticulating before her mother understood what she was looking for. There might be such a thing in the kitchen, she told her. Fanhua rushed into the kitchen, and sure enough, there was the notebook, with a few fragments of orange peel sitting on top of it. Now she remembered that she'd had it out while talking to Qingshu and Pei Zhen. She went back into the main room and slapped Dianjun with the notebook.

"You don't have to do a good job, you just have to get it done.

You maintain your army for a thousand days, all so it's ready for that one day when you need it. Someone's waiting to wear those things."

They heard the sound of a person outside rattling the chain on the gate. Assuming it was Qingshu, Fanhua refused to allow anyone to let him in. Only when she decided he'd been left to wait for a suitably chastening length of time did she put on her angriest face and step out to open the gate.

But it wasn't Qingshu. It was Xiangsheng.

"Oh, Xiangsheng – you're back. Don't you have your business to attend to in town?"

Perhaps her tone was a little too aggressive because Xiangsheng merely bit his lip and smiled in response.

Fanhua led him inside, but he paused behind her and called out to others in the house: "Who's upset this one then, hmm? Dianjun, what gust of wind blew you back into town? You must have been eating leopard gall bladder if you have the guts to make Fanhua angry."

Xiangsheng stuck around to banter for a while with Dianjun before he and Fanhua left. There was a strong wind outside, and a piece of flying debris narrowly missed them. When Xiangsheng switched on his torch, they realised it was just a plastic bag that had been inflated by the wind to look like a balloon.

"Damn," said Xiangsheng, "there's rubbish everywhere."

"On the TV they call it 'white pollution'," said Fanhua. "If our nation has so many talented people, then how is it they can't even come up with a solution to deal with plastic bags?" After that, the two of them walked on in silence. Xiangsheng's heavy footsteps disturbed the crickets living at the foot of the wall. They started chirping away, but it was cold, and the sound gradually dissipated until, after one final chirp, they were silent. Fanhua thought about what Xiaohong had told her about having seen Xiangsheng in Gongzhuang. But she didn't ask him about it. If he wasn't going to tell her himself, then she wasn't going to ask. Xiangsheng let out a long sigh.

"Surely it's just a few less bowls of cold noodles sold," she ventured, not entirely sure what he was sighing about. "Is it really as bad as all that?"

Xiangsheng clicked his tongue and stamped his feet. "What? It's the village committee I'm sighing for. I'm sighing because you lot acted too late."

Fanhua didn't understand what "you lot" was supposed to mean. There was a streetlight behind Xiangsheng that illuminated the hand he was now thrusting towards the heavens, a hand that was trembling slightly, especially the extended forefinger. He let it continue to tremble for a while before he spoke.

"Fuck, do you really not know, or are you just pretending? Xue'e's done a runner. That slut Yao has fled the village."

What? Xue'e had run away? Fanhua's forehead became hot, and she could hear a thudding sound in her ears. She hurried onwards without another word, so quickly she was almost running. Realising after a few yards that she'd left Xiangsheng behind, she stopped to give him a chance to catch up. Fanhua took a gulp and tried to calm herself down.

"No need for alarm," she said at last. "Where can she have gone, anyway? A runaway monk always comes back to the temple in the end."

THIRTEEN

From beyond the courtyard of the committee building they could hear a voice yelling: "Either bring her back, or show me the body!" Braying like a donkey – who could it possibly be? It was Li Tiesuo. Fanhua was stunned. Li Tiesuo, seriously? What a transformation. This hitherto meek, unassuming man, having failed to prevent his wife from running away, was acting like he was the wounded party here. Maybe *he* had been chewing on leopard gall bladder.

Fanhua stopped outside the entrance to the meeting room and leant against the frame of the door. She wanted to observe Li Tiesuo's antics before entering. There were so many people smoking in there that it made Fanhua's eyes water.

Tiesuo was brandishing a cigarette, but he wasn't smoking it. Fanhua hadn't seen anyone in real life pulling that kind of pose before: standing with one foot on a stool, hand clutching his shirt, neck extended – he looked like the kind of secret rebel Party member you saw in the movies. It seemed like he'd finished talking, but when Fanhua was about to step into the room, he started up again.

"I've said my piece," he said, pointing at Qingshu with his cigarette. "If Xue'e isn't back in three days, I'll burn this place to the ground. How am I going to survive?" Qingshu was leaning so far back on his chair he looked like he was on the verge of toppling over. "Tomorrow I'm going to come and eat at your house," Tiesuo continued, "and then I'm going to go and eat at *his* house, and after that, I'm going to go and eat at Kong Fanhua's house. The Party isn't going to let me starve to death!" He was getting more and more worked up. "When it gets cold, I'll be needing someone to warm my quilt up for me." So apparently Tiesuo was making plans for his sleeping arrangements right through to the middle of winter. "You decide whose house is going to be the first to host me. I'll be needing a padded red blanket, and an embroidered pillow, and a bedside table to rest my feet on." If Tiesuo liked to rest his feet on a bedside table, then he must tend to sleep with his head at the foot of the bed, Fanhua inferred.

Xiangsheng spoke up, "Tiesuo, you're frightening Xiaohong."

Xiaohong had backed up into a corner, where she was holding a book and acting like she'd heard nothing of what Tiesuo and Xiangsheng were saying. Though obviously she was actually listening to every word. Xiaohong always behaved like she wasn't really paying attention during these meetings, chewing on bubble gum or flicking through a book. A few people laughed, and Xiaohong tried to disappear further into her book. Someone let out a distinctly audible fart, and even more people joined in the laughter.

"Let's try to be serious, please," said Qingshu. "That said, it is a proper stinker. Who's been eating sweet potato?"

"A sweet potato fart?" someone said in a high-pitched voice. "There's Coca-Cola mixed in there too. Coca-Cola's all well and good, but those bubbles make you fart something rotten."

Fanhua recognised the voice as belonging to Fanqi, the committee mediator. This was no committee meeting, it was a carnival. But the one person in the room who wasn't smiling – apart from Xiaohong – was Tiesuo.

"I'm not an easy guest," he said, switching the foot on the stool. "I need two eggs every day. I suppose I could make do with one... but only if it has two yolks!"

Who'd have thought it, Tiesuo had discovered he had a sense of humour. Headmaster Xu was right: it all came down to perspective. Tiesuo had spent a few days out there working on the road and now look at him.

Tiesuo followed up his double egg yolk zinger with a bit about his stinky feet. "Let me be clear," he said, rolling up his trouser leg, "I never wash my own feet. Xue'e's the one who does that." His patter was effortless, with perfect tone and all the accompanying gestures, and no hint of a stammer. He truly brought this persona – this deadbeat character he was playing – to life. He must have been practising for this, Fanhua thought. There was no way he'd come up with all this on the hoof. But what did that imply? It implied that all this was premeditated, that it was a planned act of rebellion against the committee. Idiot! The better his performance, the more blatantly he indicted himself.

Tiesuo clearly had more he wanted to say, but – sensing that the crowd wasn't reacting in the way he'd hoped – he brought his monologue to an abrupt halt. His hand was still trembling slightly as it tucked the cigarette behind his ear.

This was the moment Fanhua chose to make her entrance. Tiesuo immediately took his foot off the stool when he saw her. Fanhua thwacked her notebook onto the table.

"If your trotter was comfortable where it was, then I see no point in moving it." Before Tiesuo had a chance to respond, she continued: "Let's move into Qingshu's office for the meeting. Tiesuo can wait for us here. Xiaohong, you just sit there and read your book. Good habit in a young person, to be a keen reader." She gave Xiaohong a look that told her she meant what she was saying. "No need to be afraid of Tiesuo here," Fanhua said, once Xiaohong had taken her seat again. "He's no Meng Zhaoyuan. When Zhaoyuan torched this place, he was answering the call of the Party to criticise Confucius and Lin Biao. But Tiesuo would be giving himself a death sentence if he tried anything of the sort." She rapped her notebook against the stool. "Tiesuo, you said something just now that really resonated with me. 'Bring her back, or show me the body!' Well, that's precisely what the committee would like you to do for us."

Fanhua stepped outside and paused for a moment in the courtyard. It was getting dark, but the animal statuettes were still visible at either end of the stage building roof. Over the years, grass had appeared in the cracks between the roof tiles. Grass that was now swaying in the breeze, like a crowd of people staring at clouds. It was the dry grass of late autumn, and the rustling sound it made was like the whispering of the crowd. From a distance came the sound of dogs barking, the kind of cautious, whiny bark that a dog makes when its tail is between its legs.

"The weather's turned," said Fanhua. "It looks like rain." No one replied. "Good for the soil," she added. Someone coughed, but still no one said anything. Once they were in the office next door, Fanhua chuckled and made a joke at Qingshu's expense: "You really have been doing womanly work. You've done a lovely job decorating this place. So pretty and clean. We all remember the state of Lingwen's pigsty of an office."

This was a pointed reference to Lingwen, Qingshu's predecessor. Fanhua had got rid of him because she wasn't satisfied with his work, and the only responsibility he had now was his flock of ducks.

Someone remarked that this office was even nicer than Township Head Bull's office.

"Never mind the township head," another voice chimed in, "hang up a world map and this place would be fit for the president of the United States."

"Well, that's as it should be," said Fanhua. "Qingshu shoulders a very weighty load."

"When the village has a bit more money, we'll get Qingshu a computer," said Xiangsheng. "With a computer, he won't need to hang his walls with all these forms and red flags."

"My sister Fanrong has a computer in her office," said Fanhua. "All ten fingers go skittering across the keys, and the words pop up like fleas." At that, Fanhua laid her notebook down on the table and turned abruptly to the real matter at hand. "Qingshu, would you be so kind as to report to the committee on exactly what the hell is going on?"

Qingshu's face went tense. He started fidgeting with his television antenna, passing it back and forth between his hands. He fully comprehended the weight of the load that had been placed on his shoulders, he said, so he'd hurried to Xiushui Town as soon as he received the secretary's instructions. In order to fulfil his responsibilities as swiftly as possible, he had borrowed Xiangmin's sedan – although he'd always driven an open-top car rather than a sedan, back in his army days – and sped off on his way. (This was the same Xiangmin who'd converted to Christianity – Xiangsheng's younger brother.)

"Official duties must follow the correct formalities," said Fanhua. "The village will pay Xiangmin a rental fee for the use of his car, in addition to the petrol money. Qingshu, get to the important bit, and we'll discuss the rest later."

When he got to the south side of Xiushui Town, Qingshu continued, well, it was pretty hectic. There were construction sites everywhere, not to mention the cranes. They were an awesome sight, those cranes. They could lift all sorts of stuff right up into the air like it was nothing.

"Is that right?" asked Fanhua. "What kind of stuff?"

Qingshu said he hadn't had a clear view of exactly what kind of stuff, nor had he had the time to make further investigations. The point was, it was a scene of bustling prosperity, which was a good thing, obviously, but a bad thing as far as he was concerned at that particular moment because it made it hard to track a person down. Qingshu had worn the soles of his shoes right down.

"Shame we're not the army," said Fanhua, "or we could give you a medal for outstanding service. So what happened when you found Tiesuo?"

It was beside a lime pit that Qingshu finally managed to find Tiesuo. He was sieving the lime, and it had turned his beard and eyebrows white, like Father Christmas in the movies. Tch, look at Qingshu, throwing out casual allusions to Father Christmas. Such breadth of knowledge.

"Get to the point," said Fanhua.

When he found Tiesuo, Qingshu said, he gave him a serious talking to. He explained the politics of the matter to him, and Tiesuo hung his head and seemed to be taking it all in. Qingshu asked Tiesuo whether he had anything to say, and Tiesuo said he'd been working all day, he was hungry and dizzy and wanted something to eat. So Qingshu took Tiesuo into town, and it was there that they ran into Xiangsheng. They had a bowl of cold noodles at Xiangsheng's place, with sesame sauce and garlic paste, it was delicious, really fragrant and fresh and tasty and just the right kind of chewy. Qingshu turned to Xiangsheng at this point in his narrative. "You didn't put any poppy seeds in the seasoning, did you?"

Xiangsheng glanced at Fanhua before giving Qingshu a playful punch. "You bet we did, you fucker, but only in your bowl."

"All right, that's enough," said Fanhua. "Xiangsheng, how much does a bowl of your cold noodles cost? I'll write out a note for reimbursement when we're done."

"It's nothing," said Xiangsheng. "What's a few bowls of noodles between friends?"

While they were eating, Qingshu continued, Xiangsheng had taken over and given Tiesuo a piece of his mind. He'd come this close to chucking a bowl of noodles in his face.

"Come on," said Xiangsheng, "the way we persuade people is with truth and reason, not by chucking noodles in their face. Not when they cost three *kuai* a bowl. But yes, I offered him a few words of advice, that much is true."

And then, Qingshu said, they all drove back to Guanzhuang. He and Xiangsheng took it in turns all the way here, letting Tiesuo have it from both sides until he was so ashamed he could barely lift his head, like he wanted to stick his head in his crotch. Qingshu put down his antenna so he could demonstrate what it looked like. Fanhua had been about to ask why they had taken a detour to Gongzhuang, but she decided against it when she remembered that Xiangsheng was present.

"All right, fine," she said. "And what happened after you got back to the village?"

Qingshu picked up his antenna again. This time he stuck it down behind his neck in order to scratch his back. "When we got back to the village, he went home, and I went home, and that was that. End of report, Village Head."

"That's it? What about Xue'e? Did she and Tiesuo see each other? Did you see Xue'e?"

Qingshu continued to scratch his back. "You told me to pick up Tiesuo. You didn't say anything about checking on Xue'e."

Fanhua felt a constriction in her chest, and the sound of her breathing became raspier. "Then tell me this," she said. "When did you discover Xue'e had run off?"

"I get home, wash my face, have something to eat, and before I even have a chance to feed the budgies, I hear the news that there's going to be a meeting tonight. So I hurry out, and then when I'm passing Tiesuo's place on the way I see someone talking to Qinglin about breeding, and I see someone laughing about some battle between geese and a car, with a bunch of people listening. So I stop there for a little while because, to tell you the truth, Secretary, I was keen to hear about it myself."

"Let me remind you again," said Fanhua, "that I am not secretary."

"Village Head, right. I'm about to go when I see Tiesuo come outside. He asks me whether I've eaten, and I tell him I have. He asks me what I've had, and I tell him I had noodles. Yum, noodles, he says, they're his favourite. Why doesn't he have Xue'e roll some out for him then? I say. And can you guess what he says next, comrades and elders? He says he damn well can't because he's got no idea where she's disappeared to. I was thunderstruck. Shivering right the way down my body. I ran inside his place, and all I found in there was his two girls, the big one crying and the little one bawling."

The expression on Fanhua's face was becoming increasingly unpleasant, but Qingshu carried on talking: "She was rolling around on the floor, the little one, rolling around like a donkey. Snot all the way down to here." Qingshu put down his antenna again so he could demonstrate exactly how far down the snot had been hanging.

Fanhua couldn't bear it any longer. She picked up the antenna and slammed it against the table. "Enough." Everyone was stunned. She took a deep breath, and then gently replaced the antenna on the table. "That would be Laddy, yes? Is Laddy a magician now? That she can be rolling around *and* have snot hanging that far out of her nose? I don't believe it. Now I'm not criticising you, Qingshu, but the fact is the fire is close enough to singe our eyebrows and you're just standing there with your dick in your hand. Is this all the intel you have to offer us, hmm? What use is any of it? I told you to bring Tiesuo back to me, and instead you take him back to Xue'e. Let me tell you now, it was Tiesuo who sent Xue'e away, I guarantee it. So please, do explain why you thought that was a good idea."

"Secretary, I–" Qingshu began.

"Comrade Director, just call me Fanhua."

Qingshu's face went red. "I'm not the director of the women's federation," he shot back. "I'm just a public security commissioner."

"A public security commissioner who can't even keep track of this one woman. Heck, even a pet dog knows how to guard the door."

Had she gone too far? If she had, then so be it. Desperate times called for drastic measures. Fanhua paused before she continued: "What was it you said just now about giving me your report? You do realise you're making your report to the entire village committee, yes? Let's speak frankly. Xue'e's up the duff, and half of the responsibility falls on you. Your comrades are here to help you. They're concerned for you. You realise that, yes? Do you deserve that concern? Shall we see what they think?"

Naturally, no one spoke. Qingshu's gaze implored them for help, but it was no use. He slowly rose to his feet, and then slowly bent over in a bow. His posture suggested he was getting ready to admit his mistake. But then they all heard the sound of someone's dog – a single bark, loud and clear, of the perky-tailed variety. Qingshu tilted his head to the side, as if he was drawn to the sound. Most likely he was reminded of Fanhua's line about how a dog could guard a door. His face flushed again. His back straightened and his beer belly rose out in front of him. His hands rooted around between his legs as though he was looking to whip out a gun. He seemed to be about to flare up in anger, but then he plopped back down into the chair and grinned. There was a hardness behind the grin, though, and a chill. Finally, he spoke. It seemed like his voice was being squeezed out of his throat, quiet but fierce. "I... I have my dignity, you know."

Oh, so now he was going to kick back, was he?

Fanhua harrumphed. "That crap's no use to you now. All I want to hear from you is this. When are you going to take Xue'e to get an abortion?"

Qingshu went silent again. If it weren't for Fanqi showing up to smooth things over, then who knows where it would have ended. Fanqi was the best talker in the committee. If Laddy's snotty nose was her inheritance, then Fanqi's was his glib tongue. When his mother was still alive she was a famous matchmaker, known for miles around as "The Number One Gab in Xiushui County". But her tongue could sprout thorns as easily as flowers. She was just as capable of killing off a seemingly perfect match as she was of resuscitating one that seemed hopeless. People said that when Zhaoyuan was in office, Fanqi's mother was the person he feared most in all the village because she could turn all the women in the village against him. She didn't even have to say anything. If she so much as smacked her walking cane against the ground, Zhaoyuan would start stuttering. It was because of Fanqi's mother that he had once become the butt of a widely popular joke. There was one occasion when Zhaoyuan had gathered the villagers together to explain what was going on in international politics. Fanqi's mother showed up, leaning on her cane, just as Zhaoyuan was reading from the newspaper about how Premier Zhou Enlai had gone to welcome Prince Sihanouk of Cambodia at Beijing Airport. The sight of Fanqi's mother made him garble the headline into a far more profane version that was considerably less flattering of the prince. The villagers found this hilarious, but then it turned scarily quiet when they stopped laughing. This joke subsequently became widely known. Zhaoyuan would have been locked up that very day if anyone had reported him, so it was lucky for him that he lived in a village as close-knit as Guanzhuang, where everyone was either a Kong or a Meng.

When it was Qingmao's turn to take charge, he very quickly gave Fanqi a position on the committee. Later, he would say that the nation ought to count its blessings that Fanqi's mother was born on Chinese soil. If she was American, she could very easily have ended up becoming their chief negotiator in the WTO talks, and then China would have been doomed. GATT? You're dreaming. Not in this century or the next. He might have been exaggerating, but it was a telling remark.

Fanqi wasn't quite at the same level as his mother, but he was certainly the smoothest talker on the committee. Which is why he retained his position as mediator. What do mediators do? They smooth things over, making sure everyone manages to get along. Fanqi had a signature catchphrase: "No one's heart is made from stone." Li Hao had once remarked that it would be a mistake to belittle this phrase. It might seem like a simple platitude, but it had real depth. In diplomacy, Li Hao said, this was called "putting aside differences to find common ground", and it was the most crucial of Zhou Enlai's Five Principles of Peaceful Coexistence. Fanqi had remained silent while Fanhua and Qingshu were quarrelling. He sat there in the corner, fondling a cigar, licking it up and down like he was in some dirty movie. Now was his moment to join the fray. He took the pack of cigars out of his pocket.

"My daughter-in-law brought these back from Beijing. They

taste like sweet potato leaves. Showing me the proper filial respect, she says. Imported from Cuba, the same kind Chairman Mao himself used to smoke, and the president of the United States too." He paused and turned his gaze towards the roof. "I also heard this is the kind Shortfur smokes."

Everyone burst out laughing. Shortfur was a dwarf who lived in the village, or a "halfling" as they called them round these parts. A travelling performance troupe once came to visit a temple fair in Wangzhai, and one of their acts was a monkey show. They'd stuck up all the posters, but then their Monkey King ended up refusing to perform because of a pay dispute. The leader of the troupe was pulling his hair out with frustration when someone suggested Shortfur Sun. During Lantern Festival, they said, on the fifteenth night of the new lunar year, he had played the Monkey King in a performance of *Tangseng Retrieves the Scriptures*, and his resemblance to a macaque was uncanny. Delighted, the troupe leader hired Shortfur for just two *jin* of sugarcane. Who'd have thought: Shortfur had never done anything to draw attention to himself before, but he seized this opportunity to occupy the spotlight. His performance was even better than their original Monkey King. That's what you call losing a sesame seed but finding a melon seed, the troupe leader said. He even gave Shortfur a stage name. The most famous of all monkey performers was Liu Xiaolingtong, "Kid Six", so Shortfur became "Kid Seven". In the end he left with them, and eventually, word reached the village that he had made his fortune. He was even glimpsed performing in a movie, playing a waiter in a nightclub. He was wearing a suit and tie and a beret, and he was in charge of serving a ravishing femme fatale with tea and drinks and cigarettes. One time, at a meeting in Xiushui Town, someone told Fanhua they'd seen Shortfur in Macau and he looked cool as fuck, perched on the arm of a sofa with one leg crossed over the other, waiting for someone to light his cigarette for him.

Fanqi's mention of the name prompted a suggestion from someone that they get in touch with Shortfur and try to bring him back to visit the village. He might have drifted away, but he was still a member of the community, and you can't go forgetting your elders and countrymen no matter how successful you are.

"We can come back to Shortfur later," said Fanhua. "Let's quieten down and listen to what Fanqi has to say."

"My daughter-in-law gave me a little grandson," said Fanqi, still holding a cigar. "I told her to bring him back home to me but she says no, the quality of education in Beijing is better. Bullcrap! If the quality of education in Beijing's so great, then how come all the emperors came from elsewhere? Screw her! I didn't want to have anything to do with her. But nobody's heart is made of stone. She brought me these cigars from all that distance away, and I could hardly decline. Come on, have a try." He gave one to Qingshu, and then handed them out around the circle. Fanhua took one too, saying she'd take it home for Dianjun.

"Dianjun? Is Dianjun back?" asked Fanqi. "Is there anything he *hasn't* smoked?"

"He did bring a few packets of cigarettes back with him," said Fanhua. "They're called Mighty Chinas, I think. They come in this red wrapper. He says they're good quality, but I don't know whether that's true or not. The man likes to exaggerate."

"He's not exaggerating," said Xiangsheng. "Those are the good stuff, all right."

"How about this? Wait until Dianjun takes you all out to dinner before you ply him with cigarettes, otherwise he'll end up smoking me out of the house."

They all pledged to fulfil this duty. Only Qingshu remained silent.

"How about it, Qingshu?" said Fanhua. "Are you in?"

Finally, Qingshu spoke: "What about drink?"

Xiangsheng struck himself on the chest. "You leave the drinks to me!"

Fanhua took the opportunity to crack another joke: "Just so we're clear, though, don't be expecting the village to pick up the tab for your drinking money!"

The atmosphere had warmed slightly, but it was still fairly tepid. The committee members were all busy people, and it wasn't easy for them to make time for these meetings. It shouldn't be a gloomy business. They were always saying on TV how there was this meeting happening in Beijing or that meeting happening in Shanghai, and whether it was in Beijing or in Shanghai there was always a "warm discussion" among the attendees before they reached any consensus. The implication was clear: all meetings should be warm.

Fortunately, Fanhua could always call on the buffoonery of County Head Zhang, the man in charge of family planning. This was a failsafe strategy for warming things up. County Head Zhang was famous for his appearance. His face was covered in pockmarks, which is why people called him "County Head Pockface" behind his back. Pockmarks that originated not in smallpox, but in the Great Leap Forward. The entire population was tasked with producing steel back then, and Zhang was one of the steel smelters who spent all day tussling with the furnace flames. The sparks left his pale face covered with scars, but only the critically wounded leave the battlefield, and his wounds were not critical. The weather was hot that year, and the furnace was hotter still, and there was no way of preventing his burns from festering. His face looked like it had bayberries growing out of it. But his leaders liked it. The top brass praised him, and before long the announcement was going out over the loudspeakers that Comrade Zhang was a model worker, a village youth who had managed to become a member of the commune revolutionary committee. Yet he always remained in Nanyuan, since he was from the area, and he had no supporters elsewhere. Up until even a few years ago, he was just the Party committee secretary for Nanyuan Township. It was then that his opportunity came along. Having handled family planning well, he was promoted to deputy county head. There's an old adage that says nine out of every ten pock-marked faces are appealing, and County Head Pockface's appeal lay as much in those pockmarks as in his words and gestures. They were highly expressive, bulging red when he was happy and black when he was angry. He could be compared to Qingshu's idol, Zhao Benshan, such was the potential comedy in everything he did.

As soon as Fanhua mentioned the name of County Head Pock-face, people started to grin. Perhaps some folk have already heard this, said Fanhua, but County Head Pockface made another long report during the last meeting, and the case he mentioned was a very similar situation to Xue'e's. County Head Pockface said there was someone from a village in the east who took his pregnant wife off abroad to have her baby. When they came back, they claimed that this wasn't their own baby they'd brought back with them, but an adoptee they'd picked up along the way. Fanhua described how when County Head Pockface mentioned the travelling abroad, his hands had started chopping back and forth like they were the oars of a little boat. Fanqi chipped in with a suggestion of his own: perhaps they weren't oars – maybe he was swimming doggy paddle. Everyone laughed. Fanhua continued: County Head Pockface asked whether it was really that easy to just pick up a random child on your travels. It so happened that the county had recently been in touch with a foreign adoption agency. They want our Chinese babies, he said, our smart, good-looking babies. They're like fun little dolls to them, with nice black hair and black eyes and yellow skin, wearing a red ribbon in their hair, and a cute red *dudou*, and tiger-head shoes, plus they do as they're told when they grow up. Splendid, let's send off our excess babies abroad. County Head Pockface's gesture to accompany "sending off" was the best of the bunch. He looked like he was doing a Cultural Revolution-style "Loyalty Dance" routine, the way he braced his torso and extended his hands out in front of his chest, before thrusting them forwards to hang momentarily in midair, as though holding a baby that he was waiting for someone to take from him. "If only Lingwen was still here," Fanhua added. "No one dances the Loyalty Dance better than him. He'd certainly be a match for County Head Pockface, in any case."

At this point, Xiaohong appeared in the doorway to report that Tiesuo had fallen asleep and was snoring loudly. And a good thing too, Fanhua said. Is he drooling? Even better. That means he's fast asleep. If he was genuinely worried about Xue'e's whereabouts, then even a bottle of sleeping pills wouldn't have knocked him out. Xiaohong jingled the keys to indicate that she'd locked the door. Somebody suggested getting Xiaohong in here to show them the Loyalty Dance, because no one could dance quite like the young folk. Xiaohong had no idea what a Loyalty Dance was.

"They're just teasing you," Fanhua said. "Leave the key here. You can head back home now, your mother'll be worried if you stay out too late."

Fanhua carried on describing County Head Pockface after Xiaohong had left. He had been pacing the stage with dainty, ladylike steps, and he rolled up the documents he was holding into a baton. This baton eventually came to rest upon a map of Xiushui County which, in his excitement, County Head Pockface treated as a map of the world. Don't imagine we'll send these babies off to America or Europe, he said. You should be so lucky. There are plenty of other countries out there, in Asia, in Africa, in Latin America. Think about Africa and Latin America. Especially Africa. They have more land out there than people, so they want our babies to do the grunt work. He demonstrated the way they'd issue their commands: Ya! Whoa! All the boys we send out there will be named Ya, he said, Ya One, Ya Two, Ya Three, Ya Four, and the girls be Whoa One, Whoa Two, Whoa Three and Whoa Four. What's that, not so keen on those names? You'd rather call them something else? Too bad. They can't be so-and-so Zhang, or Li, or even Pockface Wang. Everyone laughed. County Head Pockface may have had a drink or two, Fanhua speculated, the way he was carrying on. He had a genuine knack for making a complex idea more easily digestible, with all of his banter and sparkling witticisms.

Li Xueshi, the committee member for public welfare, ground out the stub of his cigar under his shoe. "Fuck," he said, "Xue'e won't even have to worry about choosing a name for her sprog."

Fanhua tried to quieten everyone down again. We all know County Head Pockface's trademark blend of the serious and the frivolous, she said. When he decided the time for fun and games was over, he put on a stern face, coughed and tapped his microphone. All at once, he became a completely different person. A grim look came into his eyes, and his pockmarks turned black. When the audience saw him like this, Fanhua said, no one dared laugh any more. They pricked up their ears and listened carefully. County Head Pockface had grim tidings for them all right. Family planning is no mere matter of the crotch, he said. It impacts the national economy, the depletion of natural resources, the sustainable development plan, the ozone layer, global warming and a host of other problems. Which was why, he said, if a situation like this should ever occur again, then every single official in the village would be dismissed, and the chief culprits would be forbidden from standing again as candidates in the village elections. And don't go thinking you'll be allowed to go on your way with nothing more than a smack on the bottom for bad behaviour, he continued. It's not as simple as that. Being an official isn't like being a monk. You don't just decide to give up on reciting sutras and whack the gong on your way out the door. The authorities are smarter than that. Any official who gets dismissed will have all his accounts carefully inspected, and that's doubly true for anyone dismissed over family planning. They'll dig everything out, and if they don't drive you to your death, then they'll at least drive you to your wits' ends. When the time comes, you'll need to explain exactly how much you spent, exactly how much you ate, not just to the people but to the authorities. And if you can't tell them? No problem, they'll be happy to wait until you shit out the evidence. And if you can't shit it out? No problem, they'll just tie you up. Some people might think they're protected by their connections. I'm the Buddha of a Thousand Hands, they'll say, tie up two of them and I still have nine hundred and ninety-eight free. Well, let's just see about that. Let's see whether a Buddha of a Thousand Hands like you is more powerful than the atheism of the law. At this point, Fanhua provided them with a supplementary detail: County Head Pockface had once been a local head of police, where his particular speciality was tying people up. With a rope measuring one metre in length, he could safely tie up three people at once.

Some people laughed, some lowered their heads in thought, while others stared blankly at the form on the wall. This had been an effective meeting, Fanhua thought. Everything that needed to be said had been said. The stakes had been made clear. She snapped shut her notebook. "Practically speaking, the most pressing concern for our village is Xue'e's pregnancy. Everyone have a think about where she might have run off to. We are all grasshoppers balancing on the same string, and we will all fall if we don't work together. You'll get nowhere trying to dance to your own tune. Qingshu here went out of time just now."

Qingshu's head had been bowed in thought, but he jumped and hunched up his shoulders when he heard Fanhua mention his name. It didn't take long for his grin to return, however. He must be feeling ill at ease, Fanhua thought. But she was prepared to offer him an acceptable explanation for his expression.

"Qingshu, don't smile," she said. "I know you're a little embarrassed – you've gone red in the face. That shows you've realised your mistake. But it's not too late to mend the pen gate even if the sheep have already bolted. How about this, Qingshu? You pull open that desk and bring a bed in here. You can sleep on the bed, and Tiesuo can take the desk. You're the director of public security, Qingshu, and I know you're not going to let Tiesuo disappear. Xiangsheng, you go back and tell Xiangmin that the village will have need of his car tomorrow."

"And what about you?" Qingshu asked slowly.

A solemn expression came over Fanhua's face. She gave Qingshu a provocative poke on the side of his forehead.

"What's that, worried I'm going to be sitting back and putting my feet up? I'm going to take Tiesuo's daughters back to my place and treat them like princesses for the evening. Is that good enough for you?"

FOURTEEN

Fanhua had delivered this line purely for effect. She had no intention of actually treating anyone like a princess. But she had been planning to take those two girls home even before Qingshu piped up. Work is one thing, relationships are another. Work demands steely-faced impartiality, but relationships require a bit of kindness every now and again if you don't want people to turn on you. Kindness is the yeast in the steamed bun: virtually worthless, and disgustingly sour, but essential if you want to produce anything other than unleavened lumps of dough.

"I need to go to Tiesuo's place," said Fanhua when the meeting was over. "Who's got a torch? Xiangsheng? Quit trying to hide it up your arse, I can see the thing." Fanhua was keen to have Xiangsheng go with her so she could take the opportunity to talk over this business about a foreigner coming to Xiushui. A thought had come to her during the meeting: it would be wise to send both Xiangsheng and Qingshu away from the village, to ensure they had no chance to assemble a rival faction. She could easily get rid of Qingshu by dispatching him to find Xue'e, and if he didn't succeed then that was his problem. Xiangsheng would be a tougher scalp to shave. It was possible, certainly, but it would require a bit more work. But she definitely wasn't going to let him stick around here. Wasn't he always bragging about how well his business was doing, thanks to all his connections? Well, in that case, he could put them to good use: give him some funds and have him use them to make sure this foreigner comes to Guanzhuang. It was a doomed mission, obviously. He'd have a better chance of scooping the moon from a pond.

Xiangsheng offered to accompany her, just as she'd hoped he would. "Let me go with you," he said. "We can't have that hog taking a bite out of you."

Ah yes, the pig. "Qingshu," Fanhua said, "call Hongmei and tell her to feed Tiesuo's pig."

Xiangsheng walked along behind her, flashlight in hand. He said he'd like to have a word with Dianjun when he got the chance. "Though I realise your time is precious. A couple reunited are as affectionate as newlyweds. I wouldn't want to get in your way."

Fanhua's notebook smacked into Xiangsheng's head. "How dare you talk to your aunt like that? See if I don't beat you to death."

"The nights are long enough, and it won't take up too much time. Can't the two of you spare me a few minutes?"

Fanhua was Xiangsheng's senior, in generational terms, and he rarely indulged in this kind of lewd banter with her. Perhaps he's got into bad habits up in Xiushui Town, Fanhua reflected as she listened to him carrying on. A businessman really has to swim against the current if he wants to be ethical. You're always going to end up being corrupted if you just go with the flow.

Fanhua told him she had to call in at Tiesuo's to pick up his daughters. Xiangsheng asked her why she didn't just call Xiaohong and have her do it instead. Young folk are heavy sleepers, Fanhua replied, and Xiaohong might already be in bed by now. You say the name Cao Cao and Cao Cao shows up, and at that instant, Fanhua's phone rang with a call from Xiaohong. Like the girl was telepathic. She told Fanhua she'd been worried the meeting would go on late, so she had already brought Manny and Laddy over to Fanhua's place. She had been hoping to put them to bed herself, but the two girls were crying and wailing and refusing to do as they were told. Just as stubborn as their father. Before she hung up, Xiaohong encouraged Fanhua to get some rest. Fanhua was about to ask her about the pig when Xiaohong continued: "That hog of Tiesuo's sure can eat. He got through a whole bucket of feed and still wanted more."

You see? She'd even thought to feed the pig. Xiaohong really was like a dutiful servant girl. Xiangsheng clearly thought so too, though he didn't use those exact words.

"If you're Justice Bao," he said, "then Xiaohong is your Wang Zhao and Ma Han rolled into one." He'd chosen his words well, flattering Fanhua with the comparison to the legendary judge, while simultaneously commending Xiaohong for her dependability and talent.

"Well then, what are we waiting for? Come on, you can have that drink with Dianjun."

Xiangsheng lit up the road for Fanhua with his torch.

"There's one other matter that I didn't mention in the meeting," she said. "At the county meeting, the secretary said that there'd be a foreigner coming to survey Xiushui County, though he wasn't sure whether it was because of the elections or the possibility of future investment. But I asked around, and everyone said it was about investment. You have friends in high places – could you find out how things really stand and see if you can get the foreigner to visit Guanzhuang?"

"I'm not as friendly with people in high places as you are."

"That's not true. I've heard it from Fanrong that you and the guys in the industry and commercial tax department have been calling each other brothers since way back."

"Sure, I could have a word with them, see if they can stoke the fire a bit. That would be doable. But what would these foreigners want to come and see in Guanzhuang?"

"And you call yourself a businessman?" said Fanhua. "The paper plant, of course. The place is sitting idle. If they're looking for something to invest in, we could get the place humming again in no time with some funds to pay for the pollution-filtering equipment."

Xiangsheng seemed to be thinking over what Fanhua had said. He remained silent for a long time. Taking the opportunity to strike while the iron was hot, Fanhua continued: "When the time comes, we'll need someone to send in there. What for? To be the representative for the Chinese side, of course! It's as obvious as lice on a bald head. And who here understands economics? Who's best equipped to do such a job? Why, that would be you, Xiangsheng. But we need to start preparing well in advance. Make hay while the sun's still shining."

This looked to have made an impact on Xiangsheng. He slowly inhaled, then exhaled, then inhaled again. A bit like he was practising qigong breathing.

"Everything I'm telling you now is coming right from the heart, OK?" said Fanhua. "Sure, you can make money selling cold noodles, but are you ever going to sell enough of them to be a truly successful entrepreneur? And besides, becoming our Chinese representative wouldn't necessarily affect your business – you could always rent the noodle place out to someone else."

"That's all very well," said Xiangsheng, "but the problem is..."

Fanhua gave him a playful punch. "Don't be such an old lady about it. If you've got a fart in you, then let it on out. Come on, what's the problem?"

"It's not like I'm *that* close with those fuckers in Xiushui. They're not likely to want to speak up on our behalf unless I show them some... appreciation."

"When they need some appreciation, you go right on and appreciate away."

"And if it doesn't work out?"

"It doesn't matter if it works out or not. We still need to make an effort to keep pushing things forward. We might get our hands on some jujubes or we might not, but we'll never know unless we start whacking the tree with a stick."

"But if it doesn't work out," Xiangsheng persisted, "even after the money's been spent. What then?"

Fanhua could see the calculations happening in Xiangsheng's head. He was angling for the power to spend money freely, in a way that would be impossible for anyone to track. He was a businessman all right, trying to figure out how to skim some money for himself before they'd even started.

"Well, naturally you'll need to be supplied with a stick to knock down those jujubes. You can spend away, and so long as everything's properly itemised then there'll be no problems with reimbursement, right?"

"Well then, I suppose I can try."

"Try?" said Fanhua. "What do you mean, try? I'm entrusting you with this job. What is it they say in the old play? A general in the field makes his own rules. If you can pull this off, then the whole of Guanzhuang will owe you a favour."

They passed someone walking a pair of cows. The cows had bells around their necks, and the sound of the bells only accentuated the stillness of the night. That would be Qingshe on his way home, Fanhua thought. Qingshe was a cow trader. He picked up cows all over the place and sold them to Xiushui's Muslim Hui minority. The Huis killed them and sold the meat. He'd once told Fanhua that when cows saw him coming they fled like mice from a cat, or sometimes attempted to butt him with their horns if escape was impossible. But Qingshe had a way of bringing them under control. They always turned magically docile as soon as he brought a bell out of his pocket and shook it in their direction. Fanhua asked him why, and Qingshe explained that cows love to wear bells the way women love to wear scarves.

But Xiangsheng didn't know it was Qingshe. "Who's that?" he said.

"Who else could it be," replied Fanhua. "It's Qingshe." Then she called out, "Hey, Qingshe, you in the money again?"

"Bagged myself a couple more thank you, Secretary." He came over towards them and continued more quietly: "Bought them from a blind man. One of them's pregnant and he had no idea."

"Jackpot," said Fanhua.

"Not my fault if he couldn't see it," said Qingshe.

"That's what makes you the cow connoisseur. You can tell with just a touch of your hand."

"A blessing from the Buddha, that's what it is. I'll be able to start up my own ranch if I run into a stupid cunt like that every day."

"And when that day comes, I'll cut the ribbon for you myself," said Fanhua.

When the sound of the bells had grown distant, Xiangsheng reminded Fanhua that he wanted to see Dianjun. "To tell you the truth," he said, "I want to get his advice."

"What advice can he possibly give you?" said Fanhua. "All he knows is blowing his own trumpet."

"Well, that's a talent in itself. I couldn't blow my own trumpet if I tried." Then, as though something had only just occurred to him, he went on: "Oh yes, there was one other thing I wanted to talk to you about. It's no big deal. I'd forgotten all about it, actually." Fanhua asked what it was. "It's so trivial, really, barely worth mentioning." Fanhua asked him again what he was talking about. "If I didn't mention it, I'm sure it would never have occurred to you. That's how trivial it is."

Fanhua waited for him to continue. Xiangsheng pointed his torch up into the sky. "Hey, that's weird – how come there are no stars up there?" Fanhua carried on waiting. Finally, Xiangsheng got to the point: "So, I was on my way back here today, and I called in at Gongzhuang, and I ran into someone. Can you guess who?"

"There are over a thousand people living in Gongzhuang," said Fanhua. "How do you expect me to know? Was it Caixiang?" Caixiang was an old flame of Xiangsheng's from back in the day, but the couple had been forced apart by Xiangsheng's parents because of her family's inferior status.

"Caixiang? Her stomach's as big as a keg these days, what would I want to talk to her for? No, I saw the Gongzhuang branch secretary, Gong Weihong."

"You mean Scrawny Dog?"

"Right, Scrawny Dog, though he's put on so much weight he's more like a fat pig these days. There was someone Scrawny Dog wanted to talk to me about. He went on about it for ages and ages, and I couldn't figure out who he meant. The way he was prattling on, it was nigh on impossible to work out what he was getting at. You would have struggled too, I bet."

Fanhua was wondering where Xiangsheng was going with this. She wished he'd just hurry up and get to the point.

Xiangsheng stopped, flashed his torch around them and coughed. "There's a tomb up there behind the village," he said in a quiet voice. "Do you remember?"

If she'd been asked this question two days earlier, Fanhua would genuinely have had no recollection. But it was fresh in her mind now. She pictured the tomb, and the weeds growing waist-high on top of it. It was dry sagebrush, the kind even sheep wouldn't eat, and it was a chilling image to be reminded of in the middle of the night. Not because of the dead body underneath, but because of the official policy. The dead had to make way for the living. No tombs could be left standing. No exceptions. What was

Xiangsheng getting at, bringing this up with her now? What was he plotting?

"Tomb, what tomb?" said Fanhua. "You know what a scaredy-cat I am, right? Ghost stories give me the creeps."

"I knew you wouldn't remember. I couldn't either."

"Stop waffling. What tomb are you talking about? Whose tomb?" Fanhua grabbed the torch from Xiangsheng's hand and shone it around them, as though she were genuinely afraid there might be ghosts out there.

"Gong Weihong said we hadn't levelled the grave of Qinggang's mother. Up there behind the village."

"Qinggang? Who's that? We don't have anyone of that name in our village, do we?"

"This is all ancient history," said Xiangsheng. "He died decades ago. Some people say he died in North Korea, others say he died in Taiwan. And fuck knows where that cunt of a mother of his died."

"Well, that must be why I'm hearing about this for the first time," said Fanhua. "You're a few years older than me, so you're the one who should know about all this."

"Gong Weihong said he wanted to dig Qinggang's mother out of her tomb, cremate her remains and bury her in Gongzhuang."

Fanhua didn't get it. What was this all about? A body that had been lying there for decades – even the bones would probably have rotted away by now. What did they want it for?

"What's Scrawny Dog after?" Fanhua asked.

"I had no idea until he told me. Scrawny Dog is her grand-nephew. Qinggang and Scrawny Dog's father were cousins."

Fanhua was riled. "What makes them think they can take one of our villagers and bury them in Gongzhuang? We're a village of Kongs and Mengs. We can't let Guanzhuang become a laughing stock!"

But Xiangsheng's next remark choked the words in her throat. "And if he reports us?"

Fanhua shone the torch in Xiangsheng's face, lighting up his mouth. He remained facing the beam of light, eyes screwed up tight as he kept talking. Every bead of saliva that sprayed from his mouth felt like a bullet to Fanhua.

"I asked him, when did tombs first come into the world? Whose was the first tomb in all the history of the world? Confucius, that's who. And who's Confucius? He's the ancestor of us Guanzhuang folk. But Scrawny Dog interrupted me. So, he says, you won't let us dig her up? Fine, he says, let's see how the authorities decide to deal with the matter. He said we won't have a leg to stand on if we've failed to fully implement the tomb-levelling policy. He even starts dropping in these classical allusions. You can see the sun in a single drop of water, he says, and you can see all the skulduggery of Guanzhuang in a single tomb. You've no idea how infuriating the man is. I was fuming."

That was the moment when the torch cut out. With the street-lights all dark, it was as black as the bottom of a pan when the hob turns off. They were startled by the sound of someone's pet grasshopper plunking against a metal pail. And then they jumped again at the sudden bark of a dog, like two claps of thunder. It was loud enough to activate the light under a nearby ceremonial archway. Fanhua recognised it as belonging to Xiangsheng's brother, Xiangmin. A sound-activated light? The man was burning money.

Someone carrying a hoe came along, swiftly passing through the circle of light, but Fanhua didn't see clearly who it was. They had a kind of ghostly look about them. Alarmed, Fanhua hurried over towards the light. There was a stone plaque on the arch, engraved with a line from Confucius. They'd criticised the hell out of Confucius back in the Cultural Revolution, but he was all the rage again nowadays. "Practising restraint and observing ritual proprietary", that was what they called it. But wasn't Xiangmin religious? Surely religious faith contradicted these tenets of Confucianism. Fanhua's emotions were a mess, and she stared up at the stone plaque for a long time.

"So what's your decision?" asked Xiangsheng.

"Should we just let them dig her up?"

"What do you think?"

Fanhua sniffed. "What do you reckon Scrawny Dog's goal is in all this?"

"Exactly," said Xiangsheng. "What *is* his goal in all this?"

"I still don't get it. This can't be his real objective. This is him passing a jenny off as a jackass."

"That's right," said Xiangsheng. "What's he playing at?"

Fanhua laughed. "Just think, they'll need to do the cremation, and hold a funeral. What a headache."

"Damn right," said Xiangsheng. "He's got shit for brains, has Scrawny Dog."

Reluctant to make a decision, Fanhua switched the conversation to another topic. "I've heard Xiangmin's planning to build a church in Wangzhai."

"He's burning money. It's not like he has so much of it to spare. Imagine what he'd be like if he was actually rich."

"But they say you can make money from a church as well, no? The amount you get in donations isn't too shabby. But there's one thing I don't understand – why build it in Wangzhai? Why not here in Guanzhuang? Plenty of believers round here, at least a hundred or so."

"But it wouldn't do to be making money at our villagers' expense," Xiangsheng explained on his brother's behalf. "And besides, everyone will know it was a Guanzhuang man who built it, no matter where he actually puts the thing."

Fanhua felt a sudden jolt. That foreigner would probably be religious. "Xiangsheng, when you meet the foreigner, you tell him we have a man from Guanzhuang building a church. He needn't worry about there not being any service for him to attend when he's here."

"OK, that's one reasonable argument."

"And you can say we have lovely scenery around here, and the ecological environment is superb."

"Good, that's two. Any more?"

"Absolutely. Tell him we're a village of Kongs and Mengs. Aren't they always going on about a harmonious society these days? Well, society doesn't get much more harmonious than it is around here. We've never had any conflict between labour and capital, or workers going on strike, and we never will. He can go all in, no need to hold back."

"OK, that's a good one. What's a capitalist more afraid of than strikes?" But then Xiangsheng steered the conversation back to Scrawny Dog. "So, do you agree to let Scrawny Dog dig up the tomb or not? We need a definite answer."

"Well, when would they be planning to do it?" asked Fanhua.

"I asked him that. He said they'd wait until the beginning of winter when people are less busy."

Fanhua could relax at that. Of course, she thought that Gongzhuang would be having their elections too, and there was no way a son-of-a-bitch like Scrawny Dog would have time to deal with something like this right now.

"Well, let's not answer him just yet," she said. "Come on, let's go back to my place, and you can share a bottle with Dianjun."

"Another time," said Xiangsheng. "Since we're outside Xiangmin's door, I'd better poke my head in and see what he says about building the church. It's like our great ancestor says – you should respect an older brother like you would a father."

FIFTEEN

It started raining later that night. Autumn winds and autumn showers, it got cold quickly. Tiesuo's two girls were squeezed in with Beanie. Like all young children, Laddy, the little one, was a glutton for sleep. She was whining and snivelling when she arrived, but she fell asleep almost immediately. Fanhua's father slept in the living room, and the three girls joined Fanhua's mother in bed.

Fanhua was an early riser anyway, but she woke up especially early the next day. She went in to check on her mother's room first. Fanhua's mother turned on the light when she heard her daughter come in, then rolled over to go back to sleep. She was unhappy with Fanhua for causing all this trouble. The three girls were sound asleep, like three little piglets beside their mother sow. The rainwater had come in and soaked the edge of the bed under the window where Fanhua's mother was sleeping. Fanhua mopped up the water with a cloth and then tiptoed out of the room. When she was back out in the yard, she washed her and Dianjun's underwear and hung them under the eaves of the roof to dry, before sweeping the yard and tossing a handful of grass into the rabbit cage. She liked to wander around outside in the early mornings and listen to villagers' complaints. She'd deal with them herself if she could, and if she couldn't then she'd bring them back for the committee to deal with. But the rain meant that the streets were empty this morning. It wasn't long before Fanhua reached the edge of the village. The crops hadn't come through yet, and the earth was still smooth. There was a vegetable patch where a squash trellis and a bean frame were still standing, the dark timber covered in a layer of moss. Fanhua remained there for a while, gazing at that bright glint of green through the rain. On her way back, she noticed a dead chicken in the ditch beside the field. Couldn't be a case of bird flu, could it? Using a stick, she dragged it into the field and then dug a hole to bury it in.

As she emerged from the fields, Fanhua heard the sound of someone singing. It was coming from over by the persimmon tree. It was a big tree, with branches black like charcoal and leaves red like sunset. The rainwater had turned the leaves a darker shade of red, like blood just beginning to clot. There was a little thatched cottage under the tree where a squash farmer had once lived. The voice had a husky tone that belied a hint of tenderness. It couldn't be Xue'e, whose monotone voice was as shrill as a whistle. Not Xiaohong, since it was hardly the kind of thing she'd do, and besides, her favourite song was *Who Says My Village Ain't Lovely?* Not Qingshu, surely? Qingshu's favourite song was *Ode to Beijing*, a throwback to the time he spent in the capital as a soldier. When he sang, it was invariably "Gleaming dawn clouds rise over golden Beijing". Fanhua continued in the direction of the singing

It turned out to be Lingpei. The stick he'd been using to knock down persimmons had become a microphone in his hand, and he was belting out *A Beijinger in New York*:

> *Time and time again*
> *You ask me,*
> *Ask whether I love you.*
> *Time and time again*
> *I ask myself,*
> *Ask if I do still love you.*

Lingpei was not in Beijing, and he was certainly not in New York. He'd just come out of jail, but if this was the song he wanted to sing, then no one was going to stop him. In the light from an oil lamp, his shaven head was gleaming like a greased bottle gourd. How often do you see a lamp like that in this day and age? It was strange, and somehow depressing. Fanhua didn't want to startle Lingpei, so she quietly took a few steps back before calling out: "That's a fine voice and no mistake – whose is it?"

The singing instantly ceased, and the only sound left was the rain. Plus another noise: the air bubbles popping out from the water-logged ground. A naughty sort of sound, like the chatter of children. Except as you went on listening, it started to sound more like a moan, a lamentation for some lingering pain.

Lingpei's head emerged, now looking less like a bottle gourd and more like an inflated pig's bladder. His face was as soft and tender as a one-month-old babe's. When he saw it was Fanhua, Lingpei hurried towards her, then stopped and stood there with his hands pressed tight against the seams of his trousers. Fanhua remembered that he'd inherited splayed feet from his father. Splayed feet were an advantage when it came to wielding a drill barrow, and Lingpei's father had once been his production team's drill barrow specialist. He and Fanhua's father had got along well while he was still alive. He'd surely have never imagined that his son would end up becoming a pickpocket. But a prodigal son is more precious than gold; every-thing would turn out OK if Lingpei had truly made a fresh start. Right now his toes were pointing towards each other, such was his embarrassment. He stared at them and said nothing.

"I was hoping I'd run into you," said Fanhua. "What, aren't you going to offer me any kind of greeting?"

Lingpei managed to produce one word: "Secretary."

Fanhua patted him on the shoulder. "According to family senior-ity, you ought to call me your grandaunt." She stepped into the cottage, only to discover that there were six or seven people already inside, including two girls. The light flickered with the wavering of the lamp wick, like a scene out of *Journey to the West*.

"This is my grandaunt," said Lingpei. "She's come here to see you all."

There was one man who looked to be older than Fanhua. He was so bow-legged you could have tucked a basketball between his thighs.

"Then that makes her a great aunt of mine too," he said. A smarmy reply. "After all, we're all family here. Hello there, Grandaunt."

Fanhua wrinkled her nose. She leaned in towards Lingpei and asked him what they were all doing here.

"We're here to pay our respects. To our master."

Paying respects to their master? Did that mean the old rascal who'd taught them to steal had died? That would certainly be a blessing for the people of Xiushui.

"You mean, that old guy... he's dead?" she asked.

"The old gentleman is alive and well. May he remain so until he's a hundred years old."

Fanhua was puzzled.

"The old gentleman knows the ways things are done," said Lingpei, "and he has his connections. He's the one who got us out of prison."

Fanhua lingered inside for a moment, then pushed Lingpei outside. Unsure where to begin, she eventually settled on the oil lamp. What was the deal with that? Lingpei became more talkative. He said every clan has its traditions, and every guild has its regulations. Different trades have different rituals. Some rituals involve a salvo of gunfire, and some involve fireworks. Theirs happened to involve an oil lamp.

Fanhua took in a gulp of cold air. "Are you lot planning to get up to your old tricks again? Hmm? Still hungry for punishment?"

"Don't worry, Secretary," said Lingpei. "My situation has changed. I've washed my hands in the golden basin. I'm a changed man."

Fanhua asked what the deal was with those two girls.

Lingpei was startled. "Girls? Oh, you mean the tofu puddings? They're just friends I tag along with."

Tofu puddings? An interesting name. "Tofu puddings" was what they called girls in his trade, Lingpei explained to Fanhua, sensing that she was still confused.

Fanhua gave him a punch in the chest. "Never mind all that crap," she said. "You hurry up and send these friends of yours away. I'll talk with you again another time, just the two of us. We can discuss your work situation. I've already decided we're going to give you a job, and you're going to do me proud."

An idea occurred to Fanhua right then: she could have Lingpei keep an eye on the paper plant. People were always scaling the walls of the compound to steal stuff, ever since the plant stopped operating. The township police had been over to discuss the matter with her. She acted indignant when they told her to keep her eyes peeled in Guanzhuang, refusing to admit the possibility that anyone from her village could be responsible, but that was just for show. She knew the thieves belonged to Guanzhuang.

"What work, Grandaunt?" Lingpei quickly asked.

"I want you to work at the paper plant."

"Don't try to fool me, Secretary." So it was back to "secretary" again. "They closed down the paper plant, I heard about it while I was inside."

"It's closed down for now, but it'll be opening again eventually. There have been people going in there and stealing things. We've tried to catch them but never succeeded. I'm not trying to draw attention to your shortcomings. This is the kind of job that would play to your strengths. You watch the place for me, and I'll pay you a salary."

Lingpei cracked his knuckles. "Grandaunt, just you wait. Wait and see how I handle them."

"No," said Fanhua, "you're not going to do anything like that yourself. You'll just be keeping a record of who stole what and when, and who was outside to help them get rid of the goods. Keep a record of it all. But you can't tell anyone." She peered back at the cottage. "And that includes those beanflowers of yours. If you so much as give anyone else a *hint* of this, I'll cut out your tongue, you see if I don't."

"You're good to me, Grandaunt. As good to me as my master."

This wasn't a comparison Fanhua particularly appreciated, but the sentiment was admirable. "All right, fine," she said. "A master might lead you to the door, but he can't be pious for you. Do your job, and don't cause me any more trouble."

SIXTEEN

When she got home, she went into the kitchen to fry some eggs for Manny and Laddy. In a bit, she thought, she'd go and drop them off at school. She could call in on the headmaster and ask him to keep a close eye on them. When the eggs were done, Laddy – the younger of the two – appeared promptly at the door. Fanhua asked her whether she always got up so early. Laddy informed Fanhua that she wouldn't be going to school today. Was she in a mood again? She might be little, but she certainly had plenty to worry about. Fanhua freed her hands and leant down to rub Laddy's cheek.

"Listen up," she said, giving Laddy's nose a tweak, "after breakfast, you're going to go to school. And by the time you finish school, your mum will have come back. She loves you very much, and she hasn't gone far away. She just needed to go and visit some relatives."

Laddy pointed out that the reason she wouldn't be going to school today was because it was Saturday.

Gah, she'd been so busy her brain had turned to mush. Fanhua had managed to forget the days of the week.

"So why aren't you enjoying a nice lie-in, if it's Saturday?"

Laddy moistened her lips without offering a reply. When she thought about it, Fanhua didn't know why she was saying this to Laddy. She'd been exactly the same when she was a little girl: more enthusiastic about getting out of bed on Saturday than she was on any other day of the week, desperate to ensure she could squeeze every moment of playtime out of the day. Her sister soon emerged too, and so did Beanie, following the other girls around like a shadow even though she would normally still be snoozing in bed. Under normal circumstances, Beanie refused to eat egg, which tasted like chicken poo, but she'd suddenly become more interested now her two big sisters were tucking in. From the enthusiasm with which Laddy gobbled down her breakfast, Fanhua could tell Xue'e never let her daughters eat eggs, despite owning a dozen chickens. Manny, being a few years older, knew a bit more about table manners, and she nibbled her egg yolk more slowly. Fanhua suddenly remembered what Tiesuo had said about demanding two eggs each morning, or a single egg with a double yolk if two eggs were not available.

"In a bit, you can go and give your daddy some eggs," Fanhua said to Manny. "Tell him they're all double-yolk eggs."

"Where is my daddy?" asked Laddy.

"He's been promoted," Fanhua replied. "He's working for the village committee now."

Manny yanked on her sister's hair. "You watch out, Daddy's going to smack your bottom."

Clearly, Tiesuo had threatened the girls to ensure they kept their mouths shut. When Fanhua's mother came out of the bathroom, Fanhua had her take Manny to the village committee to deliver the breakfast to Tiesuo and Qingshu. Once they'd left, Fanhua turned to Laddy.

"Laddy, does your daddy smack your bottom?"

Laddy remained silent, but her lip started wobbling, and soon there were tears spilling down her cheeks.

"If he ever dares smack your bottom again, then I'll smack *his* bottom. I'll make sure it really hurts, and I'll get your mummy to smack his bottom too. Now then, tell Auntie. Where's your mummy gone?"

"My daddy said that if anyone asks, I should tell them she's gone to Granny's house."

You can't blame a child for not knowing when to keep her mouth shut. Now Fanhua at least knew that she could scratch Xue'e's home village off the list of possible locations.

Xiaohong showed up a little while later. She was holding one umbrella and had a second tucked under her arm. She was also carrying a knitted rabbit that she said was for Laddy to play with. "What are you going to do if those girls want to play with Beanie's rabbits? Beanie will be upset if you let them, and they'll throw a tantrum if you don't." Xiaohong really had thought of everything. She handed the knitted rabbit to Laddy, and then asked Fanhua if she'd be holding another meeting, and if so whether she'd need Xiaohong to spread the word. Fanhua told her yes, but she wasn't to inform anyone until after ten o'clock.

The clothes hanging from the eaves seemed to suddenly remind Xiaohong of something. "Ohhh, what an idiot I've been," she said, slapping herself in the face. "I almost forgot – I've got two bars of soap for you." She pulled the soap out from her trouser pocket. "I can't vouch for their quality," she continued, "so don't blame me if they're no good."

Fanhua stroked the bars of soap, running her hands over them like she was caressing the cheeks of a child. She couldn't say how good they were, but it was a pretty decent brand. The name was "Fine and Bright". Not particularly sophisticated, maybe, but that was the way the guys round here liked it.

"Xiaohong, I should be reprimanding you for this. If you're not careful, you're going to turn into Sudhana, the Child of Wealth himself." But Fanhua was smiling, despite her critical words. "What's going to happen if you go on like this? I have to pay you back. How much were they?"

"I'll be making a profit if you pay me," said Xiaohong. "I was given them by someone who didn't ask for a penny in return."

"Oh," said Fanhua. She quickly hid away her smile and assumed a serious expression. "Xiaohong, was it a *boy* who gave you these? An admirer whose family owns a factory, perhaps? Come on now, give me the good news."

Xiaohong was chewing on bubble gum. Unperturbed, she looked up and replied: "Nothing gets past you. You're right, I did get them from a boy."

"Which village is he from?" Fanhua asked, lowering her voice.

Xiaohong laughed and patted Fanhua on the knee. "From Yanji-azhai. Do you see now? It was my cousin who gave them to me. He runs a furniture factory, and one of his debtors paid him back with a few truckloads of soap instead of money. They have a mountain of the stuff now, more than they could get through in a lifetime, or even two. He's grateful to me for helping him use it up. If you reckon it's good quality, then I'll go back and get you some more."

Fanhua had a brainwave: why not take some of this soap and give it out to people? Some of the ordinary villagers, especially the ones who were getting on in years, wouldn't necessarily remember who their benefactor was if you gave them money. But if you gave them a bar of soap, even if it was worthless crap, they'd be forever grateful.

"Xiaohong," said Fanhua, "go and tell your cousin that the village will buy his soap. It's not like it can be worth all that much, after all. Ask him how much he wants – it doesn't matter too much, so long as it's a bit lower than the wholesale price."

"Are you planning on giving the villagers a little bonus?" She really was uncannily sharp, that Xiaohong.

"Let's say I am. In any case, your cousin will be getting some cash in hand, and he won't end up making such a loss."

It occurred to Fanhua that this might have been what Xiaohong was secretly angling for all along. She would probably decline once or twice out of politeness, and then offer her grateful thanks on behalf of her cousin. But Fanhua was wrong. Xiaohong shook her head so sharply that her pigtails swung round and hit Fanhua.

"Oh no, absolutely not, I wouldn't dream of it. What a thought. There's no harm in taking someone's money off their hands, especially public money. But this is different. This isn't just any old public money – this is *your* public money, *our* money. I'd have bad dreams if I took it. No, absolutely not, don't frighten me saying that."

Fanhua was touched. Her heart felt squishy. There's true perspective for you. Not like Xiangsheng, who made all the right noises when he was standing in front of you, but all he really cared about was lining his own pocket. Xiangsheng was a profiteering rat, lurking in his hole, and no ordinary rat either: a demon rodent who wasn't afraid to take on several cats at once. Whereas Xiaohong was a bird of prey, a sparrowhawk, soaring with outstretched wings against the sunset clouds. Serve her up some dirt and she wouldn't so much as dignify it with a glance.

The rain had stopped. Beanie and Laddy were playing out in the yard. Beanie didn't usually have any other children to play with, and the excitement of it all had gone to her head. She was pelting around the yard and had covered herself in mud. Fanhua heard Laddy telling Beanie that they ought to sing a song. Beanie said she knew *lots* of songs. But there was one song Beanie couldn't possibly know, Laddy said. Beanie was confounded. Her shocked expression soon turned into a look of deep respect. Laddy held onto the knitted rabbit with both hands and looked extremely serious as she sang the following verse:

Beanie has been officially
Informed by imperial decree,
She can't use loo roll to wipe her botty.
If she does use loo roll, she can't talk to me,
If she does talk to me, then she can't watch TV
Until she dies from needing to pee,
Thus it shall be.

Before she had even finished chanting, Beanie had jumped to her feet. "*You're* the one who'll die from needing to pee." Fanhua had heard Beanie singing this song before. There was a time when she used to get over-excited every time they ate a meal. First, it'd be "Granddad has been officially informed by imperial decree" and then "Granny has been officially informed by imperial decree". Far from being angry at Beanie for suggesting they might die from needing to pee, they praised her performance and told her she was as talented as Princess Bright Pearl. Eventually, it was Fanhua's turn. Beanie leapt onto the table and started: "Mummy has been officially informed by imperial decree." Fanhua yanked her outside and angrily informed her that Mummy wouldn't want her any more if she ever uttered that ridiculous song again. Beanie was having none of it. She started off again: "Mummy has been officially informed by imperial decree." Fanhua lost her temper and smacked her on the bottom. And ever since then, Beanie had never dared sing the song again. But Beanie had forgotten all about the smack now that Laddy had taken the lead. She bounced up and down from the first line to the last. Where did they pick up such rubbish?

Xiaohong raised a hand to her mouth to conceal a smile. Fanhua

133

assumed she was laughing at the song. "Beanie's incapable of learning anything good," she said, "but she doesn't need anyone to teach her how to be bad."

Xiaohong continued to laugh, so hard that she eventually had to clutch her belly. Confused, Fanhua asked her what was so funny. Xiaohong was still doubled over with laughter, and it was a while before she managed to straighten up. It had just reminded her of her cousin, she explained. Her cousin, who hadn't even attended junior middle school, had now taken it upon himself to study English, and he'd referred to the soap as *saopo*. Xiaohong buckled with laughter again as she explained how her cousin's wife had suddenly lashed out at him, complaining she'd married into a family from hell, who didn't appreciate her even though she paid the appropriate respect to her husband's parents, and fed the pigs and chickens *and* found time to re-lacquer the furniture. Eventually, it transpired that she'd misheard his mangled attempt at English as the Chinese word for "shrewish wife".

Oh, so that's what was so funny. Fanhua patted Xiaohong on the shoulder and told her she shouldn't laugh. It'd be their village head who was forcing everyone to learn English, so if anyone was to blame for this farce, it was him.

"You're joking. I know their village head – he was two years ahead of me in high school. And no one hated English more than him."

"That's something I haven't had time to tell you about yet. During our meeting, the man upstairs told us there's going to be an American coming to make an inspection of Xiushui. I guess you can call this an 'international interaction'. And he gave every village head a copy of this English textbook, saying that they were the ones who should be setting an example in their studies. If you sharpen your spears at the last minute then at the very least they'll be shiny, right? Who knows if they're actually going to make it as far as Xiushui. Even if they do, I doubt they'll come to Wangzhai Township, let alone Guanzhuang Village. But since we're talking about an international interaction, we're going to fight for it. We're going to see if we can't get them to come here and interact with *us*. I've already put Xiangsheng in charge of finding some way of bringing the foreigner to Guanzhuang."

Xiaohong had been sitting down, but now she rose to her feet. "Seriously? There's really going to be a foreigner coming here?"

"Call me a cur if I'm lying."

"That's not what I meant," said Xiaohong. "I heard my cousin mention something about that, but I thought he was just trying to trick me. You don't know what my cousin's like, he's always spinning these wild stories. But I guess this one's true."

"It certainly is," said Fanhua. "I've got Xiangsheng on the job. How can it not be true?"

Xiaohong's eyes widened. "You've really put Xiangsheng in charge?"

"That's right. He's been in business so long he can convince you a square's a circle and vice versa. That's the kind of person you need to handle diplomacy. I'll need to pay him a salary as well."

"You're not worried you'll be tossing a meat dumpling to the dogs? Gone for good?"

Fanhua was confused. What was this talk of dumplings and dogs? Surely they didn't have to worry about Xiangsheng emigrating abroad with this foreigner?

"I mean," Xiaohong said quietly, "that Xiangsheng can be a bit too eager when it comes to his expenses."

Ah, so Xiaohong was worried about Xiangsheng using public funds to line his own pockets. She was worried on behalf of the village. Oh Xiaohong, Fanhua said to herself, that's exactly what I *want* him to do – I'll only start to worry if he *doesn't* help himself to the money. Xiaohong deserved praise for her concern, but Fanhua chose to act like she didn't understand the implication. "What can be achieved without money, in this day and age?" she said. "Even a dog in heat can't get what it wants for free. So long as it's spent correctly, we'll spend what we need to spend."

"I'm just worried it'll be a dumpling for dogs. Wasted."

"It still needs spending, even if it ends up being wasted," Fanhua said. "We need to be able to compete. Do you see? It'll go down in the history books if we can get the foreigner to come to Guanzhuang. And not just that. When the foreigner writes his report, you can be sure he'll want to mention the woman who's serving her second term as village head. He'll take his report back to America, and America is the home of the United Nations Headquarters. The name

Guanzhuang will be famous. Do you think we'll find it hard to attract foreign investment after that? Of course, if he doesn't end up coming then there's not much we can do about it. It doesn't do any good to push an ox's face in the water if it doesn't want to drink. Throwing a dumpling to dogs? I wouldn't call it that. I'd call it 'high pay to foster integrity'."

"What if the foreigner does come here?" said Xiaohong. "We need to start getting ready."

"No need to rush," said Fanhua. "When the time comes, we'll just hang up a couple of banners."

"That's right," said Xiaohong. "Just a couple of banners, and we'll stick up some new doorway couplets, and give every house a spring clean." Fanhua asked Xiaohong if she had any other advice. "Me? What advice could I possibly have? I'll do whatever you tell me to do. I've heard Beanie's father spoke pretty decent English when he was at school."

"Hardly. Anyway, it doesn't matter how good you are if you don't put it to use for years on end."

"He's terribly clever though, he picks things up very quickly. Why not have him help by writing a line of English on the banners? English and Chinese in parallel." Xiaohong thought of everything – she truly was Fanhua's trusty right arm.

"Forget about Dianjun," said Fanhua. "Let's get Fanqi's son Xiangchao to do it. I've heard it's foreign languages he teaches up in Beijing."

"Xiangchao? Has he come back?" asked Xiaohong.

"He will if I give him a call, won't he?"

Xiaohong laughed. "That's true. And if he doesn't, we'll tell him Fanqi's bed-ridden and see what he does then."

All of a sudden, Beanie started crying. It turned out she'd set her heart on the knitted rabbit, but Laddy was refusing to give it to her, and now they had both seized hold of the toy. Xiaohong went over and pulled them apart.

"Beanie, let go," Fanhua ordered her daughter from where she was standing. Beanie let go of the rabbit but then immediately grabbed hold of Laddy's clothes instead.

"This kid Laddy is really something," said Xiaohong. "She's certainly not intimidated by strangers."

"Beanie's been spoiled by her grandparents," said Fanhua. "She doesn't know how to compromise."

"Shall I take Laddy and Manny away?" asked Xiaohong. "It's not like there's anything else I can do to help you at the moment." She took a handkerchief from her pocket to wipe the snot from Laddy's nose. When Laddy tried to dodge away, Xiaohong pointed out the rabbit that was embroidered on the handkerchief. "Well, would you look at that, there's a little bunny on here too. Little bunny, oh so smart, with red eyes and a white fur coat. Front legs short and rear legs long, see how likes to hop along."

Laddy leant into Xiaohong, lifting up her face to be wiped. At that moment, Manny came back. Xiaohong folded the used handkerchief and tucked it into Manny's pocket, telling her she should use it to wipe her little sister's nose. Manny bit her lip and stared angrily at Laddy, as though she blamed her sister for letting the side down.

Xiaohong had a plan to cheer up Manny. "You know," she said, turning to Fanhua, "Manny is getting prettier by the day. Just look at her nose, and her eyes, and her eyebrows – especially her eyebrows. Ever so delicate. Xue'e's awfully lucky to have her." This speech was aimed at Manny's ears, and it hit its mark. The girl immediately forgot her anger. She was old enough to know how to feel bashful. A smile came to her lips, and her cheeks turned cherry red.

Xiaohong gave Fanhua a look. "I've got something," she said.

Fanhua asked what she had got, and Xiaohong told her she had an idea for how to entertain the foreigner if he did make it to Guanzhuang. Needless to say, her idea was an excellent one. She said they should group all the children in the village into a choir. She wasn't sure what song they should sing, but she would keep thinking on it. Fanhua felt like smiling when she saw how Xiaohong had got caught up in her own plans, but she went along with the idea. "OK then," she said. "There's no need for me to worry if you're organising it. You're in charge of this one."

It was still raining. Xiaohong thunked open her umbrella. "Be a good girl and come along with me now," she said to Manny. "You can carry an umbrella for your little sister."

Fanhua went outside with her. As they were passing Fanxin's cowshed, she asked Xiaohong a question: "Xiaohong, did you know Lingpei's come back?"

Xiaohong tossed her pigtails. "He didn't rot to death inside, then?"

"He looked pretty alive when I saw him," Fanhua replied. "I think he's even put on weight."

Xiaohong curled her lip. "Can't see why he didn't rot to death inside."

At that moment, Fanxin sent his cow outside. The cow was black and white, white like cotton wool and black like the cotton boll. When Xiaohong saw the cow coming towards them, she grabbed the girls and fled, her hand covering her nose. She was still a girl, after all, and she prized cleanliness. Laughing, Fanhua headed in the direction of the village committee building.

SEVENTEEN

There was clearly nothing wrong with Tiesuo's appetite since he'd not spared so much as a crumb of his breakfast. Staring at the plate, Fanhua was trying to think up some kind of cutting retort, but Tiesuo beat her to it.

"Hey," he said, "you must be pumping your hens with chemicals, those eggs were terrible. Tasted like chickenshit."

Fanhua didn't have any hens. The eggs had been bought from various families around the village, including Tiesuo's. Ignoring him, she opened a window to let in some fresh air, then picked up a pillow that had fallen to the floor. With her back to Tiesuo, she brushed the dust from the pillow. "No one's forcing you to eat them," she said. "Feel free to starve to death instead."

"You're detaining me here," said Tiesuo.

Fanhua handed the pillow to Qingshu. "Qingshu, is Tiesuo being detained?"

"Fuck me," said Qingshu. "He was sound asleep, talking to himself in his dreams, laughing too. I didn't get a wink all night."

Fanhua turned to face Tiesuo. "Oh Tiesuo, did you dream of having a baby boy?"

Tiesuo continued to play dumb. "Who's having a boy? When'll we be wetting the baby's head?"

Fanhua's ire was rising. "Quit acting the fool," she said, her voice suddenly louder. "You know Xue'e's pregnant, yes?"

"News to me."

Qingshu leapt to his feet. "Are you seriously going to stand there and tell us you didn't know your wife was pregnant?"

"First I've heard."

"You're presumably the man responsible for these glad tidings," said Fanhua. "How can you not have known?"

"Well, I didn't."

"Oh, so you're saying this is the handiwork of some other guy?" said Fanhua. "Xue'e'd tear you a new one if she heard you talking that way. How's she ever going to be able to show her face in public if you keep up like this?"

This upset Tiesuo. First, his hands began to tremble, and then he slapped himself in the face. "I, I, I haven't told you anything, have I?"

Fanhua shot Qingshu a look that told him to prepare to write this down. Instead of reaching for a notebook, Qingshu pulled a little dictaphone, about the size of a pack of cards, from inside his drawer.

"Well, you can tell us now," Fanhua said to Tiesuo.

"Tell you what?"

"You don't need to tell us about how Xue'e got pregnant. We can already guess that much. And you don't need to tell us how she evaded the tests. We can find that out ourselves. All we need you to tell us is where Xue'e is now. Just tell us that, and I'll pick her up myself."

"Don't you think I'd have told you by now if I knew?" said Tiesuo. "I truly have no idea."

It was like he'd swallowed a steelyard, the way he refused to bend. Such a shame, Fanhua reflected, that she was a woman, and a public official, otherwise she would give him a proper slap. She sat down on the table, immediately positioning herself higher up than Tiesuo, in a position of strength. As she racked her mind for some way to bring him to heel, she remembered the story Xue'e had told her about Tiesuo seeing a monk.

"Tell me, Tiesuo," she said, "didn't a monk come by your place not so long ago?"

"A monk? What monk? You're not going to try and tell me Xue'e got it on with *him*, are you?"

"If I was Xue'e I'd definitely tear you a new one, and no mistake. I'm asking *you* whether you ran into a monk." Tiesuo said he had.

Fanhua slapped her thigh. "That's bad news," she said, "very bad news for you." She was improvising. "What kind of a person is a monk? A man who can't produce an heir. Deary me, running into a monk, that's a terrible omen."

Tiesuo chuckled. "Oh? Since when do you get to decide what counts as a bad omen? Tell me this then, how did I manage to win that television set?"

For a moment, Fanhua couldn't think of anything to say. Qingshu was staring blankly, apparently also stumped. But there was no way Fanhua was going to allow herself to be intimidated by Tiesuo. She shifted to a new pose, leaning against the wall and using the pillow as a cushion. It looked like she was settling in for a siege.

"You'd have been better off not winning that TV," she said, keeping her voice as level as she could. "That was a piece of bad luck on your part. You won a sesame seed and lost a watermelon. Blessings never come in pairs, and misfortunes never come alone. Get it? I hope you do. I hope you understand how this applies to you. You're dreaming if you think you're going to have a baby boy."

"Beanie's a girl. Did you run into a monk too?"

"I didn't have your luck, I never met a monk. Which is why I could give birth to whichever I wanted. I wanted a girl, so I had Beanie. Girls are good. Very respectful to their parents when they grow up." Tiesuo produced a humphing sound through his nose and said nothing. "I've said all I need to," continued Fanhua. "You go on and think it through, and hand over Xue'e when you're done."

Seemingly unaffected, Tiesuo picked a cigarette end off the ground and asked Qingshu for a light. He drew in the smoke with relish.

As he was putting it away, Qingshu tapped on the lighter. "Haha, Latin America," he said out of nowhere. His words were so unexpected that it took Fanhua a moment to react. Then she realised that Qingshu was repeating the words of County Head Pockface. "Africa," Qingshu added. He's reminding me I need to intimidate Tiesuo, Fanhua thought to herself. But how could you take what Pockface had said seriously? Only a three-year-old would be frightened by his threats. No, not even a three-year-old, because Africa isn't a scary concept to them. Not like, say, a tiger. As Fanhua was pondering her next step, Tiesuo tossed his cigarette butt to the ground.

"That's right," he said, "Africa. Fucking bitch. Abandoned me and the two kids and ran away to Africa."

They were wasting their time. They may as well have been playing the proverbial lute to a cow. Though if Fanhua had actually played a lute to her dairy cow, it might have produced an extra few *liang* of milk, if what they'd said on TV was to be believed. But Tiesuo was apparently inferior even to a cow. Fanhua couldn't be bothered dealing with him any longer. She picked up a newspaper to read instead. After a while, she took out her phone and gave Xiaohong a call.

"When we're in the meeting later," she said to Qingshu as she waited for Xiaohong to pick up, "you propose that everyone should receive an extra fifty *kuai* mobile phone allowance this month. I'll agree to it right off."

Still no answer from Xiaohong. But perhaps she was out taking Tiesuo's daughters for a stroll, or perhaps she was dragging them with her from one house to the next as she went about informing all the officials about the next meeting. Fanhua couldn't stand the sight of Tiesuo any longer. She stepped outside. There were a couple of smells in the air, one musky, and one fishy. The musky smell was animals, and the fishy smell was the whiff of human crotches, male and female. Musky was good, it meant cows and horses getting frisky, a career in politics, a guaranteed election result. And fishy? There were both advantages and disadvantages to fishy. The propagation of offspring, that was the benefit of men and women getting busy. The downside was that all this rutting threatened to overturn the family planning policy. And that meant a swiftly curtailed career and an election lost. And Pockface turning black with rage. Fanhua couldn't say why her mind turned to the fishy smell of conjugal matters every time it rained. It revolted her, this aroma, but at the same time she found it enticing, and this incongruity brought her a shameless sense of pleasure. Fuck, if it wasn't for all this bollocks with Tiesuo, she'd leap into bed with Dianjun right now. It was on a rainy day just like this that Beanie had been conceived. She felt a twinge of sadness at the thought of Beanie, alone, with only a pet rabbit to play with. Like the one last pitiful cotton ball left unpicked on the stem, soaked

142

in rain. Honestly, she hadn't really believed all that she'd said to Tiesuo just now. She'd just blurted it out because she had no other option. She did want to have a baby boy. Fuck, if she weren't the head of the village committee – if she didn't have to set an example for all the other women – she'd bend over right now and pop out another one.

People started to show up for the meeting before too long. Xiangmin was among them. He drove his Xiali brand car into the courtyard and chucked the key over to Fanhua. Fanhua asked him how his church was coming along.

"Buddha be praised," said Xiangmin, "everything is ready, and all we need now is the east wind." Fanhua asked what exactly the east wind might be. "We still need a preacher. Ordinarily, I could just go through the motions myself, but I'm a local. Since we already have a monk who's come from far away to recite the scriptures, we need to get in an outsider. Amen." Trying her best not to laugh, Fanhua asked him where they were going to find one. "In the east, or the west, or the north. But not in the south." They sure did have a lot of special rules. Why couldn't the preacher come from the south? Xiangmin had his own explanation: "As everyone who's recited scriptures knows, *namo amitabha* – there is no Buddha in the south."

At this point, Fanqi came over. He said his wife had a craving for potatoes, for genuine Shanxi potatoes. He asked Xiangmin when he'd next be headed to Shanxi. Xiangmin said he didn't dare go back to Shanxi because the lads there tried to smash up his car whenever they saw him, as punishment for taking all their girls away. He'd already gone through several replacement windows.

"But lovers are joined by the string of destiny," said Fanhua, "even if they're a thousand *li* apart. What's the point in getting worked up about it?"

"You can't put it like that. If I sold you off to Shanxi, what would my uncle Dianjun do? Beat my legs to a pulp he would."

Fanhua went to hit Xiangmin with the keys. "Where's your respect for your elders? *I'll* beat *you* to a pulp."

Acting like his legs had been mangled, Xiangmin fled through the main entrance. But there was mud on the ground, and after a few paces, he slipped as though he'd trodden on a piece of watermelon rind. Everyone laughed, and the laughter was still echoing once they were sitting in the meeting room, discussing what to do about Xue'e's disappearance.

After a night of recuperation, Qingshu had perked up again. He fired the day's first shot, pointing out that Xue'e's family lived in Yaojiazhuang, fifteen *li* away. Women in trouble always go back to their family, it's a universal truth. Xiangsheng suggested checking out the family of Tiesuo's uncle on his mother's side, who lived in Shuiyuncun, off to the east of Yaojiazhuang. A maternal uncle will always treat his nephew like a pet dog, he reasoned, making sure he's well fed and watered and has something for the road. If his nephew's wife gets pregnant, then the uncle is bound to be helping him out somehow, so a trip to Shuiyuncun was a must. Li Xueshi said they should check on Xue'e's uncle too, because he had his uncle, and she had her uncle, and they were all one big uncle.

Everyone was cracking up before he'd even finished speaking. This was a long-standing in-joke. Back in the days when Qingmao was secretary, Li Dongfang's ambitious wife Pomegranate Zhang had come to see him about her aspiration to become a Party member. Qingmao's selfishness was not his only flaw. He was an old cow and he liked to nibble on fresh young grass. Once an attractive girl caught his eye, there was no shifting him. Fanhua didn't know whether Pomegranate Zhang's sister was really as beautiful as the Korean actress Dr Fan had compared her to, but she knew for sure that Pomegranate herself was a stunner with the looks of a movie star from Hong Kong or Taiwan. In the past, she'd worked as a shopping assistant in Xiushui's largest supermarket, and as a formal hostess, and now even when she was shlepping around the village in slippers she still strutted like she was on the catwalk. Qingmao had been drinking on the day in question, and the alcohol had loosened his tongue. When he saw Pomegranate Zhang, he blurted out the first thing that came into his head. "If you want to join the Party," he said, his head lolling back and forth, "then you'll have to join my party. The party in my pants. You've got your party, I've got my party, we've all got our parties."

Now Xueshi was pretending he didn't get the allusion. "What's so funny?" he said. "Are you saying Xue'e's uncle *isn't* her uncle?"

Fanhua tapped her notebook with her fountain pen. "Very well, we'll include Xue'e's uncle."

Xiangsheng mentioned the water pump station up in the hills. It had been built back when they were supposed to be Learning from Dazhai in Agriculture, but was never used.

"I'll ask Li Hao next time I see him, he's always up there with his sheep. Anyone else?"

Tiesuo had been standing outside. Fanhua had told him to lean up against the wall so he wouldn't get wet, but he'd continued to stand out in the rain, and now he was soaked right through. He knew how to play this game all right. He'd already employed the strongest of the Thirty-Six Classic Stratagems – escape – and now he was attempting another, the self-inflicted injury. Well, knock yourself out, thought Fanhua, if that's what you want. When they were halfway through the meeting, Xiangsheng asked Fanhua if they should bring him in. Let him soak out there for a bit longer, Fanhua said. It might wake him up. When they were nearly done, Fanhua told Qingshu to bring him inside.

As soon as he'd stepped through the door, Fanhua ripped off the tablecloth and chucked it over so he could towel himself dry.

"Tiesuo," she said in front of everyone, "do you know what the main focus of our work here is?"

"Would that be economic development?" said Tiesuo.

"Check this guy out," said Fanhua, "he knows his politics and everything. However. Because of you, all because of you, and Xue'e's belly, we've had to shift our focus. You know what that means? It means you've made a *political mistake*."

The words "political mistake" seemed to startle Tiesuo. He rubbed his head, as though trying to evaluate whether this was a hat that suited him.

"One last chance," Fanhua bellowed. "If you tell us where Xue'e is, then none of this ever happened."

"Didn't you all say she'd gone to Africa?" said Tiesuo.

Fanhua turned to the others. "You see what we're dealing with here? The man's swallowed a steelyard." Everyone agreed that Tiesuo had remained stubbornly inflexible. "Well, the village certainly won't be footing the bill to go looking for her," she continued. "I think we can all agree who should be paying. It's the sheep that produce the wool."

It was at this point that Qingshu spoke up: "Our mobile phone bills are going to be higher than usual this month."

"Well, obviously that's because our work requires it. What are we going to do about that? Xiangsheng, what do you say?"

"You decide," said Xiangsheng.

"I just want to hear some opinions," said Fanhua.

Xiangsheng's tone changed slightly, as though he was washing his hands of the matter. "I don't have any opinions."

Fanhua smiled. "Well, we can't keep putting money into it. How about this, we'll give everyone an extra fifty *kuai*. I'm sure we can find *that* on the back of a sheep."

EIGHTEEN

There was a layer of white mist across the fields and crows sweeping down through the haze. The passage of the car scattered both crows and mist, and the birds looked like they were swaddled in gauze as they soared away. Inside the car was Fanhua and the group she was leading to Yaojiazhuang. Qingshu was in the driver's seat, and he'd brought along his military belt in case they needed to tie anyone up. Fanhua knew full well that they weren't going to find Xue'e in her hometown, but she wanted to make the trip all the same. Yaojiayuan was right next to Zhangdian-cun, the hometown of County Head Pockface – both villages belonged to the jurisdiction of Nanyuan Township. An old classmate of hers, Ace Liu, was the township head of Nanyuan and a good friend of Pockface's. If they ultimately failed to track down Xue'e, Fanhua thought, then perhaps she could ask Ace to have a word in Pockface's ear and make sure he knew that Fanhua had done everything she possibly could. She took out her phone to give him a call but decided to hold back her name so he wouldn't be able to find a pretext to hang up on her.

"Hello, hello, hello," said Ace, in a voice bursting with bravado. "Who might this be?"

"Report your present position," Fanhua replied in standard Mandarin, using the exact tone of a high-level official.

Ace Liu immediately turned docile, and Fanhua could just

picture him hunching up his shoulders and retracting his neck. He reported that he was currently heading out to the fields to check on how the irrigation was holding out after all this wind and rain. He was fully cognisant, he said, of the fact that you couldn't go off running to the Buddha for help when your fields were swamped if you hadn't dug the ditches properly during the off-season. It was one smooth line after another with Ace – the man truly had the gift of the gab.

"Fine," said Fanhua, resisting the urge to laugh, "very good. But be back at your office at two o'clock this afternoon."

She was elated after this phone call, but it didn't last long. She suddenly felt a pang in her belly like a surge of stomach acid. She would be ahead of Ace Liu in life by now if she hadn't been seeing Dianjun back then. She was sure of it. If she hadn't been forever cutting class to go frolic with him beneath the green curtain of crops out back. Why had they been so utterly obsessed by that one thing, even when the mosquitoes out in the field were so vicious? Ah well. Such is life.

Xiangsheng was with them in the car too. He wanted to be dropped off in Wangzhai, where he could catch a bus to Xiushui. With his suit and tie, he really did look like a diplomat. Except he'd forgotten to shave, and a layer of stubble covered his face like some furry mask. He and Fanhua were sitting in the back. Xiangsheng wanted to talk to her about this business with the foreigner, but Fanhua held a finger to her lips to indicate that this was something they should discuss later.

"I heard you've taken a fair few of the village wives out to the city to sell cold noodles," she joked with him.

"They come begging to me, there's nothing I can do about it," he replied.

"So you arrange the work permit on their behalf, do you?"

"Bollocks I do. You think a work permit is so easy to come by? It takes at least a year to get one if you don't grease the wheels. They're all under my work permit. All the stalls are lined up together, anyway, they basically all belong to the same place. I've treated the inspectors to a good feed, so they're happy enough to look the other way."

"Fuck me," said Xueshi from the front seat. "You're a damn mothership."

"Not quite a mothership," said Xiangsheng. "One big long boat in the ocean is about right."

Qingshu twisted back his head. "No wonder they say you've got a harem of three thousand concubines."

"Qingshu, always lowering the tone," said Xiangsheng. "It's true what they say – you can't expect ivory to appear from the mouth of a dog."

"That's true enough," said Fanhua. "Anyway, a rabbit doesn't eat the grass outside its own burrow. You're doing a good deed, Xiangsheng, helping the countryside deal with its surplus labour. You've done the village a great service. Why don't I introduce you to Fanrong so she can write a puff piece about you in the newspaper?"

"Oh no, I wouldn't dream of it," said Xiangsheng, waving his hand. "It's just a small business selling cold noodles, what is there to write about?"

Xiangsheng wasn't stupid, Fanhua thought to herself. A puff piece would blow the lid right off his shady business practices. Fanhua had once heard Xueshi say that Xiangsheng was like the magpie that usurps a dove's nest. Those stalls had originally belonged to people from Shaanxi, but Xiangsheng had rounded up a few street toughs to oust them from the city.

"Xiangsheng," said Xueshi, "if my daughter doesn't get into one of the good high schools this year, then I'll send her your way."

"I wouldn't want to impede a child's future prospects," said Xiangsheng. "If she gets in, then I'll help chip in for the tuition fees."

"I'll make sure Dianjun does the same," said Fanhua.

They arrived in Wangzhai. Xiangsheng got out of the car.

"Wearing a suit to sell cold noodles," said Xueshi when he was gone. "That's Xiushui for you."

Fanhua laughed, but she didn't say anything.

NINETEEN

After hours of driving through the rain, the car left the asphalt road for a narrow, muddy track. They were bumping all over the place. Driving a tank had been less bumpy than this, Qingshu said. A farmhouse eventually appeared through the mist, along with the scent of alcohol, like the tavern bathed in apricot blossom in the old poem. This was Yaojiayuan. Compared with Guanzhuang, it was a backwards place, and poor. Though they'd put up a few two-storey buildings, most of the walls were built from mud bricks. The poorer a place was, the more it stank of booze.

Xueshi sighed. "It's like Fanhua said – we need to solve the issue of surplus labour. It's a major problem, maybe even as important as family planning. When you have nothing to keep you busy, what else can you do with yourself but eat, drink and play mahjong?" As they were all chuckling, they heard the sound of people playing the "guess the fingers" drinking game on the other side of an earthen wall. The walls round here were covered with slogans daubed in lime, mostly making proclamations about family planning. These were slogans in the style of County Head Pockface, such as "One desperate decision, two snapped tubes". The tubes in question were the seminal duct and the fallopian tube. There was a heap of rubbish under the character for "tubes", and next to the rubbish was a latrine screened off by branches, overflowing with effluence and surrounded by buzzing flies. Further in that direction was another slogan: "Don't expect anyone to untie the noose or snatch the poison from your hand". No wonder Nanyuan Township had no problems with family planning; the people here were living life poised on an axe blade between their arse cheeks. The characters were as tall as a person, and one slogan could stretch across a wall, a pig pen, a livestock shed, a pile of crops, and then onto another wall.

"This is advanced experience," said Qingshu. " We could learn from them. Shangyi writes a good grass script – let's have him produce some of these for us when we get back."

One particular wall was filled with just a single character: "bottle". And behind this wall was the home of Yao Xue'e's parents.

Xue'e's mother was in. She was a spry old woman, wearing a dark green cotton gown with her hair knotted up behind her head. Her face crinkled when she heard they'd come from Guanzhuang, and she went very quiet. She wiped her hands on the front of her gown, and her lip started to tremble. Realising the old woman must have assumed they were here to report a death, Fanhua quickly informed her that they'd just happened to be passing, and – knowing that this was the home of Tiesuo's in-laws – decided to stop by for a drop of water. Xue'e's mother relaxed, and immediately rolled up her sleeves and headed towards the kitchen to start rolling out some noodles. Fanhua held her back, saying they'd be on their way soon. The old woman asked her whether she was older than Xue'e.

"I call Xue'e 'younger sister'," Fanhua replied

The old woman tucked in her chin. "Well, Xue'e certainly *looks* older than you."

"Being a mother has taken it out of Xue'e," said Fanhua. "Two kids always following her around, demanding food and drink, and needing to go to school. Keeping a family like that going is no easy task."

"What's so hard about raising two? Xue'e had three siblings, and I managed to raise them all right. She's my youngest. Still breastfeeding at three she was. Kept sucking on that tit when all the milk was long gone. She was spoiled when she was little, and she's good for nothing now she's grown up."

So Xue'e had been a stroppy one when she was little. Not much change there then, Fanhua thought. She asked how often Xue'e came home to visit.

"A married daughter is spilt water," said the old woman. "You can't get it back. She won't come back here in a hurry. Last time was when we were planting the rice."

Fanhua took a sip of water. "Those two daughters of hers have good prospects. They're getting good scores in school."

"That's as maybe, but she doesn't have a boy."

"What's so good about a boy?" said Fanhua. "They cause you all sorts of trouble when they're young, and when they grow up you have to find them a wife."

"I told her as much," said the old woman, "but she wouldn't listen. And if she gets fined, or her house gets pulled down, then we'll be the ones who have to pay. Her three brothers won't dare help, their wives are the ones who wear the trousers."

"She's a sharp one, this old lady," Fanhua said to Xueshi. "Not like my halfwit of a mother-in-law, always grumbling about how I've not given her a son."

Xueshi was smart. He understood what she was doing as intuitively as if he were attached to her like a parasitic worm. "I don't suppose Dianjun's mother will mind you disrespecting her too much," he whispered, "what with her being dead all these years."

As Fanhua continued to chat with the old woman, Qingshu wandered around the place. Idiot that he was, he even thought it worth his time to check inside the chicken coop.

Just as Fanhua was standing up to leave, the old woman asked an entirely unexpected question: "You've no poison in the well there in Guanzhuang, have you?"

This had come out of nowhere. Fanhua was startled. "How could there be poison in the well?"

"We have poison in our village well here. Very strange it is. Every year, when it's planting time, the well water turns poisonous. Have we done something to upset the God of Rain?"

Xueshi hastily spat out the mouthful of water he was about to swallow.

"I don't know what I was thinking, complimenting that old woman," said Fanhua when they were back outside. "I tell her how sharp she is, and then she goes and brings up this crap about the God of Rain." They were standing underneath the character for "bottle".

Fanhua told Qingshu and Xueshi to check on the homes of Xue'e's three brothers.

"What about you?" asked Qingshu.

"I'm going to head over to Nanyuan. A snake can stand up to a dragon when it's on home ground. We've come to hunt in someone else's territory, so we'll be asking for trouble if I don't go have a word with the local snake."

TWENTY

It was two-thirty in the afternoon by the time Fanhua arrived at the local government headquarters in Nanyuan. Unlike the government building in Wangzhai, this place had a guard outside, as well as a sentry inside the yard. Ace Liu – the local snake in question – was waiting for Fanhua in his office when the guard led her inside. Of course, he thought he was waiting for one of his superiors, and Fanhua almost laughed out loud when she caught sight of him. He was carrying a raincoat, with raindrops beaded on his eyebrows and his trousers rolled up to the knee. There were a couple of muddy puddles on the ground. He really did look like he'd come straight here from inspecting the fields. The desk was covered with stuff, but neatly organised, and it was decorated with a little red flag, about the size of a Red Pioneer scarf. Fanhua had heard from her brother-in-law that there was a special logic to the arrangement of the desks of government officials. Crowded but neatly organised was ideal because it showed you were busy but still orderly in your thinking.

When he saw Fanhua walk in, Ace Liu's jaw dropped. He seemed reluctant to put down his raincoat to shake hands.

"I'm waiting to meet someone," he said after calling in his secretary. "Let my secretary give you a cup of tea, and I'll come find you in a bit."

"What's happened to you? You get hit by a car or something? You're all covered in mud."

Ace said he'd taken a fall and avoided all mention of going out into the fields. He rubbed his knee and made a hissing noise through his teeth like it was really sore.

Now that she'd gone this far, Fanhua didn't dare reveal her ruse. She could only keep playing along. "Hadn't you better see a doctor?"

"Please. I'm a manly man. Just need to grit my teeth and I'll be fine. Off you go downstairs now."

Fanhua went downstairs with the secretary. Seeing how clean his clothes were, Fanhua asked whether he'd gone out into the fields with Township Head Liu.

"The fields? He just finished chairing a meeting."

Fanhua quickly changed the topic. "You've done a wonderful job greening your yard here. Still flowering even when it's this cold."

The secretary told her that they'd all been planted by County Head Zhang, and he'd assigned someone specially to take care of them. Even the manure was brought down from the mountains. Fanhua didn't understand why you'd want to bring manure from the mountains. The secretary explained that the excrement of mountain dwellers was pure, untainted by pollutants. It helped the plants remain resistant to pests. Which was all very well, the secretary said, but it wasn't cheap. Cost more to ship than Coca-Cola. There was a grove behind the compound, too. In springtime, the secretary said, when the peach blossom bloomed, you couldn't see the ground for cherry blossom, and even the sago palm produced flowers. The secretary spoke with great enthusiasm – a touch too much enthusiasm, it seemed to Fanhua. She thought she detected a note of sarcasm.

"You must be an honoured guest of ours," said the secretary, "as a former classmate of Township Head Liu. Why don't I arrange for you to stay in the grove tonight?" He explained that there were several log cabins in the grove, crude in appearance but furnished with all mod cons on the inside. They were only ever used to accommodate high-level officials or old friends of Liu's. He made this confession without any pressure. Chairman Mao once said that a party without factions would be a bizarre creature indeed, and Fanhua could only infer that this secretary belonged to a different faction than Ace Liu.

"Oh, I wouldn't dream of putting you to the trouble," said Fanhua.

The secretary gave a sinister laugh. "It's only our gentleman guests who put us to trouble. Always finding fault with this and that. What possible trouble could we have from a lady guest?"

Fanhua didn't dare answer, afraid to see what monstrous moth might fly out of the secretary's mouth if they continued with this line of conversation. She changed the subject again, asking him how long he'd been working here. He extended three fingers. Fanhua thought he meant three years, but she was wrong. Three fingers meant three terms. After they'd been standing out in the yard for a while, the secretary led Fanhua into an office. There was a red silk banner on the desk, embroidered with a slogan. Fanhua gulped at the sight of it; the banner comprised a line of Chinese on top, with a line of English underneath. There was another person present, a scholarly-looking man who was in the process of grinding up ink for another slogan he was painting. Again, there were lines of both Chinese and English. This was the first time Fanhua had ever seen someone writing English with a brush. She asked the secretary what it was about. Was the American coming to Nanyuan Township? Had it all been decided already?

The secretary laughed and started to roll up the silk banner. "Township Head Liu told us we mustn't go into battle unprepared. If he does make it as far as Xiushui, then we'll do our best to get him here. Whether we succeed will be seven parts providence and three parts effort. As for the next step – whether we'll actually be able to cooperate – well, we'll worry about that later. See what you think of this. Our township head has had two fortune tellers in, a blind one and a university professor. The blind fortune teller made his prediction on the basis of the year, month, day and hour of the township head's birth, and the professor used the I Ching. More than one way of skinning a cat, I guess. Anyway, they both reached the same conclusion. The benevolence of a noble man would surely bring them to us."

Fanhua asked how they'd managed to swing it, and the secretary pointed to the wall. There, Fanhua saw a magnified print showing a group photo of County Head Pockface in the days before he was promoted, together with the officials from the township. He had the solemn expression of a duke receiving fealty from his underlings. The person standing directly behind him, in a Mao suit with a pen clipped to the breast pocket, was Ace. He looked slightly awkward, his neck bent forward like he was afraid to look directly at the camera. Fanhua understood: the "noble man" of the prediction was none other than County Head Pockface. It looked like Xiangsheng was wasting his time. But she could hardly tell him that. Let him waste a bit more of it first.

Ace Liu came in while she was still looking at the photo. He had given himself a swift makeover and was now dressed in a fresh suit.

"My apologies," said Fanhua. "I should have called in advance."

Ace asked her how the inspection tour had gone in his absence.

"Nothing but dirty jokes the whole way," she said, "each filthier than the last."

"You should sue them," said Ace as he led her out of the secretary's office. "Sue them for sexual harassment."

"Wouldn't have been much better if you'd been there."

"If I'd been there, I wouldn't have stopped at dirty jokes. I'd have given Dianjun a nice green cuckold's hat to keep his head warm on the cold winter nights."

"Behave," said Fanhua, "you smarmy git."

When they got upstairs, Ace said he'd be delighted to be of assistance if there was anything he could help her with. No, said Fanhua, nothing like that, this was just her calling in on an old classmate on her way through town. Ace leant forward on the desk and cocked his head to one side.

"Really?" he said. "Don't blame me if you come to regret it."

"Really."

Ace planted his feet on another chair and smoothed out his tie. "I'll put on a spread tonight. We'll get all our old Nanyuan classmates back together."

"Being a member of the weaker sex, I'm afraid I can't drink alcohol. It messes everything up if I do."

Ace Liu immediately straightened up in his chair and rapped his red-and-blue pencil against the desk. "You see? I knew there was something. Just say the word. So long as it's within the bounds of Nanyuan, I can guarantee you satisfaction. OK?"

"You wouldn't be able to help me," said Fanhua, "even if I told you."

"Trying some reverse psychology on me, eh? Is it a relative of yours in need of a school? Just say the word, there are still a couple of places going in Nanyuan Primary."

Fanhua finally informed him that it was to do with family planning.

"Oh, which relative of yours has had one too many? Damn, you've really gone out of your way to stump me. I can help you with anything except this sort of crap. I can only take off my official's hat."

Fanhua had been holding her laughter in as long as she could, and if she held it in any longer she'd likely do herself an injury. But she managed to restrict herself to a quiet chuckle.

"Fuck," said Ace, "you're just trying to give me a scare."

"What would I want to scare you for?" said Fanhua. "This is real. A woman in our village has had an out-of-plan pregnancy. Her family comes from Yaojiayuan. I brought a posse over here to look for her. And since we were in the vicinity of your humble abode, I stopped by to see you."

"Yaojiayuan? That's one of the Advanced Culture villages." Ace said the word "culture" in English, then swiftly offered a translation in case Fanhua hadn't understood. Apparently, he wasn't sure whether he'd said it correctly, because he pulled open a drawer and took out a book. Though it was wrapped in a protective paper sleeve, Fanhua didn't need to see the cover to know that it was another copy of *300 Sentences of Conversational English*, and Ace was checking the vocabulary list.

"Some culture. Shit and piss all over the place."

"But come now," said Ace as he continued to flick through the book. "Without the stench of shit and piss today, there'd be no scent of rice growing tomorrow. So did you catch your missing woman?"

"Did we fuck. Your Nanyuan women run faster than a hare."

Ace closed the drawer. "But hares lie down to copulate. Never heard of one running and screwing at the same time. Hence, I would point the finger of blame primarily in the direction of the male hare. Is he part of your family, the male in question? Is that why your hands are tied?"

"He's a Li, I'm a Kong. No family connection whatsoever."

"Well then, fine him and be done with it. Fine him half to death and then lop off his junk when you're done."

"Fine him? He's so poor he barely has a pot to piss in. Can't afford to pay any fine. He's got nothing to lose. The most important thing is to find the woman and get rid of the kid before it's too late. Her belly's swelling already."

"I'm still finding this hard to understand," said Ace. "Don't you do a check every month? If something slips by you, won't the machine pick it up? Is the machine broken?"

"Who knows. Anyway, she's pregnant."

"If the machine's broken, then you'll have more than just a couple of excess pregnancies to worry about. It'll be a humiliation for all of you in Wangzhai Township. He lives up to his name, your township head. Full of bull he is. There's a joke doing the rounds about you guys. Everywhere else we're striving for the Three Represents, but you guys are still figuring out the Three Basics – because in Wangzhai, communication is basically just shouting, transport is basically just walking and security is basically just guard dogs. Fuck, as poor as that, and still he brags about how your GDP has gone up fifteen per cent. Bullshit! He hasn't been quiet about family planning, either. Told everyone your township would have no problem fulfilling its duties. Looks like that was bull too. Who knows what'll end up happening to him?"

Three rosy clouds had gathered around Ace Liu's face, one on each cheek and one on his forehead. There was steam rising off him, and it was the steam of anger. "How do you get on with Township Head Bull?" he suddenly asked. "Does he come and see you often?"

"What would he come and see me for?" asked Fanhua.

"You mean he doesn't immerse himself in the masses?"

"I'm not the masses."

"If that's the way it is," said Ace, "don't count on him for any help."

"I wasn't counting on him in the first place," said Fanhua. She sighed. "It would be so much better if you were the township head in Wangzhai."

"But naturally. We're old classmates. We've eaten out of the same pot. But right now, you need to get a range of opinions so you can figure out what to do."

Fanhua asked him what he suggested. Ace took off his glasses and wiped the lenses with the little red flag on his desk. It was only now that Fanhua noticed there was another little flag alongside it. She recognised it from TV: it was the American stars and stripes. When he'd finished wiping his glasses, Ace informed her that he couldn't offer any suggestions. He'd been very busy recently, carrying out inspections in each and every village, as well as handling vital "international diplomacy", and as such he had no time to fret about such a trifling problem. Nevertheless, he had been "enlightened" while studying at the Party school some time ago, and he "happened to hear" a village head from "somewhere or other" up north talking about how to deal with family planning.

Fanhua indicated that she was very keen to learn from his advanced experience.

The thing was, said Ace, that it was a fairly harsh solution, which meant it could only be passed on by word of mouth, and not officially documented. He hadn't felt the need to pay too much attention at the time, since the family planning in Nanyuan Township was going so splendidly already, but he picked up the general gist.

By this point, Fanhua was so hungry for an answer her stomach was virtually rumbling.

It was really quite straightforward, Ace said, the method he had heard. You simply had to make the pregnant woman in question feel sick. Not physically sick, no, but sick at heart. More specifically, to make her feel that every day she doesn't have an abortion is like living a nightmare. It sounded like sorcery, the way he described it. If you did it right, he said, eventually the day would come when the woman would run to the hospital herself and you wouldn't be able to stop her getting an abortion if you tried.

Can there really be such a perfect solution? Fanhua wondered aloud. How come I'm hearing about it only now? No wonder Dianjun says I'm too insular.

Ace took a slurp of tea. "Well, there you go then. That's all there is to it. Hope that's cleared things up."

Fanhua gawped at him. Here she was still waiting for him to begin, and he'd already finished?

"You're not stupid," said Ace. "I don't have to spell it out, do I?"

Fanhua berated herself, saying she'd spent too long in the lower ranks and her brain had turned rusty.

"What does a pregnant woman fear most of all?" Ace asked her. "An abnormal birth. Kid with two heads, that kind of thing." Ace clasped his hands together and held them beside his ear to indicate a second head. "Ask her whether she's had a cold since she got pregnant. Bet you she has. Then you ask what medicine she's taken, whether she's had any injections. Then you bite your tongue. You stand up to leave without saying anything. The longer you stay silent, the more desperate she gets. She'll go crazy with worry. The next day, you send your village doctor along to ask her some questions about how her health has been lately, if her complexion isn't looking a bit peaky. You can buy off your doctor, right? He's just a barefoot doctor, after all – if you want to be rid of him, you can just throw some shards of broken glass in his way and he'll be out of commission for a while."

The way Ace showed the sprinkling of broken glass was like an opera performer tossing his white silk sleeves. His most theatrical gesture yet. Fanhua found she was unexpectedly reminded of County Head Pockface.

"You can rest assured," Ace continued, "that she'll listen to the doctor even if she doesn't listen to you. If the doctor says someone's about to die, then they'll take off their shoes today and keep them off tomorrow. What the doctor says is science. Clear now?"

Fanhua saw things clearly enough, but the problem was putting this theory into practice. When people in the village came down with a minor ailment, they tended to just disappear for a couple of days, lying down in bed like a cadaver until they were ready to get back to work. Xue'e was no different. She'd refused to go to hospital when she cut her foot on a bit of wire during last year's rice planting. And besides, Xue'e had already been in a fight with Dr Xianyu. Even if Fanhua could persuade him to go along with the plan, there was no way Xue'e would believe him.

"But if that doesn't work?" Fanhua asked.

"Look, you just need to find different ways to apply the same principle. All you have to do is make her feel sick." Ace was running out of patience. "Take water. Water gets polluted, yes? Tell them the well's been polluted. To make it credible, you can get someone in to disinfect the well. Do that and she'll have to believe it. Don't try and tell me the splendorous Guanzhuang Village couldn't even afford some disinfectant?"

Fanhua suddenly remembered what the old woman in Yaojiazhuang had asked her about poison in the well. This must have been what she was talking about. But Fanhua didn't mention this to Ace. "What if there are other villagers who've just become pregnant after getting married? Won't they be dragged down too?"

"Good question. Someone asked that very question at the Party school. And what do you imagine the reply was? 'Better to slay a thousand in error than let one guilty culprit off the hook.'" Ace drew his pencil across his neck in a gesture that was as graceful as it was callous. "I realise it seems harsh. I had a negative reaction to it myself. But you know what they say – you can't expect everything to be perfect when you're trying to effect reform."

Ach, but even the best stratagem in the world would be no use if they couldn't find Xue'e. And so Fanhua remained slumped in her chair with a furrowed brow.

Ace sighed. "Or you could just let her have the baby. If they can prove one of their previous kids has a heart defect, or is a retard, and they need another one to look after them in their old age."

"I know that one. We've used it before."

"There you go. Not so stupid after all, this Fanhua. You don't die from holding in a piss too long, right? There's always a solution to be found somewhere."

"If we really can't figure something else out, then I suppose we'll just have to try that one again. Well, I feel much better now after talking things through with you. If you were the township head for Wangzhai, then I could come and ask you for advice all the time."

Ace Liu made a hand gesture of modesty. "Don't go on like that. There are plenty of talented people in Wangzhai. I wouldn't dream of telling them what to do." He stood up.

This is my cue to leave, Fanhua thought. Ace didn't make any effort to persuade her to stay. As he was showing her out the door, he gave her a pat on the shoulder.

"Old classmate," he said earnestly, "if you need advice, you could always see Iron Crutch Li. I often consult him myself. An eccentric can offer a unique perspective. It's not sheep he's tending out there –

there are mandarins in his herd, and bureau chiefs, department heads, county magistrates and imperial ministers. You didn't know? Looks like *you* haven't been doing enough to immerse yourself in the masses. Even the least of Li's sheep is a magistrate's clerk like Song Jiang. Ancient and modern, foreign and local, all present and correct. There's one sheep named President, and the daughter of President is named Princess. That day we went to Guanzhuang, we barbecued Princess."

Ace arranged for a Red Flag car to drop Fanhua off. It had clearly once seen service at provincial level before it got relegated to county-level use, and then down another rung from there to Nanyuan Township. As she was leaving, he gave her a bottle of five-grain liquor, a bottle of Bordeaux wine and a multipack of Marlboros. Gifts for Dianjun, he said. Fanhua stopped at a market on the way to pick up a selection of cold dishes, a roast chicken and a smoked hare. She had been planning to have a drink with Li Hao anyway, but after what Ace had said, "having a drink with Li Hao" had turned into "paying her respects to Li Hao".

The driver was playing music that sounded like someone reciting scripture. A nice song about a shepherd. A fitting song for Li Hao, Fanhua thought. Fanhua asked the driver where he'd bought the cassette, and he told her it was from the church. So he was another one of these Jesus followers, this driver.

"How did you decide to believe in Jesus?" she asked him.

"I'm just a driver, me," he replied. "A scrap of meat stuck between a few metal sheets. Some of us choose the Buddha, and some of us choose Jesus. We're all just trying to stay safe."

It was then that Fanhua noticed there was a cross hanging in the car too. Fanhua considered purchasing a few crosses and tapes to take back to the believers in Guanzhuang. Maybe she'd even offer a prayer or two of her own. Couldn't do any harm. The driver told her if you kept going in this direction, then you'd see the church by the time you arrived in Beiyuan Township. This struck Fanhua as odd. She'd been along this road before, but she'd never noticed a church. She asked the driver to take her there.

The land covered by Beiyuan Township was small, but Beiyuan itself was pretty big. They drove around the outskirts for a while before stopping at a run-down old building on the west side of town.

Fanhua recognised the place. This had once been a primary school until the roof of a classroom caved in and several students were killed, and so they moved the school to a new location in the south. She assumed it had been demolished after that, but no. This old hen had reinvented itself as a duck, and it was now a church. The gable of the fallen roof had been rebuilt with halved bricks, and they'd stuck a sharpened piece of wood on the outside, which presumably was meant to represent the kind of spire you saw on the churches on TV. There was a lot going on around the entrance: a restaurant selling mutton noodles, a barber and a Goubuli dumpling house. Cassettes and pirated books were stacked on the back of a cart, with a tarpaulin to keep off the rain. Fanhua spent the equivalent of ten *jin* of eggs on tapes and crosses, and once they'd packed up her purchases, she went into the church with the driver. Everyone inside was singing a hymn, and the air reeked of bad breath. Fanhua jumped at the sight of a woman whose big arse and short hair made her look just like Yao Xue'e from behind. She couldn't help going over to get a proper look, but it turned out to be some random old woman.

Back in the car, Fanhua handed one of her new cassettes to the driver and asked him to put it on. "I want to hear that same song you were just playing, the one about the shepherd." The first song on the tape was *Away in a Manger*: "Away in a manger, no crib for a bed, the little Lord Jesus lay down his sweet head." Fanhua decided she'd give this tape to Li Xinqiao. He didn't believe in Jesus, but he did keep horses. Next up was *The Holly and the Ivy*. "The holly and the ivy... of all the trees that are in the wood... the rising of the sun, and the running of the deer..." Splendid, Fanjing would get a tape too. As well as being the village cluster group leader, she was also in charge of the group responsible for greening the village.

Then it was the shepherd song again:

> *While shepherds watched their flocks by night,*
> *All seated on the ground,*
> *The angel of the Lord came down,*
> *And glory shone around.*
> *"Fear not," said he, for mighty dread*
> *Had seized their troubled mind;*
> *"Glad tidings of great joy I bring*

To you and all mankind."

There was something decidedly lordly about Iron Crutch Li, so this was a song he was bound to appreciate. Oh Li Hao, Fanhua thought, I'm bringing you food, and drink, and a cassette of songs. Every kind of sustenance you could possibly desire. Is that generous enough for you?

TWENTY-ONE

Just when Fanhua was getting ready to go and see Li Hao, she heard a knock on the door. She shone her torch outside to see who was there. When she saw a bald head she assumed it must be Lingpei, but no. It was some kid holding an umbrella in one hand and rapping against the door with the other. When she opened the door, he went running away. That was when she noticed the car parked further along the street. The kid opened the car door, and a portly man squeezed out. He blocked the beam of Fanhua's torch with his hand.

"It's me," he said. "Gong Hongwei. From Gongzhuang."

Scrawny Dog.

Fanhua and Scrawny Dog didn't usually have much to do with each other. Fanhua had never been his biggest fan, and she remained unconvinced of his merits. There was one occasion a few years ago when some public security bureau officers had tried to round up a few gamblers in Gongzhuang just before Spring Festival. When they found they had no way of making an exit through the crowd of irate locals, they called Scrawny Dog over to one side and told him to go out there and get to work on the masses. Scrawny Dog couldn't cause too much damage when he was idle, but he could screw things up completely when he made the effort.

"Gentlemen," he addressed the crowd, "these men have had a long year. They've caught themselves a rabbit on the last day before

Spring Festival. You can't expect them to let go of a quarry they've already sunk their teeth into. Show magnanimity of spirit, and allow them to pass."

But then he turned around and tried to deploy the exact same line on the officers. "Comrades, these gentlemen have had a long year. They'd barely started playing when you showed up to take them away. Sure, you've caught yourselves a rabbit on the last day before Spring Festival. But you'd have enjoyed your holiday just the same regardless of whether you got him. Couldn't you do me this favour and let them hold onto their winnings? Show some magnanimity of spirit?" Just like that, he changes his tune completely. But the officers were having none of it, and now more and more people were joining the crowd. One of the officers took out his gun and placed it on the table. He said they'd never had to worry about being surrounded by a mob when they went to arrest people in Guanzhuang. And even if they did, you could be sure they'd disperse at a word from their village head. No need to ever take out a weapon.

Fanhua heard about all of this later. She found out that one of the policemen had given Scrawny Dog a dressing down, telling him a woman was doing a better job than him, and he was letting down men everywhere, and wasn't he ashamed of himself? Hmm? Scrawny Dog's reply had also reached Fanhua's ears. "Well, of course we can't all compare to Kong Fanhua," he said. "She's the Empress Consort Wu, and her merest fart has the authority of an imperial decree." This was an unpleasant thing to say, not because it imagined Fanhua farting (or at least, not only because of that) but because it betrayed his jealousy. Only the incapable were jealous of others. Which was why, ever since hearing this story, Fanhua had lost all respect for Scrawny Dog.

It went without saying that Scrawny Dog was here to discuss the tomb. But Fanhua certainly wasn't going to be the first to raise the subject. She led him into the side room.

"You've put on weight, Secretary Gong."

Scrawny Dog slapped his belly. "You're mocking me, Secretary Kong. I'm just bloated, that's all."

Fanhua asked him whether he'd like some water, but instead of answering in the affirmative or negative he just said thank you. So

Fanhua had to pour him a cup. Scrawny Dog sipped his water and started talking about the weather.

"Rain's been coming down like cat piss."

From inside the main room came the sound of the news on TV. There'd been an earthquake in Taiwan, they were saying. Scrawny Dog's ears perked up.

"Taiwan, oh my, Taiwan."

"Sounds like they had an earthquake," said Fanhua.

Then the news moved on to America and Iraq.

Scrawny Dog sighed. "Taiwan, America, Iraq. It's not looking good, is it, Secretary Kong?"

"Can't see any sign of it stopping," she replied.

"Seems like there's an election on the way in America. Soon as the president realises he isn't going to win, he starts shooting off guided missiles. Things get messy for everyone else whenever they have an election."

What was he talking about? Fanhua wondered. How had they got onto guided missiles? But Scrawny Dog hadn't finished.

"Soon as they hear the sound of explosions in the Middle East, his popularity at home shoots right up. Is that messed up or what?"

It might be messed up, Fanhua thought, or it might not, but either way, it's no concern of yours. Might as well be fretting over the flavour of someone else's pickled radish. After that, Scrawny Dog somehow got onto the Three Communiqués that had been issued by China and America.

"Secretary, the Three Communiqués have been around for ages. I heard it was Kissinger who came up with the expression 'the Chinese on either side of the Straits'."

Oh look, now Kissinger had appeared. Fanhua was trying hard not to laugh. Was this like one of those summits between two heads of state, where talks inevitably had to begin with a discussion of Taiwan? Fanhua wasn't much of a historian, and she had no idea whether it was Kissinger who'd come up with the phrase.

"I think so," she said. "But I wouldn't want to draw a definite conclusion without seeing the evidence."

Scrawny Dog tilted back his head and took a large gulp of water. As he did so, his eyes widened, and Fanhua suddenly noticed how big they were, those eyes. In Xiushui parlance they'd be called "bull gonad eyes". But remembering Scrawny Dog's childhood nickname, Fanhua decided "dog gonad eyes" would be a more fitting description.

"It was Kissinger, for sure," said Scrawny Dog. "That guy knew what was what."

It was at this point that Dianjun appeared. He pulled back the door curtain and stuck his head inside. "Are we going or not?" he asked.

Dianjun was referring to the visit he and Fanhua had just agreed to pay Li Hao.

Before Fanhua had a chance to answer, Scrawny Dog replied, "Secretary Kong and I are just talking something over."

Fanhua had no choice but to introduce Scrawny Dog to Dianjun.

"I know him," said Dianjun, "he's Scrawny–"

"That was my childhood nickname, yes. But names aren't too important to us children of the workers. And you're Mr Zhang. I've heard so much about you. A master engineer."

"He had to pass through Xiushui on a work trip," Fanhua said, "so he stopped by briefly to see us."

"Xiushui's developed so quickly these last few years," said Dianjun.

"You go and get on with your work," Fanhua said to him, concerned that he might start shooting his mouth off. She spoke in a very respectful tone of voice, as though Dianjun was genuinely over-whelmed with work.

"How about you?" Scrawny Dog asked Fanhua. "Have you been busy?"

"This old monk keeps on clanging the bell. You?"

"Who isn't?" said Scrawny Dog. "But recently, I have been even more busy than usual. I feel like I've been spinning round in circles, like a dog chasing its own tail. And likely to be busier still in future, now that I'm in mourning for one of my elders."

Fanhua didn't respond. Let's wait and see what emerges from this dog's mouth, she thought to herself.

Scrawny Dog sighed and told her they had one family who'd had three sons in three years. Three! He extended three fingers. But they were all stillborn. The desperate turn to any doctor they can find, but no doctor could provide them with any logical explanation. In the end, they found a holy man. From Shaanxi he was, blind, and very sharp. When he heard their story he refused to tell their fortune, no matter how much money they offered him. He said he would only do it if they gave him several objects.

"Secretary Kong," asked Scrawny Dog, "can you guess what those objects were?"

"No I can't," Fanhua replied. "Seeing as how I'm not blind."

Scrawny Dog said that this blind man had a long list of demands. And then he burst into song, just like the blind man had:

One *liang* of stars, two *liang* of moon,
Three *liang* of autumn wind, four *liang* of cloud,
Five *liang* of water vapour, six *liang* of smoke,
Eight *liang* of fog and nine *liang* of zither sound,
And one last request I have to make,
Give me half a *liang* of dried snowflake.

"So greedy," said Fanhua. "I can't imagine the Buddha would be terribly impressed."

True enough, said Scrawny Dog. They tried everything they could think of to reason with him, and finally they managed to persuade him. In the end, it was like they were forcing their money on him. Five hundred *kuai*. Enough to buy a donkey. The blind man rolled back his eyes and pinched his fingers together, and a gurgling sound emerged from his throat. After a very long time, he asked an unexpected question: did the Gong family have a great aunt who had died without an heir? Everyone was dumbfounded by the question, said Scrawny Dog. No one could think of the great aunt he might be referring to. The blind man pointed and said it was in a northwestern direction, very close, just two or three *li* away from Gongzhuang. This great aunt was living in the wilderness, he said, a wandering ghost, her cries to heaven unanswered, her cries to the Earth ineffective. She was just looking for someone to talk to. Like who? She had a good heart, this old aunt. At first, she was hoping to find a grown-up to talk to, but it was hard because all the grown-ups had families to look after. So she decided to settle for a child, a newborn, a blank slate. Leaning on her stick, tottering along on her bound feet, she

170

began to scurry from house to house. Thus this fatal phantom had stolen away one, then two and finally three children.

Scrawny Dog's voice was fluctuating wildly, high and then low, raspy and then breathy. When he was describing the old aunt tottering between houses on bound feet, he tapped his fingers against the table. Tap tap tap. Tap tap tap. It was so vivid it made Fanhua feel a chill down her spine. When the blind man had finished speaking, Scrawny Dog continued, one of the aunties of the family sprang to her feet and announced that there was just such a great aunt, who had indeed died without an heir. She was the mother of Kong Qing-gang in Guanzhuang Village.

Fanhua wanted to take the opportunity to point out that this was all news to her, but when she opened her mouth, Scrawny Dog suddenly made a gesture like a basketball referee indicating time out. At the same time, she noticed the presence of a tear trembling in each of his eyes. Scrawny Dog bit his lip. He was clearly making a considerable effort to hold it back, to encourage those tears to return where they had come from, but in the end they came trickling down his cheeks all the same. It was quite a performance, Fanhua thought, for the sake of someone who'd been dead for decades.

Scrawny Dog said this auntie had bent down to pick up a cornstalk and whopped him over the head with it, cursing him for a worthless wretch who'd neglected his ancestors in the pursuit of power and money. What good is being an official, really, no matter how powerful? What good is making money, no matter how much? If he didn't put Qinggang's mother to rest, he was letting down his forefathers and future generations alike, and he may as well die and keep his great aunt company personally.

"Secretary Kong," said Scrawny Dog. "As you can see, it's like my auntie says. If I don't rescue her, then I put my own pitiful life in peril." His face bore such a pained expression that Fanhua found herself hurrying to comfort him. "No matter what it costs me," he continued, "I have to save her. It was so convincing, the way they described it. I was convinced. I know we're Party members, materialists, and we're not supposed to believe in these crooked old superstitions. But you never know, do you? What if something bad *does* happen? How am I supposed to explain it to the masses?"

Fanhua remembered what Xiangsheng had told her: if she didn't let Scrawny Dog excavate the tomb, he'd inform the authorities that Guanzhuang had schemed to avoid implementing the "The Dead Shall Make Way for the Living" policy with sufficient diligence. This made Fanhua mad. She despised no one more than snitches who thought they were still living in the Cultural Revolution.

So she would try her best to deny him his pretext. "Now that you mention it, I do remember there was such a person in the village. But I couldn't tell you where she's buried. We razed all the tombs long ago, as you surely must have done in Gongzhuang too. There was punishment for anyone who didn't."

"We did," said Scrawny Dog, "we razed them all. Call me a cur if I'm lying."

"Well, exactly. You razed yours. We razed ours. How are we supposed to find it?"

"If you just give me the nod, you can leave that to me. I wouldn't want to cause Secretary Kong any unnecessary trouble."

"Easier said than done," said Fanhua. "We can't have you digging holes all over our good land like you're harvesting sweet potatoes, now can we?"

"Secretary Kong, you can rest assured, we'll leave your land as smooth as a mirror. I guarantee it. My name's not Gong if we don't."

Fanhua continued to stall. "What about all the plants? They're all public property. How am I supposed to explain *that* to the masses when you've up and vanished? I'll drown in their angry spittle. It's not like I have the power of an Empress Consort Wu."

"We won't forget the Three Rules of Discipline and Eight Points for Attention. Any damage will be compensated. Call us thieves and whores if we don't."

What crap the man was talking. Who was supposed to be a thief and who was supposed to be a whore?

They had a small gift for Secretary Kong, Scrawny Dog continued, which he hoped she would deign to accept. He gave her a smile that was intense and furtive. He took his bag out from under his arm, placed it on the table, and then, after glancing towards the door, he pulled open the zip. What could this be – not a bribe, surely? Scrawny Dog lifted out an exquisite little box bound in red silk. Not money then, to Fanhua's slight disappointment. Then what? Mooncakes? The box slipped on Scrawny Dog's knee, and the lid opened just enough for Fanhua to see something glinting inside.

"What treasure might this be?" she asked. "Not that it matters, because you'll have to take it back with you regardless."

"Hardly treasure," said Scrawny Dog. "A mere trinket, nothing more. Everyone knows Secretary Kong is entirely incorruptible. Like Zhao Benshan said to the aliens – 'everyone on Earth knows it'." He opened the box. "This isn't from me, it's from the mother of the still-born son. And she said if you don't take it, she may as well just run her head into a wall and die."

Neatly positioned inside the box was a commemorative coin to mark the return of Hong Kong to China. The face value of the coin was one *kuai*, but it was actually worth something like fifty. Barely enough to buy Beanie a new doll. Fanhua blocked Scrawny Dog with her arm.

"Even if you plucked me the stars from the sky, I wouldn't take them."

Scrawny Dog proffered the gift to her with both hands. "Don't you like it? If you don't, then I'll wrap it up and take it away. Secretary Kong, oh Secretary Kong, so hard of heart. Can't you show some pity?"

"How about this? I'll bring it up in tomorrow's meeting and see what the others say. You and Qingshu get along well, yes? I'll send him along with an answer for you the day after tomorrow."

That was the hint for Scrawny Dog to depart, but he showed no sign of leaving just yet. "What's that?" he asked, placing the box on the table. "My old comrade-in-arms, Qingshu?"

"Yes, Qingshu told me the two of you crawled out of the same trench."

"Don't mention his name to me. I was humiliated because of him."

Fanhua made a surprised noise. "Humiliated? How?"

Scrawny Dog rubbed a hand across his nose and chin, apparently reluctant to speak. But speak he did: "You can't judge a man from his appearance."

Fanhua didn't understand what he meant. She asked him what he was talking about, and he just repeated the same line. She eventually realised he was implying that Qingshu might act like a simpleton, but there's more to him than meets the eye.

"Surely not," said Fanhua. "Qingshu's a good man."

Scrawny Dog gave a snort of laughter. "Good? A dog that bites doesn't bark, and a dog that barks doesn't bite."

Again with the insinuations.

"Qingshu might be a little petty," said Fanhua, "but deep down he's all right."

Another snort from Scrawny Dog. "Back when we were fresh recruits, he was the one who used to tip out the bedpans for us. Piss all over his fingers. He said he was learning from the example of Lei Feng, but we all knew better than to believe that. Once he squats down, you know exactly what kind of turd he's brewing. He was tipping out the bedpans so that someday he'd be tipping out the bedpans of the senior officers so that eventually *he'd* be in a position to have someone else tip out *his* bedpan."

Fanhua laughed. "You shouldn't mock someone for wanting to learn from Lei Feng."

Scrawny Dog shook his head. He had an unnatural smile on his face, partly showing his disapproval and partly laughing at Fanhua. Then, gesticulating, he produced a line from TV: "Secretary Kong, it is in order to comprehend the future that we must understand the past."

What exactly was this fart that Scrawny Dog was encouraging her to sniff? She knew full well the kind of person Qingshu was and certainly didn't need *him* to explain it to her. But she was astonished by what he said next.

"Secretary Kong, Qingshu told me he already has a hold on fifty per cent, and he's confident he can obtain another twenty per cent. Because he has a *secret weapon*."

Now Fanhua was the one snorting. "Is that so? Well then, let him be the village head, and maybe then I can finally enjoy a rest."

"Do I have to spell it out? I know I shouldn't speak out of turn, and it's no business of mine. But there's nothing I hate more than people who plot and scheme. The toad fancies he can sleep in the emperor's bed. If you don't nip this in the bud now, who knows where it'll end. No village'll be safe."

"The position's open to all. It's just a village title. We're hardly talking about the imperial throne."

"It's still a throne, never mind the size. Aren't you interested in knowing what he's up to?"

"It's just Qingshu," said Fanhua.

"And you think you don't have to worry about his shit until the moment he squats down?" There was that line again. "I bet you don't realise what he's up to now. Think about it. You can't know what kind of turd he's brewing if you don't know when he's planning to squat. And then, by the time you realise, it's already too late. He's already finished, there's shit all over the floor, and the cherry tree's already starting to grow. Simple as that. I'll take another glass of water. To the brim."

Fanhua had to admit she was intrigued. She smiled as she poured Scrawny Dog another glass, thinking maybe she wouldn't mind hearing what he had to say after all.

Scrawny Dog took a couple of gulps of water and licked his lips. "Secretary Kong," he said, "if you're really not interested, then I'll up and go right now." He was lording it over her now.

"Finish your water first. No need to rush."

Scrawny Dog put the glass down on the table. "Do you know why I told you this?" he asked.

"You told me already. Because you're worried the rot is going to spread to Gongzhuang."

Scrawny Dog extended his pinkie like he was ruminating on some philosophical conundrum. "That would be the first reason, yes. But there is a second."

Fanhua had picked up a porcelain ladle, and she traced the shape of a "2" on the ground with its handle. "Go on."

Scrawny Dog bowed his head like he was confessing a crime. It was because he felt partly culpable, he said, and he regretted it terribly. He hadn't anticipated the way Qingshu would latch onto his mention of the three stillborn sons. Qingshu immediately extracted all the details from him. Apparently, Guanzhuang had also had several stillbirths. Could it be that theirs had something to do with Qinggang's mother too? She'd hanged herself. She had a grudge. Besides, they'd levelled all the other tombs apart from hers. This was a problem.

"Let me be straight with you," said Scrawny Dog. "I already knew all about the tomb. I knew there was a tree on top of it. Qingshu told me everything." He shook his head and said he couldn't help but admire the man, for his attention to detail if nothing else. Once upon a time, he had admired him for the steady hands with which he carried a chamber pot, and now he admired him for his mind. It had somehow occurred to him to ponder the social interactions of the dead. That very same day, Scrawny Dog said, Qingshu had gone to get a divination from a blind fortune teller.

"I was there," said Scrawny Dog, "and so was that guy from your village who sells cold noodles, Xiangsheng. After Qingshu had explained everything to him, the fortune teller gurgled away for ages, eyes wide as a chicken's arse when it's just laid an egg. Yes, he finally announced, these incidents were surely related. Because what little ghost would dare pay Qinggang's mother a visit? She's the only one out of all of them who has a tomb. And there's a tree on top of it, and a dead tree at that. A gallows just waiting for a victim. Who'd be so bold as to risk dying all over again? Hmm? Which leaves her all by herself. A solitary, neglected ghost. No way of finding anyone to talk to, so she has no choice but to set her sights on the living. Gongzhuang was her family home, and Guanzhuang was the home she married into. Between the two she wanders. When she isn't at Gongzhuang, she'll be at Guanzhuang, and when she isn't at Guanzhuang, she'll be at Gongzhuang. Doesn't matter much to her where she ends up. She's in the dark. Can't see her. Can't stand in her way. Nothing you can do."

At this point, Scrawny Dog glanced at the door and clamped his hand over his mouth, as though he'd heard the walking stick of Qinggang's mother herself rapping against the ground outside. Fanhua dropped her ladle to the floor, where it smashed in two.

"Qingshu told me he was going to bring the blind fortune teller to the village before the election," Scrawny Dog continued, bending down to pick up the broken halves of the ladle, "and have him reveal his divination. Xiangsheng asked him exactly what he was planning. Secretary Kong, think about it now. Who was the one who forgot to level that tomb? You'd not be able to explain yourself even if you were covered with mouths from head to toe.

Any family who's lost a child will blame it on you, even if they don't have any relationship with Qinggang's mother. And no one will be separated by more than one or two degrees from someone who's affected. You can't disentangle the families round here – they're stuck together as tight as rutting dogs. You're going to drown in the angry spittle of the people, my dear. Nothing you can do about it, we can't expect our people to suddenly turn sophisticated overnight. You can't curse them, you can't get angry with them, and you can't shift the blame. I'm very worried on your behalf, my dear."

Fanhua shook her hand like she was waving away a fly. Dig her up then, she said, hurry and dig her up, quick. But Scrawny Dog didn't seem to be in any rush. We'll need to wait for the right weather, he said. Not when it's fucking raining like this, mud everywhere.

Scrawny Dog asked her one last question as he was leaving: had she had any luck finding Yao Xue'e? Oh, said Fanhua, so he'd got wind of that too. Such sensitive ears. They haven't yet built a wall that doesn't let in some draft, said Scrawny Dog. But she could rest assured, he said, he hadn't mentioned it to anyone else. If we see her in Gongzhuang, we'll be sure to bring her right to you. A disgraceful woman, disrupting village stability and making a mess of the election with her antics. Deserves a spanking.

Fanhua carried the umbrella for Scrawny Dog on his way back to the car. When the door was closed, he rolled down the window to shake hands with Fanhua. His hand was plump, but strong, as you'd expect from a former military man. Neither of them said anything in the presence of the driver. Their silence was a mixture of mutual respect and tacit complicity.

Fanhua remained standing there for a while after the car had left. When she turned back towards the house, she jumped at the sight of a shadowy presence. When the shadow coughed, she realised it was her father.

"I heard everything," he said.

"What do you think you heard?" Fanhua said. "I thought you said your ears were going."

"That Qingshu's a son-of-a-bitch. Rotten just like his father. He was a double-crosser too. Worked as a farmhand for Tiesuo's father, then after Liberation, he struggled against him as a landlord.

Wouldn't rest until he was dead. Double-crosser. Runs in the family."

When she got back inside, Fanhua saw that her father was clutching a hearing aid.

"An unexpected problem has emerged," he continued. "The proverbial Cheng Yaojin on the road. And he doesn't wish you well. I think we need to hold a family conference."

This made Fanhua smile. There had been a time when family conferences were a regular occurrence, organised and chaired by her father. He generally had the final word. The last family conference had been when Fanhua had decided to stand in the village elections. They had eventually come to two resolutions: even the chewiest of bones must be chewed, and even the stubbliest of heads must be shaved. These resolutions, collectively entitled "the Two Superlatives", should indicate how thoroughly they had thought through the potential challenges.

After the conference, the whole family was mobilised. Fanrong was in charge of propaganda, which meant penning a newspaper article under an assumed name, praising Fanhua's work and high-lighting the good example she had set by having just the one child. For a countryside woman, especially one who had given birth to a girl, this was an achievement without precedent in Xiushui County. Thus, Fanhua became the first person in Guanzhuang to have their name appear in print. Fanrong's husband was in charge of arranging a loan to repair the road, as well as borrowing a seed drill from Xiushui Town to help families short of labour to plant their crops. Fanhua's father went into action too. His bone, to use his own anal-ogy, was the chewiest of all. He was responsible for highlighting Qingmao's shortcomings. But you can't go hitting a man smack in the face, and you can't go shouting about his flaws in the street. You had to find the correct temperature: not hot enough, and you wouldn't get the required result; too hot, and you could end up starting a feud. The strategy Fanhua's father employed was to praise Qingmao, to commend him for his many years of work. Everyone knew Qingmao had been toiling away diligently, he said, which counted for more than getting actual results, in many ways. Even though some folk had their complaints about the way he'd handled the paper plant, Qingmao had always tried his best, there was no denying that. The reason he hadn't done a better job was that he was just too nice, and he hadn't wanted to displease his superiors. Had Qingmao received any personal benefit from the paper plant? Some people said he had, some said he hadn't. Fanhua's father said he believed Qingmao had not. And even if he had, they were surely mere trifles, barely worth having. Old ginger has the sharpest taste. Every one of the old man's words was just and reasonable, and every one concealed a dagger.

Could Fanhua's father be planning to resurrect the Two Superlatives policy, now that he was calling for another family conference? It's late, said Fanhua, and Fanrong's not here. What kind of a meeting can we hope to have? We could give her a call, said her father, have a phone meeting.

And where was Dianjun anyway?

"He went off to pay a call on Li Hao," her father informed her. "Took some booze along with him. Said it was your idea. Now, I'll go and see that blind fortune teller myself. This stubbly head is mine to shave. If money can compel a ghost to turn a millstone, then it's certainly capable of convincing a blind fortune teller. Don't pay attention to his 'three *liang* of autumn wind, four *liang* of cloud' nonsense. You remember Charter, from our village? He practised divination too, back in the day, and he was always spouting the same kind of crap. It's what they're taught to do. Just another way of squeezing a few extra pennies out of you."

The Charter he was referring to was another blind man. He'd had smallpox when he was a child, pustules all over his face. The pus went into his eyes when he scratched them, and that was that. Blind. He could play the erhu, too, and during the Cultural Revolution, he'd accompanied the Mao Zedong Thought Dissemination Team. Later on, he'd left the village. Someone said they'd seen him at the entrance to a subway station in Beijing, still playing that erhu, still doing divinations. Fanhua hadn't seen him for years and had no idea whether he was even still alive.

"Scrawny Dog paid him five hundred, right? Well, we'll pay him five-fifty. Screw that cunt. We'll just have to write this one off."

Fanhua held back the urge to laugh at her father's stinginess. Only prepared to beat Scrawny Dog's price by fifty *kuai*. He was clearly getting into the spirit of things, but Fanhua didn't need him

179

to saddle up on her behalf this time. She was quite capable of shaving this head herself.

"You take a rest," she told her father. "Don't go exhausting yourself."

All of a sudden, the old man stamped his feet. "I've got it!" Beanie was so startled by the volume of his voice that she toppled to the floor. Fanhua asked him what exactly he thought he'd got.

"When I see the blind fortune teller," he said, "I'll have him do a divination first, to find out how Qinggang's mother died. If he can't work it out himself, then I'll tell him she was struggled to death. Then I'll ask him who killed her, and if his divinations don't tell him the answer, then I'll let him know it was none other than Qingshu's own father who drove her to death."

Fanhua helped him back into his chair. "Didn't you tell me before that it was Qingmao's father who took the lead?"

"Did I say that? Don't think so. I definitely remember it being Qingshu's father. He was an expert when it came to the struggle sessions, was Qingshu's dad. Like father, like son. Oh yes, he had quite the talent for it. Ask Qingmao if you don't believe me, he'll back me up for sure. It was Qingshu's dad. Hell yes, that settles it. Anyone who dares say it was Qingmao's father will have me to answer to."

TWENTY-TWO

L i Hao lived on the west side of town. There was straw stacked up both inside and outside the yard of his house. Fanhua could hear the sheep bleating before she arrived. It was easy on the ear, the sound of sheep bleating. A kind of tenderness to it, a childlike curiosity, like a baby crying for the teat. When she got inside the yard, she heard Dianjun talking to Li Hao about camels. A starving camel is still bigger than a horse, said Dianjun, and a horse is bigger than a cow, and a cow is bigger than a sheep. Keeping one camel was as good as keeping a whole flock of sheep.

"I'll do it myself, if you won't," he said. "Just try not to be too jealous of me when the time comes. I don't want to be an engineer any more. I want to find a partner to raise camels with me."

Hmm. It seemed like something had changed in Dianjun this time. Had he got his nerves crossed or something? Why this incessant talk of camels? Fanhua coughed, and Dianjun stopped talking. He switched to another topic when she stepped inside, pointing at a poster on Li Hao's wall and asking Fanhua if she knew who it was. It was a girl, not exactly pretty, but certainly sensuous. Her tits were squeezed up so tight they looked ready to burst her top and send the button flying. Like a pair of bunnies they were, ready to bounce away at any moment.

"It's an excellent film," said Dianjun. "We should arrange a screening in the village. Liven up the cultural life around here."

181

"You seen any of her films then?" asked Li Hao.

"Fuck, do you think so little of me? *Titanic*, obviously. She was Rose in *Titanic*."

Li Hao chortled. "Look more carefully."

Dianjun came as close to the wall as a gecko, his nose touching the girl on the poster. "That's Rose all right. Like the flower. She got an Oscar."

"The Titanic?" said Li Hao. "There's no denying it's worth learning about. One of mankind's greatest calamities. But that's not her."

"Want to bet? Win and you get to finish this bottle of five-grain liquor, and I'll switch to the local rotgut."

"You're definitely losing because that's not Rose. I'm not interested in Hollywood. That's Monica Lewinsky. Recognise her now? She's the one who managed to get inside Clinton's trousers. I find her fascinating, this girl. Quite fascinating. Almost as fascinating as the legendary beauty Xishi."

Fanhua wasn't much inclined to listen to this back-and-forth between the two of them. "I've a little present for you," she said to Li Hao. "I think you'll like it."

She passed him the tape. "Religious music?" said Li Hao. "I shall study it thoroughly."

"There's a song on there about shepherds. I found it quite touching. Made me think of you. I reckon you'll like it." As she spoke, she took out the cold dishes she'd brought with her, opening up the roast chicken and smoked rabbit.

"Most people don't really understand a thing like religion," said Li Hao. "You need to still your heart, approach it gently."

"Well, you have a nice quiet place here," said Fanhua. "Not like our place. Quarrelling parents and a squalling kid."

"Well, they both have their pros and cons. It sticks in your teeth, this rabbit. Let me get some toothpicks."

Mindful of Li Hao's limited mobility, Fanhua followed him outside with a torch. Out on the porch, he picked up a broom and snapped off a few of the bamboo twigs. A fresh sheep turd rolled across the ground, like a six-ingredient rehmannia pill.

"You put up with a lot, living like this," said Fanhua. "How can you keep getting by without a woman to help you handle things? I worry about you, Li Hao."

"Sheep turds aren't dirty. Sheep are the cleanest animals going. There are people in the West who keep them as pets. Why would they sing songs about them otherwise?"

Fanhua knew how to handle her drink. "The elections are approaching," she said, clinking glasses with Li Hao, "and I'll be needing you to saddle up for me this time. Take some time off from your sheep. I want to pay you a retainer and put you in charge of the common reserve fund, the administration costs, the public welfare fund. All of it. I need a true friend in my team. Eventually, the village will be founding a people's finance cluster group, and you'll be in charge of that when the time comes too."

Li Hao picked at his teeth. "What about Xiangsheng?"

Fanhua made a dismissive noise. "Him? He's busy with his business in town. Making money's the only thing that matters to him. As far as I can tell, he's quite ready to have the load taken off his shoulders."

"Are you sure?"

Fanhua laughed and shrugged. "He barely comes to the meetings. You know what my boss calls someone like that? A day-school cadre. That's what he said during the official meeting, and when the meeting was over he called them an even less flattering name. Randy dogs in springtime, that's what he said they were. Randy-dog cadres."

Li Hao blew the residue off the end of his toothpick and continued scratching at his teeth.

"Are you saying he's got something else in mind?" Fanhua asked him.

"Why, the hearts of the people."

Fanhua put down the chicken foot she'd just picked up. "You mean Xiangsheng wants to be village head?"

Li Hao truly treated his words like pearls and nuggets of gold, too precious to squander. "What do you reckon?" he replied.

Fanhua picked up the chicken foot again, but this time she rapped it against the saucer to punctuate her words. "Come on. Speak up. You spent so long with the sheep, you've forgotten how to talk?"

This may have loosened Li Hao's tongue, but it was sheep rather than people that he proceeded to talk about: "When I'm with my sheep, I can talk all day and not get bored. Sheep are the best. Very considerate. They'll listen to whatever you have to say to them."

"Li Hao, you've truly transcended mortality," said Dianjun. "Let's drink."

"I really doubt Xiangsheng has any aspirations of that sort," said Fanhua.

Li Hao slurped down his liquor. "Xiangsheng will come to see me before too long."

Oh, said Fanhua, was he back from the city already? Then how come he hadn't showed up to make his report?

"Don't fret," said Li Hao, "the sheep will announce him. I have one particularly sensitive sheep named CIA Chief Sheep. Soon as he hears the sound of Xiangsheng's footsteps, he starts bleating. And he's not like the other sheep who only know how to bleat – he can communicate through his horns as well. He knocks his horns against the door, *rat-a-tat-tat*, like a telegraph."

"Is Xiangsheng's business not going well?" said Fanhua. "I thought he was recruiting new underlings?"

"And where do all these underlings come from? Our village. He's recruiting an army, doing people favours, getting ready for battle." Li Hao's voice was quiet and cold. Cold like a steel blade gleaming in the moonlight.

"Recruiting an army? Battle?" Fanhua shivered.

"Think about it," said Li Hao. "Who is he recruiting?"

"They're all women. Sanhu's wife, Xianqiang's wife, Qingxi's wife, Tiedan's wife. A bunch of wives."

"Now count on your fingers how many of them are on your side. Haven't they all been punished by you at some point? Some of them you've forced to have an abortion, others you've fined for stealing plants. Qingxi's wife only stole a few shoots of maize, but you came down on her hard in the meeting."

"I didn't mention her by name, though."

"You talked about a woman with a wasp waist, and everyone knew that meant Qingxi's wife, who can't have children. Each of these women has a man at her back, and each of those men has a whole family at his back. In the end, it comes down to a popular vote, right? Whoever wins the most ballots is the one who'll be in charge."

Fanhua shivered. She felt like a current was flowing across her scalp. Outside, a sheep suddenly bleated. She remembered that Xiangsheng was supposed to be coming to talk to Li Hao about the water pump station, one of Xue'e's potential hiding spots. Plus, she still wanted to ask him if there was any progress with the foreigner situation. But Li Hao informed her that the sheep bleating was not CIA Chief Sheep, but Madonna Sheep. Madonna Sheep was the loudest and sauciest sheep in the flock. Her arse jutted out provocatively even when she was asleep, not unlike some department head at the art and literature bureau of a TV channel, and at this moment she was surely attempting to woo one of the other sheep.

"Fuck me," said Dianjun, "it's like the United Nations in here."

"But the delegates at the United Nations are all from the Earth," said Li Hao. "Whereas we've got a Chang'e Sheep, too, representing the moon."

"Fascinating," said Dianjun. "Truly fascinating."

Men were always like this, never further than a sentence or two away from the subject of women. But this wasn't what Fanhua was interested in. "Hey, where's Xiangsheng gone?" she asked. Apparently, this was now her most pressing concern.

"He'll be here before too long," said Li Hao. "I bet he's chatting to Shangyi."

"What does he have to chat to Shangyi about?"

Li Hao leaned back. "I'm only telling you this because we're old classmates. Shangyi's a man with a banner arrow in his brush pot. He has power. Shangyi is the one who decides who gets to be a Three-Good Student, who receives a scholarship, who's an Outstanding Student Cadre. An Outstanding Student Cadre gets an extra point of merit – how much do you think that might be worth? Three thousand, at least, maybe as much as ten thousand. What parent can afford not to think about that? You haven't had to worry about this yet, because Beanie hasn't started school." He paused. "You were born in the year of the dragon, yes? Well, Xiangsheng's a tiger. So that makes this dragon versus tiger, a battle too close to call."

Dianjun had kept on drinking, and he was slightly the worse for wear by this point. When he heard Li Hao mention a dragon versus a tiger, he thought he was referring to food. Dianjun asked him whether he'd eaten this particular Guangdong speciality. Li Hao, despite the considerable breadth of his knowledge, had not. Gesticulating with a chopstick, Dianjun explained that the dragon was snake and the tiger was cat, and when you stuck them in the pot together you had yourself a dish of dragon versus tiger.

Fanhua told him to be quiet and reached out to knock the chopstick from his hand. "What about Xiaohong?" she asked Li Hao.

Li Hao finally had some good news for Fanhua. "Xiaohong is a golden phoenix," he said. "The two of you are like a dragon flying and a phoenix dancing, harbingers of prosperity just like we have carved up there above the stage. She was born to take the mantle from you."

Fanhua was happy with his reply, but she was curious about Li Hao's choice of words. Why did he say Xiaohong was born to take over from her?

"Having a woman in a position of authority makes us famous throughout the whole of Xiushui County. There are two reasons why it's such a good thing. First, because it's so rare, and scarcity increases value. Second, because society is all about putting ladies first these days. A woman is always going to be first in line for any potential benefits. A rabble of men competing with one woman? They don't stand a chance. Wangzhai have the township Party committee HQ, which is one advantage they have over us. So they live off the Party committee, just as mountain dwellers live off the mountain and sea dwellers live off the sea. But you're the committee representative at the National People's Congress, whereas the village head of Wangzhai is a mere dog fart. So women are on top. We're heading for a matriarchal society."

Fanhua didn't object to this conclusion but wasn't entirely comfortable with Li Hao's reasoning. "A what-now society?" she cautiously asked. "Matriarchal? I don't recall seeing any mention of that in the Party constitution."

It was complicated, Li Hao explained. Too complicated to summarise, but the basic idea was that even though it had already been decided that women held up half the sky, well, now women had a change of heart and fancied a bit more than half. How much more, exactly? They hadn't quite made up their minds about that yet, but they'd take what they could get.

"Now I'm confused," said Fanhua. "Should I be insulted?"

"Insult you?" said Li Hao. "I wouldn't dare, even if I were a braver man than I am. I'm just saying, women are on top, which makes it easier to get things done. So Xiaohong would definitely be the most fitting choice of successor."

As if I need you to tell me that, Fanhua thought. "OK, that's enough about her," she said. "How about Xueshi?"

"Xueshi is the icicles hanging over the precipice in the Mao Zedong poem, and you're the indifferent sprig of plum blossom below. You don't need to worry about him."

"And Fanqi?"

"Since he's always telling us that no one's heart is made from stone, we can safely assume that his is no exception. He's soft. Won't ever amount to anything."

"What about old Uncle Qingmao?"

Li Hao clicked his tongue in disdain. "He's said it himself, an old horse knows when it's reached the end of the road. Beef is worth less than donkey meat, and horse meat's worth even less than beef. But it can be sold off as donkey meat once it's dead. Some people are still alive when they die, and some people are already dead when they're still living. Qingmao's already dead. Not actually dead, obviously. But when he does die, you should pull out all the stops for his funeral."

Having gone inside for a lie-down, Dianjun suddenly piped up: "Well, check you out!"

Li Hao assumed Dianjun was praising his expertise. "I'm just a drunken shepherd shooting his mouth off," he said modestly.

But Dianjun shot out of the room with a book in his hand. The cover was so crumpled it looked like an unwashed nappy. "You've actually been researching feminism?" he said.

"That book belongs to Ace's girlfriend," Li Hao said. "She left it behind when they were here for the lamb barbecue. I've just been flicking through it." He took the book and sat on top of it.

"What girlfriend?" asked Dianjun. "Has Ace got a divorce?"

"Has he bollocks," said Li Hao. "It's his mistress."

"Damn, he must be doing all right for himself then," said Dianjun, "if he's got himself a mistress."

"Jealous? What cheek." Fanhua wasn't sure she liked Dianjun's attitude. "How come Xiangsheng still isn't here?" she asked Li Hao.

"He'll be in a meeting by now," said Li Hao.

Startled, Fanhua asked what meeting this might be.

"Just a little get-together." He had turned taciturn again.

Fanhua remained quiet, deliberately allowing an awkward silence to extend. She knew how to deal with Li Hao. Begging him just inflated his ego. But he wouldn't be able to bear it if you just stayed quiet for a couple of minutes.

Sure enough, it was Li Hao's cough that broke the silence. "Has Qingshu spoken to you about shouldering a weightier load?" he asked.

Fanhua didn't reply. The reminder of Qingshu was as unwelcome as swallowing a fly.

"Did you know what books Qingshu's been reading?" Li Hao asked, oblivious to the fly Fanhua was digesting.

She spat onto the floor. "What decent books could he possibly be reading?"

"He's been borrowing books from me."

"Well, I suppose his taking up reading can't be a bad thing," said Fanhua.

"He's been borrowing books about Lin Biao. About Jinggang-shan and the Pingxing Pass, and the Liaoxi-Shenyang Campaign, and the Lushan Conference. Learning lessons from positive examples and negative case studies. About how long the red flag can keep flying, and how someone might end up becoming president. That's what he spends his days researching. I can tell from the way Qingshu bends over what kind of turd he's brewing. Lin Biao wanted to be president, and Qingshu wants to be head of the village committee."

"Well, it doesn't look like it's going to be his turn just yet," said Fanhua. "As you said, when I decide to call it a day, there's Xiaohong. Not to mention Xiangsheng."

Li Hao stayed quiet as he bit into the chicken head, and used his makeshift toothpick to spear the brains inside. The once white chicken brain had darkened as it was cooked, and it was now the colour of a sheep's turd. The look in Li Hao's eyes was similarly opaque.

"But Xiangsheng could handle the rudder," he said at last, "while Qingshu takes the oars. One branch secretary, one village head."

The drink had clearly gone to Li Hao's head. He was talking nonsense. In every village in Xiushui County, the positions of secretary and village head were held by the same person. There were a few villages where the jobs had once been separated, but the secretary and village head invariably ended up fighting like dogs. It caused such a ruckus that they changed their policy to one person shouldering both roles. Xiangsheng would either become secretary and village head, or he'd remain in charge of culture, education and public health. That much was obvious.

But they could let this topic rest for now. Worried that Xiangsheng might show up at an inopportune moment, Fanhua turned the conversation towards Xue'e. She asked Li Hao whether there was any way someone could hide out at the old pump house up in the hills. She hadn't had any time to think about the elections recently, she said, because Xue'e's belly was taking up all her attention.

"The calmest spot," he said, "is the eye of the storm."

"You mean...?"

"Hiding in broad daylight."

Hiding in broad daylight? Fanhua couldn't see what Li Hao was getting at.

"Tell me what's closest to the eye," said Li Hao.

"Eyelashes," said Fanhua.

"Eyelashes don't bloody count, they're part of the eye. It's the nose! The nose is closest to the eye. But can you see your own nose? Only if you're an elephant."

At this point, Li Hao stood up. He rubbed his hand against his hair, and his trousers, and then opened the door. In came the sound of rainfall and the cracking of branches, and sheep bleating like newborns wailing in the delivery room. Qinglin's wolf was crying too, howling and whimpering like a widow wailing at her husband's grave.

Li Hao raised his finger to his lips and shushed Fanhua. "Xiangsheng's here."

A figure burst through the door of the yard and raced inside. Tch, wasn't this supposed to be a mere social call? Why such a rush? Think you're so special? Give it up.

This person stopped at the door and knocked. Fanhua remained seated as Li Hao went to the door. But it was not Xiangsheng, after all, it was Shangyi. As he gawped at Fanhua, clearly surprised to see her here, the reek of booze diffused around him. Fanhua realised that he'd come to take Li Hao out for a drink. Sent by Xiangsheng, unless she was much mistaken.

Fanhua spoke first. "Teacher Shangyi," she said, "are you out visiting the parents of one of your students?" She made a point of avoiding the real reason for his presence. "I believe you've come to the wrong house. This is Li Hao's place."

Shangyi took a gulp and recovered his composure. "Actually, I'm here to borrow a book from Li Hao."

Shangyi explained that he was here to borrow a book to help him with the job Fanhua had given him: putting together a quiz on family planning. My my, this was above and beyond the call of duty, rushing about the village in the dead of night, so busy he didn't have time to sleep. Truly outstanding service. Fanhua took his hand and pulled over a chair for him to sit down.

"I'm lacking in relevant materials," said Shangyi. "So I came to borrow some."

"Why don't you pour a glass for Teacher Shangyi?" Fanhua said to Dianjun.

"My deepest respect to a man of culture," said Dianjun as he poured out the liquor.

Shangyi, who had clearly already had a lot to drink, initially flinched from the glass that was proffered in his direction. But he quickly recovered and accepted the drink with two hands. "Well, no harm if it's just the one," he said. "But my stomach's been bothering me recently, and I can't drink too much." He put down the glass and patted his pockets, saying he'd already come up with a few questions, no harm in checking them over. He produced two sheets of paper from the pocket of his blazer and passed them to Fanhua. Fanhua took them but didn't look at them yet. She told Shangyi to sit down and informed him that she had to make a trip to the toilet. "Could I borrow your umbrella?" she asked him. She wouldn't have to worry about him doing a runner if she was in possession of his umbrella.

Fanhua dialled Xiaohong's number as soon as she was squatting down over the latrine. She wanted her to go over to Xiangsheng's house and find out if he was hosting some kind of banquet. She'd be able to hear well enough from outside, so there was no need for her to actually go in. The raindrops were pattering against the umbrella, and Fanhua's heart was pattering with them. How had she ended up like this, sneaking about as though she were up to no good? Xiaohong had either fallen asleep or silenced her phone and failed to notice it ringing. Either way, she didn't answer. Young people are fierce sleepers, Fanhua thought. Her face was getting hot. Good thing Xiaohong didn't answer anyway, because Fanhua might have been too embarrassed to even say anything.

Back inside, Fanhua picked up the sheets of paper Shangyi had brought with him. "Shall I take a look?"

"I hope you'll point out any infelicities," said Shangyi as he took a sip from his glass and then returned it to the table.

Obviously, Li Hao knew the real reason Shangyi had come here, and how impatient he must be to leave, but Li Hao chose to play along with Fanhua. "I hope you realise, Fanhua," he said, "that I paid good money to purchase these resources. I'm happy for Shangyi to borrow them because you need to put your best steel in the blade of the knife, but I wouldn't lend them to anyone else."

"We live in a market economy, you know," said Fanhua. "You should start charging a fee."

"But that'd just be spiting my own face. We're all a part of the same community, after all. Let's call this my contribution to the cultural development of the village."

Shangyi was still holding his half-empty glass. "A friend from afar is a special pleasure." He clinked his glass against Dianjun's. "Cheers." After downing his drink he stuck out his tongue, like it was too hot for him to handle. "It's been a while since I last had a drink. Hard on the throat."

Protesting far too much. He may as well have put up a sign saying "No treasure buried here", thought Fanhua.

"Do you have any books here about asexual reproduction?" Shangyi asked Li Hao, in all seriousness.

Li Hao was stumped. "Asexual reproduction? What's that?"

"Like how a hen carries on laying eggs even without a cock," Shangyi replied.

"Is this for the quiz?" asked Fanhua.

191

Li Hao rubbed his hands together. "I was just thinking. If a man and woman have both been sterilised, but their child dies and they want to have another one, what are they supposed to do?"

"Why would both be sterilised?" said Fanhua. "One's enough."

"But that's how it is with Xiangning and his wife. He's sterilised, and so is she."

The Xiangning he was referring to was a butcher from the west side of the village. His wife hadn't wanted to undergo the operation due to her health problems, so Xiangning got the snip. But before long his wife died. Then it gets really weird: after just six months, his two sons were travelling back from the Wangzhai market when they got hit by a coal truck. Both killed. Xiangning ended up marrying a widow, but it wasn't until after the wedding that he realised she'd been sterilised. There were some in the village who said Xiangning was being punished for his profession: Yama, the King of Hell, had taken the lives of his family to pay for all his killings.

"That's just one case out of ten thousand people. Are you a member of the Communist Party? Then you should know that Party members need to think about how to benefit the majority. Don't mention Xiangning again."

"I feel the same way," said Shangyi, "but Xiaohong was the one who brought it up. She wanted to give him some grounds for hope, make him understand that heaven always leaves a window open. So that's why I thought of it."

So considerate of Xiaohong, Fanhua reckoned, even thinking about Xiangning's problems. As she looked over the questions, Fanhua decided she'd go and visit Xiangning one of these days. Asexual reproduction was all very well, hypothetically speaking, but a realistic solution might be adoption. Fanhua even worked out what she'd say to Xiangning when she saw him: "I just have the one Beanie, but if I had two I'd let you have one of them to adopt. A child's basically like a dog. They give all their love to whoever brings them up."

Fanhua couldn't help chuckling when she actually started paying attention to Shangyi's quiz questions. The first question was multiple choice: why are women of childbearing age in rural areas permitted to have two children, while women in urban areas are not? There were four possible answers:

A. Country folk eat off the land, while
city folk don't soil their hands.

B. Since country women work the farm, an
extra birth won't cause them harm.

C. Country folk are a higher priority, so
they get a "have-one-get-one-free".

D. Raising a city child is dear, double
what it costs round here.

"Have one, get one free?" What was this, a shop getting rid of excess stock? But Shangyi's questions were certainly catchy. Which was the right answer, though? Fanhua was confused.

"Beautifully worded, Teacher Shangyi," she said, "but all four of those answers sound good to me."

"But 'good' isn't always good enough," said Shangyi. "There has to be one answer that's better than the others."

Fanhua laughed. "That's all very well, but some of the specifics still need a bit of work. Are we saying giving birth is potentially harmful for city folk? Are they not a priority for the government too?"

"It's about the country folk scoring one over on the city folk. We get to have two children, but do they? No. We get to choose their village head, but do they get to choose their mayor? No."

"It's not about scoring points," said Fanhua, "it's about heightening the self-esteem of country folk."

"That's right," said Shangyi, "the self-esteem of twenty-first-century country folk."

The second question concerned the Organic Law of Village Committees in the People's Republic of China. This was a document Fanhua had studied during her time in village cadre training, and it defined the rules of the village elections. The question was this: in what year was the Organic Law of Village Committees adopted by the state? This time there were no multiple-choice answers to choose between.

Fanhua couldn't come up with an answer.

"There's a clue in the question," Shangyi explained. "It rhymes with the answer, you see."

"Oh?" said Fanhua. "How so?"

Shangyi repeated his question in an actorly voice: "In what year was the Organic Law of Village Committees adopted by the state? The answer is 1998. You see? When you read it aloud, the answer suggests itself."

"Damn," said Li Hao, "last time it was 1818, this time it's 1998. You've got a thing about the number eight. But it's a lucky number, so I suppose it's all for the best."

"Not too shabby, Teacher Shangyi," said Fanhua. "Not too shabby at all."

"Oh, it's nothing," said Shangyi. "You're the ones building the Great Wall. I'm merely supplying a brick." Turning his wrist to look at his watch, Shangyi announced that it was time for him to be on his way. Pei Zhen would worry about him if he was too late.

"Wait a while and I'll walk you home," said Fanhua.

Alarmed, Shangyi dismissed her offer with a wave of his hand. "I couldn't. I wouldn't dream of troubling you."

"Well, let Dianjun go with you then," said Fanhua.

"Mr Zhang? Absolutely not. As our headteacher said, Mr Zhang is a pioneer, surfing the waves of the oncoming market economy. I certainly wouldn't dream of troubling Mr Zhang."

Though it was only a moment ago that Fanhua was worrying about how much Dianjun had already had to drink, now she was encouraging him to have a few more shots with Shangyi.

Dianjun picked up his glass. "Teacher Shangyi, do tell me where you stand on the subject of camel rearing."

There he goes again. Always with the camels.

"Being a mere teacher," said Shangyi, "I have a very limited view of the world. I wouldn't know where to begin. All I know is that we're all crossing the river by feeling for the stones, and some people end up drowning while others barely get their shoes wet."

Dianjun flopped back down and drained his glass. "I'd be a dead man were it not for camels. It was a camel that carried me out of the desert."

Fanhua gawped at him. Clearly, something had gone very wrong in his brain. Someone starts talking about water and shoes, and you respond with deserts and camels. What had set him off? As Fanhua stared at him, flustered, Dianjun moistened his lips and scratched at his head. She remembered the scar. There must be some other explanation for it. Was Dianjun hiding something from her?

Still scratching away, Dianjun rose shakily to his feet, pushed open the door, and stepped outside. He was going for a tinkle, he announced, but he slurred his words and it ended up sounding like "going to fight evil". The wind came in through the open door and swept the tiny bones from the table, along with the toothpicks Li Hao had improvised. When Dianjun eventually came swaying back in, he picked up his chopsticks and started moving them back and forth between the plate and his mouth, despite there being no food left on the table. He reached for the jar of liquor again. Forget it, thought Fanhua, no more for Dianjun. He was far drunker than Shangyi, and if he made a fool of himself now, then the whole village would hear about it. Time to get him home and figure out what'd happened to him.

Fanhua grabbed the jar from his grasp. "Teacher Shangyi, we can't have Pei Zhen worrying about you. Let's call it a day for now. We can get together another time. Fine food, wine and cigarettes, on me. After you."

To her surprise, Shangyi answered in English: "Lady first. After you."

TWENTY-THREE

Dianjun fell into the slumber of a dead hog when they got home. He threw up once during the night, and then went back to dead-hog sleep when he was done. It was light outside by the time Fanhua nodded off, but she was immediately woken up by the presence of a foot on her calf. Dianjun was lying sprawled on his back, splayed limbs trembling like he'd had an electric shock or pulled a tendon.

"Village elections."

Dianjun was talking in his sleep.

"Repair the road."

Fanhua was touched. Dianjun was preparing her election speech in his dreams.

"Camels."

Wait. What did camels have to do with the elections? Fanhua couldn't figure it out no matter how hard she tried. Then, Dianjun suddenly started crying. It was a muffled sob, like he had phlegm blocking his throat. Patience running out, Fanhua grabbed hold of him. Instead of opening his eyes, he began to tremble, hunching his shoulders and begging for his comrades to spare him, babbling about how ships travelled by water and camels travelled by land.

Fanhua gave him a slap. "Open your damn eyes. This is your wife."

Finally, Dianjun could breathe easy. He relaxed his shoulders and opened his eyes. Fanhua demanded he explain to her what was going on, and what the hell all this was about camels.

At first, he was stubborn. Camels are just camels, he said. There are dromedaries and there are Bactrians.

"Do you have a bit on the side, a girl out there named Camel, is that it?" said Fanhua, deliberately trying to rile him.

Dianjun sprang to his feet. "I've done nothing to be ashamed of," he said. "Camels are just camels."

Fanhua had given him a slap, but now it was time to show him some tenderness. Tried the rod, now for the carrot. She pulled him close to her like she was placating a child. Stroking and kissing his face, she told him to tell her the truth. Finally seeing that there was nowhere else he could hide, Dianjun told her everything.

Dianjun revealed he'd received no salary for the last four months. "In the end, the workers turned on the factory director. They beat him up. They had weapons."

Fanhua continued to caress his face. "Did you have a weapon?"

"Do you think I'd be here with you if I did? They were all caught."

Fanhua sighed in relief and lay back down. "Dianjun, remember this. Anyone who tries to take on their superiors is asking for trouble. Doesn't matter if there's a good reason. You'll pay for it when they settle things up in the end." Nevertheless, Fanhua was outraged. "That son-of-a-bitch. Why didn't he pay his workers? Does he think he can take all the money he's made with him to the grave? Man like that deserves a good beating."

"He gave it all away. In donations."

"Gave it away? Who to? Can't be donating it all to Africa, can he?"

"He made a contribution to the road repairs in town. And to Project Hope. And to pay for bamboo to be airlifted here from Japan to feed hungry pandas. He even gave away his mistress. You have to be willing to sacrifice your child's life if you want to catch a wolf, and you have to be willing to sacrifice your mistress if you want to win over a sleazebag. He donated her to his local department head."

Fanhua was so suffused with bile her belly had swollen like a toad's.

"That shitbag," Dianjun continued. "Dreaming of becoming a

member of the Political Consultative Conference. Well, if you keep at it long enough you can make a needle from an iron rod. Fuck him, and his mum, and his grandma too. He actually did it."

"Well, he's not a stupid shitbag, I'll give him that much. Taking from the people and using it to make a power grab."

"We saw him on TV," said Dianjun, "hugging a bouquet of flowers and waving a certificate. Face was red like a monkey's arse. Made the workers so mad they went and picked up stones from the latrine. Shitty stones for a shitbag. It was nearly dark when he got back, so pleased with himself in his BMW, flowers fastened to the bonnet. They stop him the minute he comes through the factory gate. Go find the accountant, he says. The accountant's dead, someone says. When did he die? asks the shitbag. His whole family died, the workers say, they ate themselves to death. One of them who's been drinking says it looks like you've had plenty to eat, maybe it's time for you to die too. That makes the shitbag mad. He tries to run this guy down, and his car hits a few people. One of them goes flying through the air and smashes the windscreen when he lands. So then the people at the back, who can't see what's happening, they hear the sound of breaking glass and they think it's on, the fight's started. They all pile in. With their weapons. And they beat the crap out of him and smashed his windscreen to bits."

"Good. He was asking for it, the shitbag. And did you do any smashing?"

"Well, of course I did. With a brick."

Fanhua tweaked Dianjun's ear. "Oh I see, and you weren't worried about getting caught? Weren't worried about what me and Beanie would do if something happened to you? So heroic. Someone gives you a pinch of colour and suddenly you think you're ready to start a dye shop."

Dianjun stroked Fanhua's breasts, and her nipples stiffened until they looked like chilli peppers. Under normal circumstances, she'd climb on top of him, or let him climb on top of her. But now she knocked his hand away.

"Tell me the truth. Did you get that scar on your head from someone hitting you?"

"Fuck no," said Dianjun, "I skedaddled after one whack of my brick. Think they can catch hold of me? No chance."

Fanhua guided Dianjun's hand further down her body and grabbed his other hand. "And how about the camels? Camels this and camels that, you're always going on about them."

"I have this friend," said Dianjun. "He's from Ningxia, a technician like me. He did a bit of whacking too. But he's a coward, got no guts. Or they're no bigger than sesame seeds if he does. The more he thought about it, the more scared he got. He wanted to run away that very night. He used to raise camels, he told me, and now, screw this, he'd go back to raising camels. If he can raise camels, then why can't I? I went with him on a trip to Ningxia to check out the camels. They're worth their weight in gold, camels. The only problem is the smell. Knocks you right off your feet."

"Never mind the camels. I don't want to hear any more about them tonight. But there's one thing you need to remember. From now on, you're not to mention what happened at the shoe factory, OK? I can't afford the disgrace."

"Disgrace, what disgrace? I whacked my brick. I can hold my head up high."

"Wouldn't make a difference even if it was two whacks."

"Well, I wasn't going to tell you, but actually it was three."

"I don't have the time to go on about this. Let me be clear. If you mention what happened at the shoe factory again, I'll make you live to regret it, you hear?"

Fanhua was going to say more, but in the end, she held her tongue. The reason she'd taken Dianjun off on their tour around the village was to let people know that he'd been making lots of money, more than he knew how to spend, which guaranteed that Fanhua would be an incorruptible politician who wouldn't embezzle a penny from the public purse. She'd be done for if they found out he was actually a penniless good-for-nothing. Even if she was as honest as the legendary Lord Bao, they'd suspect her of corruption just the same.

TWENTY-FOUR

I t was bright outside. Fanhua was usually out of bed by this time, but today she stayed lying there a bit longer, having not slept all night. Then Beanie came rushing in, tweaking her nose to wake her up. Beanie wanted her mother to see the pigtails she now had jutting off the top of her head, tied with red bows.

"Who did that for you? Granny?"

Beanie shook her head.

"Daddy?"

Beanie shook her head again. She pointed out the window and then sprinted away again. People from around the village often used to try to give Beanie treats of snacks and toys. Fanhua had taught her to always say: "No thank you, we have some at home already." Fanhua pulled back the curtain and saw Xiaohong outside. That was all right then. If it was anyone else, Beanie would be due a smacked bottom. Xiaohong was talking to Fanhua's parents, and she'd made them laugh so hard they were bent over double. And Beanie was clutching Xiaohong's clothes and bouncing around. Fanhua tugged on some clothes and stepped outside.

"What are you all laughing at?" she asked.

"Xiaohong can tell you," said her father. "It's hilarious."

"It sure is," said Xiaohong. "Funnier than *Journey to the West*."

"What?"

"Shortfur's come back," said Xiaohong. "And he's got himself a girlfriend."

This cheered up Fanhua immediately. "Shortfur? A girlfriend?"

That's right, said Xiaohong. She'd thought there was something funny about it from the beginning, because some people said Shortfur was at a Beijing nightclub, and some people said he was in Macau, and *some* people said he was in both Beijing and Macau because he frequently flew back and forth between the two cities. "Just like the Monkey King," she quipped, "living on the Mountain of Fruit and Flowers by day and the Water Curtain Cave by night." Since when had Xiaohong discovered she had such a sense of humour?

"He never comes back for New Year's or any other festivals," said Fanhua. "What's he doing here now?"

"I was wondering the same thing," said Xiaohong.

"And he has a girlfriend? Have you met her? Is she a midget too?"

"That's what's so funny. She's about the same height as me. Hair dyed the colour of monkey fur. Walking down the street, they look like a mother monkey with her little baby monkey." Xiaohong started laughing again.

"Could they be here to get married?" said Fanhua. "Hurry up and check whether midgets are legally permitted to get married."

"It's for a performance," said Xiaohong. "He's in Xiushui Town, apparently. Lots of people have seen him."

Obviously, Xiaohong wasn't here just to tell Fanhua the news about Shortfur. She started with Xiangsheng. She'd bumped into him on her way here, she told Fanhua, and he'd said there was still a glimmer of hope. He'd heard the so-called foreigner was, in fact, a man from China who had fled to America with his tail between his legs after the nation's liberation. Now an old man, he was returning home with his tail sticking proudly in the air like some returning hero.

Fanhua was combing her hair. "Good. Tell Xiangsheng to keep on making enquiries."

"Did you call my phone?" Xiaohong asked unexpectedly.

Fanhua remembered that she had made the call while squatting over Li Hao's latrine, and – fortunately – Xiaohong hadn't picked up.

"Oh, that," she said, "I was calling Qingshu but his phone was switched off, so I thought I'd give you a try. How has Qingshu been getting on with his work?"

"I've heard he's been running all over the place trying to find Xue'e," said Xiaohong. "What a piece of work that Xue'e is. Running away all this time, abandoning her children. Heartless. Worse than any wicked stepmother."

By this point, the very mention of Xue'e's name was enough to infuriate Fanhua. "Worse than a dumb animal. At least they know to look after their own brood."

Another voice suddenly chimed in: "Surely you can't be saying Xue'e's heart is made from stone."

Fanhua was expecting to see Fanqi when she turned around, but no, it was Xueshi. Fanhua continued to comb her hair as Xueshi produced his report. He said someone had seen Xue'e. Fanhua's hand slipped when she heard the news, and the comb pulled a clump out of her head.

"Who saw her?" she asked, indifferent to the pain.

Xueshi repeated the same thing: *someone* had seen her. He didn't say who. That was how Xueshi was, never wanting to get anyone into trouble.

"There's no one else here," said Fanhua. "Just tell me."

After prevaricating for a while, Xueshi eventually came out with it. "Last night," he said, "Tiesuo went out. I doubt you've noticed, but in the last couple of days Tiesuo has been eating and sleeping so well that he's come out in pimples." A sly expression appeared on Xueshi's face. Fanhua waited for him to continue, but he didn't say anything else. Instead he chuckled, and his chuckle was as sly as the look on his face.

"Well, wouldn't that be because his nutrition has improved?" said Fanhua.

"Perhaps," said Xueshi, "but in any case, the pimples appeared."

Still not explaining himself. "Yes, pimples, understood. And?"

Xueshi glanced at Xiaohong, then turned away from her slightly and continued in a quiet voice: "And then, *they disappeared*."

Now Fanhua understood. Xueshi was implying that Tiesuo had engaged in sexual activity. Xiaohong seemed to understand too, because her face went red and she turned away.

"You didn't hear anything from me," said Xueshi. "But those pimples on his face were plain for everyone to see."

"Do you know where it was he went?" asked Fanhua.

"I asked him where he'd been gallivanting about, and he said he'd been on a jaunt to Xiushui Town. But I don't know whether he was telling the truth."

Fanhua's face filled with anger. "Does Qingshu know this?"

Xueshi snorted. "Qingshu?" He licked his teeth, like Qingshu was a nasty bit of grit that he'd found in his dinner. Fanhua appreciated the gesture. "How am I supposed to know? It's not like I'm attached to him like some worm in his belly."

There were multiple levels to this seemingly throwaway remark about parasitic worms. It aimed a veiled criticism at Qingshu for his lack of team spirit and failure to take responsibility for his work, while also serving as an indication from Xueshi that he had no desire to be dragged down with Qingshu. It might be government policy that determines direction, but it's where you plant your arse that decides your perspective, and Xueshi was letting Fanhua know that he'd planted his firmly on her side of the fence. He was here to help.

Fanhua looked at Xiaohong and then looked at Xueshi, before giving a satisfied laugh. "Excellent. No need to bring him up so early in the morning. That piece of grit!"

TWENTY-FIVE

Xiaohong's information was out of date. Shortfur had already arrived in Guanzhuang. A good pair of ears and eyes aren't enough to keep you informed of everything, clearly. It was Xiangning's wife who told Fanhua the news. It was late in the morning, and though Fanhua was nominally visiting to buy some of Xiangning's meat, the true purpose of her visit was to demonstrate her concern for him. Xiangning was certainly not a man to be underestimated. There were always plenty of people trying to curry favour with him. A twitch of his cleaver in either direction would decide whether your meat'd be mostly lean or mostly fat. His butcher's shop also served as a hub of news and gossip, where people chatted away about this and that as they waited for him to chop their meat and bones. Which meant he had access to more news than anyone else, not unlike those "websites" Fanrong had mentioned. No wonder Xiangsheng had set his sights on Xiangning, Fanhua thought. He had a good eye.

Xiangning had gone out, leaving the widow he'd married at home. When Fanhua saw her, she was wearing wellington boots and leather gloves as she busied herself cleaning pig intestines in the yard. There were enough shiny white serpentine coils to fill the whole tub. Xiangning's wife was bending over to tip baking soda onto them, which is what you need to do if you want to get those intestines clean. The woman's arse was as big as a panning sieve. An arse that size surely came with boobs to match. Such a waste if she could never have a child.

"You've got a customer," Fanhua called out.

When she saw it was Fanhua, Xiangning's wife brushed back her fringe, embarrassed, and called her "aunt". Fanhua was about the same age as her, so it felt strange to be addressed that way. But Fanhua couldn't just ignore it now she'd said it.

"You may be able to call me aunt in terms of seniority, but I'm definitely your junior when it comes to money-making ability," Fanhua replied tactfully. "I'm the one who should be calling you aunt."

"But an aunt is an aunt," said Xianging's wife, "no matter where you might be."

Fanhua laughed. "I'm here to buy some meat." To Fanhua's surprise, Xiangning's wife frowned, apparently not pleased to have a customer. Fanhua detected resentment in her eyes. "What's the matter? Don't you want to sell to me?"

"We've nothing left but tripe," Xiangning's wife replied.

"Business is *that* good? The quality of life round here really *is* improving."

She should tell Dianjun to include this in the speech. No mean feat for so many people to be able to afford meat and fish. "Excellent," she continued. "If the village can get through a pig in a single day, then I can't have any objections when there's none left for me."

But Xiangning's wife dispelled her happiness with a stamp of her feet. "No," she said, "it's that dwarf." She drew a line in the air at breast height. "He bought the lot."

Dwarf? Surely she couldn't mean Shortfur? Was he back in the village already? "Was it Shortfur?" she asked.

"I think so," said Xiangning's wife. "Lingpei was there too. Xiangning knows the two of them well. He helped them cart the meat away. I heard the neighbours talking about how Lingpei is a..." She mimed the act of picking pockets.

"He's young," said Fanhua, "and he's gone a bit off the rails. Still time to change his ways, though."

What can you do when you came to buy meat, but there's no

meat to be had? You take what you can get. Fanhua asked what tripe they had left. Intestines and pig liver, Xiangning's wife replied. There'd been a bit of pig kidney left over, but Qinglin had snapped that up already. Wolves work just the same way as people, according to Qinglin. Eat kidney to give your kidneys a boost. Xiangning's wife, who was actually a very friendly woman, chuckled as she told this to Fanhua.

"Well, in that case, I'll take some liver," Fanhua said. "My father's a fan of liver."

"It's good, pig's liver," said Xiangning's wife. "The best. Boosts your eyes as well as your liver."

When she came to weigh out the meat, Xiangning's wife made a point of adding enough extra to make the weight on the other end of the steelyard beam swing up in the air. This, Fanhua knew, was the woman's way of giving her face. Under normal circumstances, people said, it was only her deftness of hand that prevented the weight from sliding right down off the beam. She picked up the liver and wrapped it in a plastic bag. "Here you go," she said to Fanhua. "Take that away and don't even think about trying to pay."

Fanhua brought out her money and drew in her chin. "Don't be like that, or I won't come here next time. Come on, how much?"

"But how could I possibly take my aunt's money? How about this, it's one *jin* and six *liang*. Let's just call it one *jin*."

"Let's call it exactly what it is," said Fanhua. "I'm grateful to you that people don't have to leave the village to buy meat any more."

Xiangning's wife took the money and put it down beside the tub, tucked under the steelyard, as though she was too embarrassed to put it in her pocket.

"What do you plan to do next?" Fanhua asked. "When you've made enough money."

"Plans? What plans could I possibly have?"

"How about Xiangning? Men don't think about problems in the same way that women do. We have a built-in account book."

Xiangning's wife wiped at the corner of her reddening eyes with her top. "Thank you for looking out for me, Aunt."

"Of course I look out for you. I wish I could do more. But you need to learn to look out for yourself."

A light came into the eyes of Xiangning's wife. "I heard... I heard they have a very talented doctor at Hanzhou Hospital, who can maybe reconnect the tubes after they've been snipped?"

"Who told you that?" said Fanhua. "Was it Dr Xianyu?"

"Xiangsheng told me."

"What does Xiangsheng know?" said Fanhua. "When I asked Xianyu, he said he was sceptical. So how can Xiangsheng be so sure? Childbirth is a very different business from selling cold noodles. But how about this? When I'm not so busy, I'll go there with you."

On the inside, she was cursing Xiangsheng. Not because he didn't know when to keep his mouth shut, nor even because he was scurrying around trying to canvas votes, but because he didn't know how to behave appropriately. Oh, Xiangsheng. Xiangning is your kin. What were you thinking, broaching conjugal matters of this sort with his wife?

"Did Xiangsheng tell you this himself?" asked Fanhua, smiling.

"He sure did," said Xiangning's wife. "Described it all very vividly."

Fanhua laughed. "Oh, Xiangsheng."

Xiangning's wife's eyes widened. She didn't know what Fanhua was going to say next.

"Don't be taken in by him," she said. "He may seem like one of the lads, but in truth he knows a bit too much when it comes to women's affairs. You never know when it comes to people. Sometimes you'll bite into a nice seed and find a nasty bug inside." Fanhua stuck to a jokey tone as she vented her anger, just to be on the safe side. Then she wiped the smile from her face. "But you need to have a back-up plan. If the hospital can't help you, then..." She paused, as if waiting for suggestions. Xiangning's wife drew closer, clearly very keen to hear about possible back-up options. "Then you could always think about some of the nephews in your family," Fanhua finished.

"But who could bear to be parted from their own flesh and blood?" said Xiangning's wife.

"Why? An aunt's hardly going to mistreat her own nephew, is she?"

"I appreciate your concern. But I don't think that's an option."

"Well then, that leaves the hospital," said Fanhua. "Don't be stingy when the time comes." Fanhua suddenly felt like this had been an entirely unproductive conversation. She put down her liver and took the other woman's hand in hers. Leading her into the main room, Fanhua sat down on one chair and sat her down on the other. "There's something I've been wanting to say to you for a long time," said Fanhua, still holding on to her hand.

"You're welcome to say whatever you like, Aunt," said Xiangning's wife.

"Are you sure? If I'm speaking out of line, then just act like you didn't hear me. In one ear and out the other, OK?"

"I'm listening."

"If the doctor can fix up your tubes, well, then of course that would be perfect. And if he can't? Then just tell everyone he did, all the same. No one else can see inside your belly, so they'll be none the wiser. Keep the truth to yourself. Then disappear for a little while. Not too long, maybe four or five months. Adopt a child. Bring him home, and say he's your own. Who's going to know? Kids grow up to look like whoever raises them. No one will have any doubt he's Xiangning's sprog."

Xiangning's wife listened and gaped.

At this point, a dog climbed over the wall and picked up one of the intestines in its mouth. It was a black-and-white dog, and Fanhua recognised it as belonging to Lingwen. Xiangning's wife saw the dog too, but she didn't react. It was long, the intestine, and as the dog scampered this way and that it soon found itself helplessly entangled. Now it looked like it was trailing an intestine from its own belly. Fanhua suddenly remembered that Li Tianxiu's yellow dog had gone missing a few days ago. It couldn't have ended up getting trapped like this, and killed by Xiangning... could it? The dog was panicking now and starting to whimper. Finally, Xiangning's wife responded. First with laughter, then anger.

"Whose damn mutt is this?" she said. But she didn't stand up.

The dog finally managed to extricate itself, and leapt back over the wall, leaving the intestine behind.

"But would that work?" Xiangning's wife asked Fanhua. "I can't see how it would. Where would we disappear to, for a start?"

That was a good question, and Fanhua didn't have an immediate answer. If Dianjun had still been working in Shenzhen, then it'd be simple. They could just hire a room in the shoe factory and stay there. But Dianjun wouldn't be going back to the shoe factory.

"Let me think about it. I'm sure I can come up with somewhere. How does that jingle go? 'In the end, everything will work out, the current will always take care of the boat, and you'll find a Toyota on every road.' Don't worry about it. And don't tell anyone else. Let's keep it between me, you, the sky and the Earth, OK?"

Xiangning's wife moistened her lips. She was staring blankly ahead of her, clearly lost in thought. After a while, her eyes lit up again. But in the end, she sighed. "Let's just leave it to fate. If we're destined to have a child, then we will. And if we're not, then it'll be just the two of us."

As she left Xiangning's house, Fanhua shook her head and smiled to herself. Such a sly one, that woman. Think I can't see what you're playing at? Fanhua could tell she had decided to do exactly what Fanhua had suggested: adopt a child without telling anyone else, including the person who'd given her the idea in the first place.

Carrying her pig's liver home, Fanhua walked along a little way before she was struck by another idea: why not go and see Shortfur? But where would Shortfur be? He'd had no home in the village for a long time. His parents' old mud-brick home had been pulled down to build the new road back when they'd redistributed the residential land. She would have to explain what had happened to Shortfur when she saw him. But he wasn't wanting for cash, in any case, so they could give him a new plot of land and let him build whatever kind of house he liked. The plots were big enough for a decent-sized yard. Not quite big enough to build a Mountain of Fruit and Flowers, or hollow out a Water Curtain Cave, admittedly, but more than enough space for a dozen or so Shortfurs to live comfortably.

Fanhua's guess was right. She found Shortfur at Lingpei's place. Lingpei was still living in the house he'd paid for in picked pockets. There was an old scholar tree out front, with new twigs growing out from the dead twigs. They were normally festooned with a rainbow of plastic bags, these twigs, rustling every time the wind blew, but right now there were several monkeys crouching in the branches, plus a dog crouching on the ground below. Not actual monkeys, obviously, but bare-arsed kids. Kids love nothing more than monkeys, and so of course they were going to love Shortfur, who played a monkey. They'd clambered up into the tree just to get a glimpse of him. Fanhua counted seven bare arses. At first, she was going to yell at them to scram, but then she worried they might fall down if she startled them, and possibly get bitten by the dog if they were to land on its back. So she remained silent as she made her way towards the gate.

There were several more kids outside, trying to peep inside through a crack between the gates. Fanhua pushed a couple of their heads out of her way so that she could peer inside.

Fanhua saw Shortfur sitting sprawled across a chair. He was speaking, and Lingpei's rotten band of cronies were sitting around him. The girl Xiaohong had mentioned was there too, and she was busying herself cleaning Shortfur's ears, would you believe it. Xiaohong's description was accurate in that her hair was dyed as red a coxcomb, or a monkey's arse. Xiangning was there too – he was the one boiling the meat. Being the host, Lingpei was scurrying about, trying to listen to what Shortfur was saying while he helped Xiangsheng with the big pot of meat.

Shortfur began to speak more loudly. "Standards," he said, "the most important thing is to have standards." His voice sounded a bit like the quacking of a duck. "Nothing can be achieved without standards." Fanhua had no idea what standards he might be talking about. "And then there are foreign languages," Shortfur continued. "Even my dog can understand foreign languages. My dog's nickname is Pipi, and his full name is Peter, P-e-t-e-r. Got him in Hong Kong. Purebred Pekinese, completely white, every single hair of his coat. Super cool. If you find one dark hair on his body, then my name's not Kid Seven."

Fanhua was finding it hard not to laugh. This was Pigsy seeing himself as a human when he looked in the mirror. She rapped the door knocker.

It was Lingpei who came to open the door. "Aunt, what are you doing here?"

"I just happened to be passing, and I thought I'd drop by. Oh, quite the party you have going on in here." She looked at the girl with the red hair. "Including a tofu pudding."

Lingpei quickly gestured for Fanhua to avoid that kind of talk. It was only then that she cast her gaze towards Shortfur.

"Well now, surely that isn't..."

Shortfur sat up and squatted on the seat like something out of *The Carnal Prayer Mat.*

"Shortfur?" said Fanhua. "Kid Seven? Are my eyes playing tricks on me?"

"That's right," said someone nearby, "it's Kid Seven himself."

"Oh my," said Fanhua. "Why didn't you come and greet me?

Shortfur ran his hand through his beard before extending it towards Fanhua. His arm was no longer than the handle of a noodle-slicing knife, and Fanhua had to take another half a step towards him just to shake hands. Then he sprang out of his seat and gestured for Fanhua to go inside with him for a chat. Fanhua tried to make him go first.

"Secretary, please, after *you*," he said. Despite spending so long wandering away from home, it looked like he'd kept himself informed about which dynasty held power in the village.

As she followed Shortfur inside, Fanhua turned back and called out: "Xiangning, why don't you come in with us for a talk?"

Xiangning declined with a hasty wave of his hand. "Oh no, I couldn't possibly." He pointed towards the pot, indicating that he was still busy boiling meat. Fanhua didn't say anything to Lingpei and his band, and they knew better than to try to follow her and Shortfur inside.

Once they were sitting down, Fanhua asked Shortfur where he'd been drifting all these years, except she changed "drifting" to "improving yourself" at the last minute. This was a phrase she'd learned from the television. Stars from Hong Kong and Taiwan were always going on about improving themselves.

"People used to say 'wherever there is oppression, you'll find resistance'," said Shortfur. "Now they say, 'wherever there is money to make, you'll find Kid Seven'."

"We're always thinking about you here in the village," said Fanhua. "We all saw that movie you were in. It was superb. Five stars."

Shortfur made a dismissive gesture. "Oh, that was no big deal. Just a special guest appearance."

Momentarily unable to think up a reply, Fanhua just looked at Shortfur with a gaze that blended solicitude with pleasant surprise.

"Since you're here," she said eventually, "why don't you stick around for a while? The village has changed a lot. See for yourself. Have a wander around and check it out."

"OK," said Shortfur, "I'll see what I can do."

Fanhua pointed outside. "It's nice of Lingpei, cooking all this meat for you. Very loyal is Lingpei."

"They want to go with me to Hong Kong, to Macau," said Shortfur. "To 'improve themselves'."

Fanhua was alarmed. Lingpei's band of crooks were good for nothing but stealing. It would be a calamity for the comrades in Hong Kong and Macau if they were to show up there. "And did you agree?"

Shortfur shook his head like a rattle drum. "No, no, no, I haven't given them the nod. I want to keep an eye on them for a bit longer."

"All right then, you do that," said Fanhua.

At this point, the girl with the dyed red hair came in with a glass of water for Shortfur. When she was about to leave, he made a cigarette appear in his mouth like a conjuring trick. Shortfur was irritated by her failure to notice its presence. He slapped his hand against the chair, and she quickly pulled out a lighter and lit it for him. Gosh, you certainly get to act the big man when you have cash to spare. Shortfur waved the girl out of the room.

"And this would be...?" Fanhua asked tentatively.

"One of my fans," he said. "I guess we could call her my girlfriend."

Shortfur said the word "fans" in English, but the way he said it sounded more like *fanshi*, which means "breakfast time" round these parts. Apparently, Shortfur had spent so long living nocturnally he'd got the times of day mixed up, Fanhua thought.

"It's not so easy for you to get back to these parts," she said. "Why don't you get married while you're here?"

"I'm a busy man," said Shortfur, "too busy."

"But even a busy man needs a wife. I wouldn't have to worry about you if I knew you had someone to look after you."

Shortfur picked his ear. "Andy Lau doesn't have a wife. Nor does Leslie Cheung. Andy Lau once said 'one must cast one's eye across more distant vistas'. Cool, huh?"

Fanhua almost laughed out loud. How had a line of poetry by

Chairman Mao turned into an Andy Lau quote? Shortfur was a bit too brash, she thought, and would end up getting himself into trouble eventually. When that day came, he'd be a laughing stock round here – but beyond the village, it'd be Guanzhuang that was the laughing stock. That wouldn't do. Fanhua would have to put some pressure on him. Not too much, obviously – she didn't want to hurt him.

"You know, Shortfur," she said, "you should be happy. A nice tall girl like that, with you. You're lucky."

"What? Because I'm short? So what if I'm short? Size doesn't matter, it's technique that counts."

Shortfur was *definitely* going to get into trouble someday.

"Well, why don't I leave you to it. If you need me, just give me a call."

Shortfur hopped off his chair when Fanhua stood up. "And I shall certainly consider your request, and do my utmost to find the time."

Fanhua was puzzled. When had she requested anything of him? "You mean...?"

"Xiangsheng told me. He said it was coming from you. I intend to take it very seriously."

Fanhua was compelled to stay and talk with Shortfur for a bit longer. She leant against the doorframe as he explained that Xiangsheng had told him they wanted to put on a show before the elections and were hoping he would be able to help.

"I'll have my troupe here in a few days," Shortfur said. "They can put on any show you like. Not just the monkey show – we can do a model show." He pointed at the girl with the red hair. "We have a model who's much hotter than this one. You have a Pomegranate Zhang in the village, right? Pretty good-looking? When everyone sees my model, Pomegranate will want the earth to swallow her up."

"Is she a goddess? I wouldn't mind seeing that myself."

Fanhua stepped out into the yard. Lingpei was gnawing on a bone, grease smeared all over his mouth. He's another one who's bound to run into trouble, Fanhua thought, if he carries on hanging out with these no-gooders instead of watching over the paper factory.

"Enjoying your meal?" she asked.

Lingpei wasn't stupid; he caught her drift at once. "I'm just on my way," he explained. "I'll be leaving once I've finished eating."

A buddy of Lingpei's drifted over, holding onto the hand of one of the tofu puddings. "You need a good meal inside before you can get to work. You don't chop firewood any quicker by not sharpening the axe." Indecent *and* idle. What a bunch of reprobates.

TWENTY-SIX

The weather forecast predicted more rain, but a clear blue sky stretched in every direction the following morning. The grass at the foot of the wall had turned from a withered yellow to a more greenish shade after the recent rainfall. There were even a few fresh tips peeking through, a tender green and slender like beansprouts. Several branches were scattered across the street, blown down by the wind. Fanhua shifted one of them out of the way and then headed in the direction of the school. She wanted to check the records of Xiangsheng's accounts. Li Hao may not be entirely credible, but she couldn't ignore what he'd said. Did Xiangsheng want to be secretary and village head? Well, don't imagine nothing can stop you once you've been voted in. There's still a tiger blocking your way. A tiger in the form of the accounts books. County Head Pockface had got one thing right: a man shits just as much as he eats. Well, before we move on to the question of shitting, Fanhua thought, let's find out exactly how much you've eaten.

In the distance, she saw Xiaohong with Manny and Laddy. The two sisters looked very fashionable, dressed up like little cowgirls. Fanhua caught up with them and tugged on Manny's sleeve.

"Did you buy this?" she asked Xiaohong.

"Where would I've found the time for that?" Xiaohong replied. "These are old clothes of mine from middle school I've just altered for them."

Fanhua pulled on Laddy's collar. "That figures. Can't find a fit like that off the shelf."

"I'm not sure how good a fit they might be," said Xiaohong, "but I've done the best I can, with my limited abilities."

"I want you to go and have a word with Qingshu. Tell him to make a trip to Shuiyun Village. The river splits Shuiyun in two, South Shuiyun and North Shuiyun. Tiesuo's uncle lives in North Shuiyun."

It was only when she saw the slogans stuck on the school gate that Fanhua remembered the township education authorities were coming to sit in on a class. She was about to turn and go, but the sharp eyes of Headmaster Xu had spotted her from a distance, and he insisted on bringing her inside. The people from the township hadn't arrived yet. While Fanhua chatted with some of the other teachers, Headmaster Xu climbed onto the concrete table tennis table and began to make a speech. After a couple of sentences, he blew a whistle and asked the students whether they understood, and the students bellowed a reply in unison: "We! Under! Stand!"

The headmaster blew his whistle again. "Raise the flag! Play the music!" The national anthem blared and the red flag soared. The children faced the flag, right hand raised to the crown of their head, arm bent like a drawn bow. When the flag reached the top of the pole, the headmaster blew a whistle for the students to lower their hands and stand still.

"Students," he said, "welcome Secretary Kong, who is here to give you a speech."

This was news to Fanhua. Fortunately, she was a woman of experience, and if she could give a speech to the county magistrates then she wasn't going to be fazed by this.

"At ease!" she commanded. The mountain you stand on determines the song you sing, or so the proverb says, so this seemed like an apt way to begin. Then she encouraged everyone to study hard for the sake of the Guanzhuang of tomorrow, for the sake of the glorious Xiushui County of tomorrow, and for the sake of the splendorous China of tomorrow, to absorb each and every marvellous fruit of human civilisation, to strive to surf the tide of the twenty-first century. The sound of applause rippled around, then ceased as abruptly as if it had been sliced with a knife.

The headmaster blew his whistle again. "Dismissed!" Presumably, this had all been arranged in advance, because everyone now left except for the one class that the township officials would be joining. It was Manny's class.

Headmaster Xu put on a stern face. "Anyone who forgot to wash their face today should raise their hand now." Nobody raised their hand. Fanhua was reminded of the County People's Congress, where a moderator with a microphone said that anyone opposed to the motion should now raise their hand. No one ever did, for much the same reasons that these students chose not to admit that they'd neglected to wash their faces. Which is why every motion ended up getting passed unanimously.

The headmaster tried another tack. "Who *has* washed their face today?"

Fanhua couldn't see the point of this, but one of the other teachers explained it to her: "The ones who are raising their hands the highest are the ones with the cleanest faces, see? And the handful who are barely raising their hands at all are the ones who *haven't* washed their faces. They're still kids, after all, they haven't learned to lie convincingly yet."

Obviously, this didn't escape the notice of Headmaster Xu. "What did I tell you last week? Everyone needs to wash their face. So why do we still have some washed faces and some unwashed faces?" He stepped in between the ranks of students and roared, "*Why?*" He bent down towards the ground when he discovered one hand that was raised particularly high. It was Xiangmin's son, Olympic, who was standing directly in front of Manny. Olympic's jaw was clenched, and his hand was raised high and getting higher as he raised himself up on tiptoes. The headmaster gave him a nod without looking at his hand. It was the state of Olympic's armpit he was interested in.

"Personal hygiene is not merely a personal matter," said Headmaster Xu. "It is also a matter for the collective. There is a dialectical relationship between the two. Olympic here has grasped the connection between them." A cloud of confusion passed across the face of Olympic, who, needless to say, had no idea what a "dialectical relationship" might entail.

Then, Headmaster Xu discovered a hand that was not raised so high. This was someone who had neither washed their face nor grasped this crucial dialectic. This was Gawp's son, Fisher. Fisher's hand was raised, but it had already sagged down to ear height. His head was facing the floor and he was too afraid to look up.

"Fisher," said Headmaster Xu, "your classmates have their faces, and you have your face. We've all got our faces."

Fanhua smiled to herself, and the teachers who recognised the allusion smiled too.

"Fisher," said Headmaster Xu, "did you choose to besmirch the face of the school on purpose?"

"I, I'll wash it tomorrow," said Fisher.

Headmaster Xu rapped a curved index finger against Fisher's head. "Tomorrow? Don't you think it might be a bit too late by tomorrow? Hmm?" He glanced at his watch. "Very well, I think we've all learned a valuable lesson here. Enough criticism for today. Anyone who has not washed their face should go to the well and do so now." At this, seven or eight students rushed off.

"And don't forget to wash your neck while you're at it," Fanhua heard Shangyi add. Shangyi was wearing a suit and tie. He'd have looked just like one of those university profs on TV if it weren't for his coarse, farmworker's skin. He kept fidgeting with the knot of the tie, probably because he wasn't used to it. Fanhua asked him if he was ready, and he said he was, yes, he'd memorised everything backwards and forwards, patting his belly to show how securely the knowledge was stowed inside of him.

Shangyi went off to his class when the bell rang, and Fanhua went for a walk around the school in the company of Headmaster Xu. With the inspection today, she said, and the competition tomorrow, the school's outgoings must have gone up, no? Xu immediately pulled out a handful of invoices and said Comrade Xiangsheng had signed them already, and they could go and get the money from him as soon as they had the secretary's signature. Glass, stools and coloured chalk. Good, very good. A piece of glass costing twenty *kuai*? They'd only paid two *kuai* last time they'd replaced the windows in the committee office, and it came to no more than ten even including the price of the installation. Was this bulletproof glass, or the kind they used for X-rays? The stools were even more suspiciously expensive. They were just plain wooden stools, but somehow they'd ended up costing more than a chair with a backrest. Were these stools, or thrones?

"Was it you or Xiangsheng who made these purchases?" Fanhua asked.

It was Xiangsheng himself, Xu replied, and what's more, they'd discovered yesterday that they were two stools short and had been forced to borrow a couple more from Shangyi's house. Consider this his contribution to the furnishing of the school, Shangyi had said.

"We must be very grateful to Shangyi," said Fanhua. "Let's make sure to give them back to him in a couple of days."

"His wife, Comrade Pei Zhen, sent a bouquet of flowers, too."

"Good. Very good. You can tell she's made her living as a teacher."

Fanhua folded up the invoices and put them in her pocket. "If there's anything else you need to spend money on, just say the word. We can deal with them all at once."

There was a big smile on Headmaster Xu's face as he nodded, chin going up and down like it was hoeing the soil.

Fanhua noticed a hole in the wall of the school. Laughing, she pointed it out to Xu. "Is that for dogs?" she asked.

Xu smiled. "Our latrine overflowed not so long ago. Some of the boys dug their way out through here to relieve themselves." Fanhua was reminded of the toilet in Yaojiazhuang with its dense layer of black flies. It was a nauseating thought.

"Is it still overflowing?" she asked.

"That depends on the inclinations of God," replied Xu, laughing. "When it rains, it overflows. When it doesn't, there's no problem."

"It rained yesterday," Fanhua pointed out.

"It wasn't such a big rain yesterday, so we're still about a bowl's worth of water away from overflowing."

"You hurry up and draw up a plan," said Fanhua. "Give it me, and I'll pass it on to Xiangsheng as soon as I've signed it. Act quickly while he's still around, and we'll have him fix it as soon as possible."

Fixing a toilet wouldn't come cheap, Fanhua thought to herself. Let's see how much finds its way into your wallet this time, eh Xiangsheng?

At that moment, the school PE teacher came whizzing over on a bike. He was almost out of breath, he'd been pedalling so fast.

"They've entered the village," he said to Headmaster Xu. "The devils have entered the village." So, Xu had put him on sentry duty.

Xu gave a long whistle, and all the teachers came outside to line up on either side of the school gate. One of the women was carrying the bouquet of flowers that Pei Zhen had supplied. Soon enough, the officials from the township education office had arrived. They were riding in a Red Flag sedan that looked like it'd been driven here all the way from the other end of the country. It was in even worse shape than the one she'd seen in Nanyuan Township. When Fanhua heard Xu making the introductions, she realised this was the actual office director and not the deputy who was still biding his time. Definitely no chance of avoiding a lunchtime banquet then, Fanhua thought. She gave Xiaohong a quick call and told her to jump in a taxi and wait for her at the entrance of the school. Then she phoned the wild game restaurant on the west side of the highway and told them to be ready.

TWENTY-SEVEN

fter that, she went along to listen to the class. Shangyi's topic turned out to be "Covering One's Own Ears to Try to Steal a Bell".

"Today's class is a very significant one," Shangyi said. "It will teach you an important lesson about establishing a correct moral perspective." First, he had the students silently read a text and pick out all the tricky characters they didn't recognise. Then he got the boy named Olympic to stand up and recite the whole thing out loud. A little over-excited, Olympic started off loud and got so much louder as he went on that his voice began to resemble the chirrup of a cicada.

Shangyi felt compelled to interrupt.

"Olympic has done a splendid job reading out the first passage," he said. "Now we'll have another student read the second passage. Let's have one of the girls. Manny, why don't you have a go?"

Manny's voice, however, started off quiet and got quieter. She sounded like the drone of a mosquito. The other students were growing agitated. Fanhua could see the ears of the children in the back row turning red. But Shangyi knew how to make them relax. Once he took over the reading himself, they were transported to the scene of the crime and forgot all about the strangers listening in on their class. Shangyi's enthusiasm brought the story to life, especially the description of the theft itself. His gestures were perfect – the way he bent forward, legs splayed, and used his chalk as a prop to demonstrate the motion of a cartwheel. Remarkably lifelike. Even a master of the trade like Lingpei would appreciate the performance, Fanhua thought.

There was something about the way he leant backwards that Fanhua found particularly familiar. Eventually, she realised it was an action she'd often seen Pei Zhen perform. According to Pei Zhen, this was to check the size of a jumper; if it pulled back to her belly button, then it was just the right length. But Pei Zhen would have a vaguely alluring expression on her face when she did it, her midriff rippling like she was some kind of belly dancer. Which Shangyi did not. Shangyi always had the same solemn expression, no matter what he was doing, and it was the solemnity that came from knowing that his was the most glorious profession under the sun. Playing his current role, however, this expression contrived to make the would-be bell thief seem decent and brave, like he was some misunderstood renegade.

Fanhua suspected some of the more mischievous boys in the class would find this thief a rather admirable character, and perhaps even be tempted to give his trade a try. A few of them were already starting to fidget under their tables.

When he reached the end of the reading, Shangyi began the process of dissecting and summarising the story. Then he asked the students what they thought the main idea of the story might be.

"He knew he'd made a mistake," said one of the boys, "but he carried on doing it all the same. What an idiot."

"Very good," said Shangyi, "let's see if we can't find a slightly less offensive word than 'idiot', and perhaps we could come up with a more formal alternative to 'doing it' while we're at it."

"He knew he'd made a mistake," said another student, "but he persisted all the same. How foolish of him."

Shangyi was so delighted he switched briefly to English: "*Yes, very good!*" he cried. "Such a good answer. Does your classmate deserve a round of applause?" The students clapped. Shangyi wrote the answer on the blackboard, and told them to copy it down and remember it deep in their hearts. Then he asked them what they could learn from this story. Some of them answered that they had learned to establish a correct moral perspective. Others said they had learned the importance of being a clever child and also of dedicating their talent to the motherland. Shangyi asked Fisher to stand up and tell everyone what he had learned from the story.

"If you're stealing a bell," said Fisher, "don't cover your ears."

All the students laughed, and the visitors joined in. There's one of them in every class, isn't there? That one student who can't resist clowning around, who'd whiten the tip of his nose with chalk to get a laugh. Except this wasn't Fisher playing dumb and giving a deliberately stupid answer – or if he was, then he was an actor of preternatural talent.

Fanhua laughed, but when she thought about it she realised Fisher's answer wasn't entirely wrong. But it was wrong as far as Teacher Shangyi was concerned.

"Fisher, why don't you try again? Think deeper. Maybe something about moral perspective?"

"Don't steal bells," said Fisher. "You're a bad student if you steal bells."

Fanhua thought this was an entirely reasonable answer, but Fisher had still not done well enough for Shangyi's liking, or rather, for the demands of the curriculum.

"But *why*, Fisher, why does that make him a bad student? Is it perhaps because he has failed to establish..."

Fisher finally produced the correct answer: "Because he has failed to establish a correct moral perspective."

A peach blossom sprang to Teacher Shangyi's cheek. "Students!" he said, smoothing out his tie. "Is Fisher's answer correct or incorrect?"

Once again, the students' voices sounded like they had been cut off with a knife: "Corr-rect!"

"Tell me," Shangyi continued, "is your classmate Fisher holding the rest of you back, or is he not?"

Some of the students decided he was holding them back, while others disagreed. Shangyi used his tie as a prop to demonstrate "holding them back", first yanking it tight and then loosening the knot.

"I say he is not," Shangyi said. "Or we might say that though it may *appear* he is, he is, in reality, not. Though Fisher may not be as bright as some of the rest of you, with the help of his teachers and classmates he is striving to keep up. This allows the rest of you an opportunity. What opportunity might that be? The opportunity to assist him, and to demonstrate to the rest of your classmates how one may take pleasure in helping others. What do you say, shall we give Fisher a round of applause?" Shangyi's timing was perfect. The bell rang just as the sound of applause was dying down. Not a second of class time wasted.

The township education officials were apparently very diligent in their work because they launched straight into their evaluation session without pausing for a break. Fanhua was invited to sit in. Their appraisal of Shangyi's class was highly favourable. "A perfect synthesis," they said, "of knowledge, ideology and fun."

"In order to thank our prominent comrades for the support they have given Guanzhuang," Fanhua said, "and in order to grant us a lengthier opportunity to learn from your wisdom, I have arranged you all a meal. Don't worry, it'll all be very basic – you won't be doing anything wrong. And please, don't waste any time objecting, because everything has already been arranged. Now, why don't you continue with your meeting, and I'll go and make sure it's all ready."

When she left the meeting room, Fanhua saw Shangyi walking circles around the table tennis table like a donkey round a grindstone.

"That Fisher is a true numbskull," he said when he saw Fanhua. "He could have ruined everything. I came this close to giving him a good slapping."

"That's hardly necessary," said Fanhua. "We can't expect all five fingers to be the same length."

"That's true. At least I can use him as a negative example for the others to learn from."

"Shangyi," said Fanhua, "I've loosened the purse strings on your behalf today. I've arranged to take them to eat game for lunch. Come with me now, and you can join them for lunch."

"Would that be appropriate?" asked Shangyi.

"Come now, so long as I'm head of the village committee, it's appropriate if I say it is. That's settled then."

The taxi took them out onto the highway. While they were driving along, Fanhua asked Shangyi whether he'd finished the family planning quiz yet. It was basically done, he replied, but there were just a few particulars in need of polishing. Family planning was a fundamental policy of the state, he added, and it wouldn't do to be sloppy about such things. In order to come up with the best possible questions, he had made several trips to the Xinhua Bookstore and purchased a whole heap of books, as well as the ones he'd borrowed from Li Hao.

"Give me the receipts when I see you next, and I'll make sure you're reimbursed."

"Maybe I'll slip in that question about Marx's birthday again. It's not like Marxism-Leninism ever stops being relevant, after all."

Fanhua laughed. "That's your call."

Just before reaching the tollbooth, their taxi left the highway and took a dirt track heading west. After travelling for another five hundred metres or so, they caught sight of some trees, and after passing beyond the trees they saw water. Between the trees and the water, there was a little wooden house, so crudely constructed it might have been a cowshed. The two chefs were out by the waterside, butchering turtledoves and sparrows. Some cicada pupae had been removed from the freezer to defrost. They'd already gutted a pheasant and wrapped its tail feathers up in cellophane to serve as a dazzling gift for the guest of honour. Fanhua's sister Fanrong had just such a collection of feathers in her study – the last time Fanhua came here was with her and her husband. There'd been a kerosene lamp inside back then, which was meant to be "atmospheric", according to Fanrong's husband. All the game birds had their own special names round these parts: sparrows were "wheat-chicks", turtledoves were "lesser pigeons", while pheasants, oddly enough, were "house sparrows".

"We can talk more freely now that you've had a chance to relax," Fanhua said to Shangyi as they walked between the trees. "I don't want to bring up a sensitive subject, but just think how exhausted you'd be right now if you'd had that child. Forget about having any sort of a career."

Shangyi sighed. "Cao Xueqin got it right when he said girls are made of water. But dammit, I need some water in my life."

"We always want what we can't have. As you've probably heard from Pei Zhen, Xue'e is pregnant. She wants a boy. But is it up to her?"

This remark caused Shangyi visible consternation. His hands started tugging at his tie, and his face turned red. He eventually loosened the tie, before finally pulling it right off.

"You must be joking, Secretary. How could Pei Zhen know a thing like that? She couldn't possibly. I'd be willing to bet on it."

"Are you saying this is news to you?" Fanhua asked.

Shangyi swallowed. "I suppose I must have heard *something* about it."

Suppose? A peculiar choice of words.

"Well, where did you hear it from?"

Shangyi turned his gaze up towards the tree branches. "I can't presently recall."

"Did Xiangsheng tell you? He's a good man is Xiangsheng, in every respect, except he doesn't always know when to keep his mouth shut."

"I guess I must have heard it from him," said Shangyi, "but I honestly don't really remember. These last few days I've been so busy preparing for the demo class, I haven't really been able to absorb anything else."

"Well, your work paid off. You did an excellent job. The students are lucky to have you as their teacher. Headmaster Xu says you do a better job than the professional teachers. Actually, a thought occurred to me about that just now, though I didn't have time to mention it to Headmaster Xu. Starting next year, regardless of whether you end up getting an official position or not, we'll make sure you're paid as much as they are. Equal pay for equal work, am I right? We're sacrificing ourselves for nothing if we do a better job than them but take home less money."

On hearing this, Shangyi clapped his hands to the side of his head, though this time it was to show he couldn't believe his ears, not because he was pretending to steal a bell.

"Don't mention it to anyone else yet," Fanhua said. "Not even Xiangsheng."

"Don't worry," said Shangyi, "I'm not one to move a rock just so I can drop it on my own foot."

Fanhua had originally been planning to take the taxi back to the village once she'd delivered this crucial speech. But now she felt it would seem a bit abrupt to just up and leave so soon, as if she'd only come here to demonstrate her own ingenuity. So she brought up Tiesuo and Xue'e again. "If you have time," she said, "you could do worse than to have a word with Tiesuo. Tell him to quit being stupid and hurry up and deal with Xue'e's belly. You're an educated man, and a model of family planning. He'll listen to you."

"He won't listen to me," said Shangyi. "I'm no doctor. You should try Xianyu."

"But Xue'e had a fight with Xianyu's wife. She'll trust him no further than a chicken trusts a ferret." This mention of birds reminded Fanhua of the pheasant's tail feathers. "Did you see the feathers back there?" she asked Shangyi. "That's right, the ones wrapped in cellophane. The kind of plume you'd see sticking out of a general's helmet in the theatre. You give them to the head of the education office later on. They're an emblem of good luck. Like the peacock feathers officials attached to their hats in the olden days."

TWENTY-EIGHT

A call came down from the township: the number one in each village was to come in for another meeting. Apparently, Township Head Bull was getting addicted to the sound of his own voice. He lived up to his name all right. No one liked chewing the cud more than him. The difference was that his cud comprised county leader reports, not grass. Of course, he did occasionally add some additional content to his ruminations. Such as? Fanhua was fairly sure it'd be something along the lines of how important it is to synthesise the essence of the county leader's instructions with the practical reality of Wangzhai Township, to walk a road that embodies the unique quality of Wangzhai. This "unique quality" was manifested primarily in the form of a number. In a percentage, in fact: twenty per cent. If the county leaders were talking about reforestation, and they'd instructed every village to restore one hundred *mu* of agricultural land, then the Bull would demand one hundred and twenty *mu*. Always an extra twenty per cent. If the leaders were telling everyone that cash crops should comprise thirty per cent of every village's agricultural output, then the Bull would turn that into fifty per cent.

Of course, this rule could occasionally backfire. Like last year, when there was a change in the village tax allotment. Originally, the county authorities were planning to bring it down ten percentage points, to twenty-five per cent of the total, but then they changed their plan and announced that they would in fact be reducing it by just five, to thirty per cent. This was announced as a measure that would make life easier for rural folk. Township Head Bull came back and made his usual speech about synthesising with the practical reality of Wangzhai Township, and announced that the village tax allotment was now fifty per cent. Which, being an increase and not a decrease, totally contradicted official policy. The county head had ripped him to shreds. A bull you certainly are, he said, with horns sprouting out of your head. Too bullish by half. If the entire county were to follow your lead, how would we eat? How would we drink? Can we eat the northeast wind? Can we drink the northwest wind? Hmm? If the whole county does what you've done, will the peasants still leave home for work once they've got a taste for the easy life? Hmm?

Later, in private, Township Head Bull complained that the percentages had been whizzing up and down during the county head's speech. A fart in the pants goes in two separate directions, as the saying goes, and his problem stemmed from having paid attention to one direction but not the other. In the days that followed, the Bull's eyes were permanently red. Whether it was out of rage or a sense of injustice, no one could be sure, but it was most definitely a frightening sight. He looked like he was this close to headbutting someone.

What sort of thing would he be chewing over this time? Fanhua wondered. Elections were approaching fast, so it would probably have something to do with safety issues during the voting period, to ensure there was no trouble. Presumably, he would be expecting twenty per cent less fighting and brawling than they'd seen during the previous elections.

Qingshu was out in his car looking for Xue'e again, so to get to Wangzhai, Fanhua would either have to hire a taxi or take one of the privately-run minibuses. There were several other Guanzhuang folk out waiting for a ride. They asked Fanhua where she was headed, and she told them she had to get to Wangzhai for a meeting. Then she unleashed a stream of abuse at Township Head Bull: "Such a damned nuisance, that Township Head Bull. Never content. Always finding new ways to pick on us."

The township-level officials were generally the least popular figures in Guanzhuang. Not a single redeeming feature, as far as the villagers were concerned. Always looking to screw over the village. Nobody had any faith in the people directly above them. The villagers mistrusted the township officials, but they had confidence in the county leaders; the township officials mistrusted the county leaders, but they had confidence in the municipal leaders; and the county officials, well, naturally they had no faith in the municipal leaders, but they did believe in the provincial leaders. There are no errors in the scriptures of the Buddha, only misreadings by neglectful abbots.

Sure enough, someone soon picked up where Fanhua had left off.

"Township Head Bull is a grasshopper at the end of autumn. The county head is going to sort him out eventually."

"You've got that right," said Fanhua. "His hopping days are numbered."

But of course, the Bull was not really a grasshopper at the end of autumn. A grasshopper at the end of autumn hops madly around at random, whereas his hopping was of the highest calibre. When Fanhua stepped into the yard of the township government building, he was playing badminton with his secretary. He leapt into the air to return a high shot, smashing the shuttlecock with a grunted expletive. He was dressed all in white – white jumper, white trousers, white trainers. His hair would have been white too, except he dyed it black. All the onlookers applauded, and the vanquished secretary told him he played like the Olympic badminton champion Li Lingwei.

He was a keen-eyed one, this secretary. Fanhua could tell he'd registered her presence, but he didn't initially make any move to greet her. Instead, he made sure that the shuttlecock went promptly out of play and just so happened to land at Fanhua's feet.

"Oh," he said, acting like he had only just noticed her arrival, "you're here. The bossman has been waiting for you." It was at this point that Fanhua discovered that none of the number ones from any of the other villages was here. Just her. The "bossman" dropped his racket to the floor. A typist handed him a towel, which he used to wipe his face and neck and clean the insides of his ears. Then, after combing his fingers through his hair, he greeted Fanhua and indicated for her to follow him. Fanhua went into his office. The typist brought in a glass of water, and Township Head Bull took a gulp, tilted his head back and gargled loudly. He swallowed the water afterwards rather than spitting it out, possibly out of consideration for the water conservation policy, or possibly not. Then he took another gulp, gargled again, and this time spat it out. After wiping his mouth, he finally spoke.

"Secretary Kong, were you planning to stand there all day if I didn't ask you to sit down?"

Something felt off. In an attempt to lighten the mood, Fanhua replied in a jokey tone of voice, "How could I possibly dare sit down when the esteemed township head is still standing?"

"How are things?" Township Head Bull asked as he took a seat. "Everything going well?"

An extremely vague question. Fanhua wasn't sure where to begin answering it, so she chuckled. "Not bad."

But the Bull remained serious. "Be specific. Which areas are less bad, and which are more bad?"

"Well, we can't expect all ten fingers to be the exact same length," said Fanhua. "There are always going to be some areas where the work isn't quite perfect."

Township Head Bull riffled through a book – it looked like *300 Sentences of Conversational English* – but then immediately shut it again. "More specific, if you please. Which exactly are those parts where the work isn't quite perfect?"

Fanhua felt uncomfortable. She'd dealt with everything, she thought, except for the mess of the paper plant. And she could hardly mention that without making it seem like she was insulting the Bull. This was a hornet's nest all right, and she couldn't go poking it at random.

"Go on," said Township Head Bull. "A problem is nothing to be afraid of. It's the problems we don't know about that we should fear the most. If there's pus in the boil, why not squeeze it out?"

This damned son-of-a-bitch, what the hell is he getting at? But no, it was better to take the lead herself. Pull the bull by the nose instead of letting the bull pull her.

"Township Head Bull, am I to assume you have paid an incognito visit to Guanzhuang? Please inform me of any problems you

231

discovered. Rest assured, the village committee and I will carry out your instructions in full."

Township Head Bull's hands had been lying on the table in a loose fist. Now they suddenly flattened and rose into the air. When his palms reached the height of the little red flag on the desk, they sank back down again. Then they came up again. Was this some kind of qigong exercise?

"Secretary Kong, oh Secretary Kong. When we push a gourd down into the water, we must not allow the ladle to bob back up to the surface."

What was this now about ladles? The man sounded like some old aunt spinning riddles.

"I'll be sure to amend whatever faults you point out," said Fanhua.

"Is there not a woman in the village named Xue'e," he asked, "who had run off with a pregnant belly?"

Fanhua was stunned. The man must have ears sharper than any dog's to have picked up Xue'e's name. Before she had a chance to reply, he slammed his hands down onto the table.

"An out-of-plan pregnancy. You lot really have some nerve."

Seeing that there was no way of covering this up, Fanhua could only come clean. Yes, there was a baby in Xue'e's belly, but—

Township Head Bull leapt to his feet before she'd finished speaking. "But? But what? Screw your buts. A belly! One belly! How is it that you're incapable of managing a single belly?"

"I only just found out about it myself," said Fanhua. "But it's not too late for action. We can still get rid of it, and that'll be the end of it."

"Well, that does sound simple. But good news stays indoors, and bad news travels a thousand *li*. The whole world knows about this already." He slapped himself in the face. "I'll never be able to show my face again once you lot are through with me."

It was Li Tiesuo who did the deed, thought Fanhua, not you. What do you have to be ashamed of? But then she quickly saw how things stood: someone must have gone over the Bull's head and reported this to the county. But who had connections at the county level?

Township Head Bull's next line provided Fanhua with an

inkling: "Look, no township is completely clean. Here in Wangzhai, there in Nanyuan, there's dirt everywhere. But that's just the way it is. We throw a sheet over it and it disappears. But you – the whole world knows about you now."

Nanyuan Township? Wait, so it was that fucker Ace Liu who let the cat out of the bag? Well, Ace, you've truly fucked me over this time.

There was nothing Fanhua could do beyond reiterating her good intentions. She could only tell the Bull that she shouldered the blame for Xue'e's belly herself, and that she would resolve the situation as soon as possible. "Just leave it to me," she said. "I'll find a way."

When she'd said her piece, Township Head Bull called through for his typist to bring Fanhua a glass of water. Once it was just the two of them again, he shook his head and smiled, and the change in his expression was so abrupt it made Fanhua jump.

"Fanhua," he said – not "Secretary Kong" now – "honestly, I only ever get mad at myself. No one else can make me angry. Don't take it to heart. I may be Bull by name, but I have the temperament of an ass. Irritable and stubborn. Irritable when I find my work isn't up to scratch, and stubborn when other people tell my work isn't up to scratch." Then for some reason, he brought up Fanrong: "I often read your sister's articles. She has a sharp pen. You'd never imagine they were written by such a fine-looking girl. A touch of the Lu Xun, I think. But let me be straight with you, Fanhua. I'm concerned you don't understand the way things are done. You might end up getting into serious trouble. Operating in the realm of officialdom is like buying a cat in a sack. You don't know whether you're getting a he-cat or a she-cat, black or white, tabby or yellow, leopard or Persian. So you need to be careful. Watch what you say."

This amounted to an instruction that Fanhua was not to have any more to do with Ace Liu. To her surprise, after all this talk of cats in sacks, Township Head Bull actually offered her some praise: "You did very well today. When I didn't tell you why I'd brought you here, you played dumb. Very convincingly. Sometimes you need to play deaf as well as dumb. Don't think I'm angry. I'm not. I'm happy. How can I not be, seeing what progress you've made? Happy! It's like that song they once sang in the New Year Gala. 'Today is happy, truly happy.'" The Bull switched from local dialect to standard

Mandarin for this ditty, but his accent turned the word "happy" into "harpy".

Fanhua swallowed and tried not to smile. Township Head Bull told her to let him know if she encountered any other difficulties in her work. He was here to help, he said. How was she feeling about the upcoming elections?

"I'll do another term if they pick me," she said, "and if they don't, then I'll give it up."

This earned fresh praise from the Bull. "A true Communist is prepared for every eventuality. Very good. But I'm sure you'll be re-elected. Actions speak louder than words, and you've proved in the field that you're a horse, not a mule. I wouldn't feel confident about entrusting Guanzhuang to anyone else. I mean, we're talking about being responsible for over a thousand mouths."

"Well, I'm ready either way. If I lose, I'm going to head to Shen-zhen. My husband is doing business down there, and he could use another pair of hands."

Township Head Bull's face turned stern at this. "What's that? Don't talk nonsense. I read something in the *Eastern Times* recently that made me think of you. It said 'prosperity isn't one man getting rich, but a whole village getting rich'. I can't believe you'd abandon the village to go make your own fortune."

This was music to Fanhua's ears. He would never be going on like this if he wasn't truly confident she was going to be re-elected. Just you wait, she thought. Let's see how you change your tune when I start my second term with an attack on the paper plant.

TWENTY-NINE

Slogan banners had been pasted up around the village by the time she got back. And just like that, election season had arrived. There was one banner skewed across the railings of Fanxin's cowshed proclaiming "The People Choose the People's Village Officials, Wow!" A few steps further and you got to Linghui's place. Linghui was the village barber. The original name over the door – "Pacific Hairdresser's" – had later been replaced with "Atlantic Hair Salon". Fanhua had once asked him why he changed the name, and he told her "Pacific" sounded a bit tacky, whereas "Atlantic" had a more of a fashionable, foreign-sounding ring to it. How was "Atlantic" more foreign-sounding than "Pacific"? It was lost on Fanhua. There was also a poetic couplet flanking the door, carved out of wood. On one side it said, "A raven-haired scholar on arrival", and on the other, "A pale-faced novice on departure". Linghui periodically filled in the etched characters with a fresh layer of red paint. It was a well-turned phrase, and Linghui said he'd given himself high blood pressure with the effort of thinking it up. But now they had been covered by a fresh couplet on red paper: "Arrive trembling and fearful" and "Leave happy and relaxed". It was hard to grasp the logic on first reading, but when you thought about it, Fanhua decided, it was perfect: a profound message about the nature of officialdom, conveyed in plain language. Linghui wasn't stupid, he had ink in his veins.

As Fanhua was passing by, Linghui stepped outside to toss out some water.

"Linghui," she said, "that's a nice couplet you've written there. Did it affect your blood pressure this time?"

Linghui looked in Fanhua's direction, then turned to regard the couplet and snorted in laughter. He'd written that for the sake of the children whose parents bring them in here, he explained. Always crying and wailing about how they don't want their head shaved. It was to let them know that they didn't need to be afraid, that the stubble of a shaved head wouldn't prickle against their ears, would feel quite lovely, in fact. "Didn't mean anything by it but that," he insisted, in a way that made it hard not to conclude he definitely *did* mean something by it.

Fanhua laughed and continued on her way. After a few steps, however, she turned back and bowed towards Linghui, wishing him a prosperous business.

After walking along a bit longer, Fanhua started to feel like things weren't quite right. The streets were too quiet. She'd not seen a trace of anyone else, nor heard even a dog barking. When she passed Qinglin's yard, she noticed there was a lock on the gate. Had someone died or something? The entire village congregated whenever anyone died, under the pretext of consoling the family of the deceased, but actually because they wanted to enjoy the spectacle. To observe the tears of the mourning offspring, and judge whose were genuine and whose were fake. Whose tears were the fiercest, and whose were the most moving. Then, in the evening, when the funeral musicians arrived, the sons would prostrate themselves before them, and before their foreheads hit the ground, the musicians would strike up a screeching fanfare with accompanying drums and woodblocks. The fanfare was so mournful it could pierce you right to the core, and the percussion was so thunderous it could crush your insides. Then the musicians divided into two groups and squared off against each another. When one group played *Slowly, Slowly* the other played *Bitterly, Bitterly*, and between all the slowness and the bitterness, you could hear the weeping of mourning sons and the sighing of spectators. When one group played *Red Plum Over the Wall*, the other played *Flying Snow Covering the Sky*, and that got the sons weeping and the spectators sighing again, because what image could be more evocative of decay than a sprig of red plum exposed to drifting snow? When one group played *Goddesses Scattering Flowers*, the other played *Petals Falling Profusely*, and if divine petals were fated to turn to mulch, then what could a mere mortal hope for? But now the spectators would be consoling the mourning sons. Don't cry, they're gone, your tears aren't going to bring them back to life. And then, the final song, *Dragon and Phoenix, Harbingers of Prosperity*, and it felt like the deceased was up there in heaven already, become dragon if he was a man, or phoenix if she was a woman, but either way, definitely an emblem of auspiciousness.

Now Fanhua did seem to hear the faint sound of someone crying, but it was distant and hard to pinpoint. She ran through all the village elders in her mind, but couldn't work out who might have died. As she continued on her way, she got the impression the sound was coming from somewhere behind her. She retraced her footsteps, and it became slightly clearer. Wait, that meant it was coming from Qinglin's place. Weird. She walked slowly back to his front gate and peered through the crack into the yard. There was no one inside, just a few bones strewn across the ground. They were very clean, these bones, gleaming like jade. Clearly, they'd been licked clean by the wolf. When she looked at the bones again, it seemed to her that they didn't really look like pig bones or cow bones for that matter. But no... surely they couldn't be? Fanhua wasn't prepared to follow that line of thought any further. She took a few steps backwards. No, she thought, there was no way the wolf's belly was big enough to hold an entire person. Even if it had eaten someone, it couldn't have licked the bones as clean as that. She stepped forward and rapped on the door knocker.

Qinglin's wife came out from inside, almost at a run. She had tears in her eyes, but a smile on her face. "You're back, you're back," she said as she approached. "Hello Grey, hello."

Fanhua realised she'd mistaken her for Qinglin, returning with Grey. When she saw no Qinglin and no wolf, she started crying again.

"What are you crying for?" asked Fanhua. Qinglin's wife started sobbing even harder once she saw who it was, saying she needed the secretary's help. When Fanhua enquired what the hell she was talking about, she pointed in one direction, then in another direction, before stamping her feet twice, all without speaking. When Fanhua asked her again, she sank to the floor, squatting on her haunches and sobbing with her hands over her face.

"No more crying!" shouted Fanhua. "Stand up!"

Qinglin's wife rubbed her eyes with the front of her clothes and stood up. Fanhua eventually managed to decipher her incoherent babbling. It turned out Qinglin had taken Grey off to a fight. Where was this fight? She pointed this way, then that way and then up into the sky. Was that why the village was so quiet? But surely they couldn't have *all* gone to this fight, could they? A chill crept up Fanhua's spine, and when it reached the back of her head, it turned and went back down to her trembling legs.

She raced off towards the paper factory. From a distance, she could see that there was no one around the entrance, but her legs continued to carry her in that direction all the same. When she got there, she ran her hands across the sentry lion outside, and the stone ball inside its mouth. Children loved to play with that stone ball, and it was as smooth as an abacus bead from all the hands that had touched it. Cool to the touch. There was a leaf caught in the crack in the lion's paw, a scholar tree leaf. She picked it up, looked it over and put it back. Eventually, she decided she'd better go back to the village. If everyone had gone to this fight, then her father might be among their number. Dianjun would definitely be there, but having learned from his experience in Shenzhen, he would surely know better than to rush to the front line.

She started running back towards the village. Since becoming village head, she'd walked everywhere with restrained, steady footsteps, and hadn't run anywhere. Back in primary school, she used to run like this every day. But she pretty much stopped running when she reached high school, except for the group exercise routines. In those days, she could feel the slight swell of her breasts as she ran, bulging a little like melons growing on the vine. Her clothes would rub against her nipples, like thorny branches against wild jujubes. Wild jujubes that Dianjun had held in his mouth when they snuck out to the copse behind the school. But now her breasts felt less like melons and more like bottle gourds at the end of autumn, juddering back and forth with enough force to shake down their frame. Her frame was certainly ready to fall apart by the time she got home. Fortunately, there was no padlock on the gate. No one inside except the rabbit, standing up on its hind legs with its paws across its chest, its little red eyes watching her curiously like she was some unfamiliar interloper.

Then Fanhua heard a noise that sounded a bit like the hubbub from a nursery school playground. She could hear it clearly now, coming from the direction of the school. She raced off again, past the school and towards the hills, where she was able to see Li Hao's flock. There was fear in the sound of the sheep's bleating, and unease, and then there was another kind of noise mixed in, coming from further up the hill. Fanhua heard the name Qinggang. And then, all at once, she understood everything. Oh no. This had to be a fight against Gongzhuang.

THIRTY

The Gongzhuang folk had already dispersed by the time Fanhua got there. It was getting dark, but not so dark that Fanhua couldn't see the cheerful expressions on every Guanzhuang face. The cheerful expressions of the victorious. No one was empty-handed. The men were carrying picks and shovels, while the women were armed with rolling pins and frying pans. Beanie was the first person to spot her. Beanie had a weapon of her own in the form of a stick from a willow tree. She waved her stick and jumped around, and then ran over to her mother. She wrapped her arms around Fanhua's legs, but Fanhua didn't have the energy to pick her up. Beanie started crying, and the noise drew attention to Fanhua.

"So you're finally here." This voice belonged to Linghui. What's *that* supposed to mean, you stupid, braindead butcher? Are you suggesting I've been keeping away from here on purpose?

"Have you been up there?" she asked him.

Linghui scratched his scalp. "If I had, we'd have torn them to pieces a long time ago." So that meant he had basically been a spectator on the sidelines, then.

"Oh, here to inspect the fruits of victory are you?" said Linghui's cousin Lingwen. This was an even more obnoxious remark, implying she had come down from the mountain to pick their peaches and take credit for their achievements.

"Did you suffer any battle wounds?" she asked Lingwen.

"Pfft. Those pathetic runts think they can come at me? As if."
Which meant he hadn't been involved either.

"Well, so long as you're not hurt," said Fanhua. "That's the main thing."

At this point, Qingshu came over. He was carrying his military belt again, and blustering loudly: "A great victory won, without so much as bloodying our blades!"

Fanhua was tempted to ask him what he was doing here when he was supposed to be out looking for Xue'e. But she didn't. Instead, she praised him: "Wherever Qingshu is needed, that's where he'll be!"

"Well, we sure cut that Scrawny Dog down to size, and that's what counts," said Qingshu.

This mention of a dog reminded Fanhua of Qinglin's wolf. "What about Qinglin? And his wolf?"

"The wolf did us proud too," said Qingshu. The wolf was, in fact, right next to Fanhua, locked inside a cage. How was he supposed to cope with a battle like this? He had his head tucked under his tail, and was shivering like a chaff shaker, rattling the cage. A defeathered phoenix is no better than a chicken, and a terrified wolf is definitely nowhere near as useful as a dog. He was whimpering so hard it sounded like he was having an asthma attack.

"He did us proud," Qingshu repeated, "he truly did."

Qinglin affected modesty on behalf of his wolf. No more than his duty, he said. And he doesn't like to be praised, he added, it makes him blush and hide his face behind his tail.

"How, exactly, did he do us proud?" Fanhua asked Qingshu.

Qingshu explained that among Scrawny Dog's forces was someone who'd brought along a dog, a fierce one, but just the whiff of a wolf was enough to make him piss himself and run away.

Fanhua was desperate to ask how exactly the fight had gone down, but she restrained herself. Instead, she quietly asked Qingshu which other village officials had been in attendance. Qingshu told her that everyone who was able to come had been there.

"Xiangsheng?" asked Fanhua.

"Xiangsheng wasn't there," said Qingshu. "Isn't he off on a diplomatic mission?"

That was something, Fanhua thought. It would have been potentially disastrous for her if he'd been here, bragging just like Qingshu, and somehow succeeded in convincing the villagers that he was the hero of the hour.

Suddenly, someone started crying. A man's fitful voice, and a voice Fanhua recognised: it was Xiaohong's father. She raced over, and beside the tomb of Qinggang's mother, she found someone lying down and another squatting on the ground beside them. The latter was Xiaohong's father, and the former was Xiaohong. She was covered in dirt and curled up like a dried shrimp. Fanhua called out her name but got no response. She tried again, and Xiaohong stretched out her body just a little bit before curling back up again. Fanhua grabbed hold of her hand and tried to pull her up, but someone was pushing her away. It was Xiaohong's father, and he had seized Fanhua's collar.

"This is your fault," he yelled at her, "you did this to her. She did this for you." Dianjun came hurrying over, but Xiaohong's father grabbed onto him before he'd had a chance to speak. "Why didn't you jump down? Call yourself a man? Then why didn't you jump down there?"

Fanhua understood what had happened. Xiaohong must have jumped down into the tomb. Night had almost fallen by now, and the tomb was a black hole whose depth it was too dark to gauge.

"Oh no," murmured Fanhua. Please don't let it be a broken back.

At this point, Xiaohong managed to open her mouth, but her voice was too indistinct for Fanhua to understand. Fanhua lay down close beside her and asked her what she was saying, but Xiaohong's father pulled her out of the way and lay down in her place. Then he was back at Fanhua's collar again.

"Look at the condition my daughter's in," he said, "and still she's thinking of you, still she's thinking of other villagers." What did she say? Fanhua asked him urgently. "She said you didn't need to trouble yourself about her, and she asked if anyone else had been hurt."

At that, Xiaohong's father started crying again, beating his chest and stamping his feet against the ground, wailing to the heavens. But one hand was still clutching Fanhua tight. Fanhua tried to detach herself, but she couldn't loosen his grip.

"Get the doctor here," she said, as she attempted to prise open his fingers. "Where's Xianyu?"

Dr Xianyu was gone already. They pulled over his wife, Cuixian, who was basically equivalent to half a doctor. She felt Xiaohong's forehead, and then put her hand under her nostrils. When she tried to pull back her eyelids, Xiaohong batted away her hand, which then landed in her mouth instead.

"There's blood, it's bleeding," Cuixian cried when she took away her hand.

A wheelbarrow had arrived. Fanhua climbed up and sat on the wheelbarrow, cradling Xiaohong. Then Xiaohong's father pulled Fanhua off and took her place himself. But not before Fanhua'd had a chance to see the trace of blood in Xiaohong's mouth for herself. The barrow set off, but no sooner had it left the crowd of onlookers than Xiaohong's father called it to a stop.

"Oh no," he said, "I wouldn't dream of troubling a master engineer." It was then that Fanhua realised Dianjun was the one who'd been pulling the wheelbarrow. So now they just stood there, with no one to pull the thing, until Lingwen came over and more or less grabbed the barrow out of Dianjun's hands.

Fanhua followed them to the clinic. Strangely, Xianyu was still nowhere to be found, and even Cuixian had no idea where he'd got to.

"Hurry up and get over to Wangzhai Hospital," said Fanhua.

Xiaohong was able to speak again by this point. She looked at Fanhua and attempted a smile, but the effort of it turned the smile into a grimace. Fanhua hurried over to hold her hand.

"I'm not going to die," said Xiaohong. Fanhua was immediately in tears. "I haven't let you down, have I?" Xiaohong asked. Her voice was quiet, but Fanhua heard her clearly. Fanhua's knees went weak, and she almost crumbled to the ground. "You need to tell the secretary you were wrong," Xiaohong said to her father. "It wasn't her fault."

It usually irritated Fanhua whenever anyone called her "secretary" because it sounded like they were insinuating something. But right now she couldn't think of anything she'd rather hear. Not "Fanhua", or "village head", or "chairperson", or "auntie" or even the celestial music of the heavens.

THIRTY-ONE

Fortunately, Xiaohong had only sprained her back. The skin on the back of her head was broken, but there was no serious damage. They said she would be fine to leave the hospital the next day, but Fanhua overruled this decision and insisted they keep her under observation for longer.

Fanhua asked Xiaohong whether she wanted to see the numerous villagers who were keen to pay her a visit. Xiaohong said she'd do whatever Fanhua thought best.

When the villagers showed up, Fanhua exaggerated the severity of Xiaohong's injuries, telling them the doctors had insisted she rest and recuperate and avoid speaking too much.

"You shouldn't have said that," Xiaohong said to Fanhua a bit later. "You really shouldn't."

"Why not? I want them to know that the women in our team are stronger than the men. The women aren't afraid to risk their lives when trouble comes knocking, while the men are all hiding away like cowardly tortoises."

Some of Xiaohong's relatives had come to visit too. This time Xiaohong insisted on downplaying the damage, saying she didn't want people talking about her injuries. As she hid her face under the quilt in embarrassment, Fanhua understood her concern: she was worried her injuries would get more and more severe in the retelling,

244

and any talk of long-term health effects might affect her future marriage prospects. But surely Xiaohong wasn't thinking of marrying outside the village, was she? Fanhua would have to have a word with her once she was out of hospital.

Xianyu was one of the people who'd come to the hospital to see Xiaohong. Fanhua was going to let him in, seeing as how he was a doctor, but Xiaohong's father refused him entry.

"Where were you?" he said, pointing at Xianyu. "Xiaohong was in trouble, and we wasted precious time because you weren't there, you realise that?"

Fanhua hastily drew Xianyu off to one side. The old man's upset, she said to him, there's no point arguing with him. Xianyu just smiled and said nothing.

"But come to think of it, where *were* you?" said Fanhua. "Normally you're always there, hanging around the village, but when you were needed, you couldn't be found."

Xianyu raised his palm to his mouth and whispered from behind it, "I went to Xiushui Hospital."

"What, was someone else from the village hurt?"

Xianyu lifted his hand again. "Scrawny Dog was hurt too."

"Really? Hurt where?"

"I don't know," said Xianyu, "but I know he was hurt. They conscripted me. Put me in Scrawny Dog's car and drove off to Wangzhai. But once they arrived, they decided they may as well go to the hospital in Xiushui Town. So off we went to Xiushui. Don't worry, it's not going to be fatal. He'll be out of hospital in a couple of days." If Scrawny Dog runs up a big medical bill, Fanhua thought, and charges it to Guanzhuang, what would they do? But it wasn't long before she felt calm again. Fine, if that's how you want to play it, then Xiaohong's medicals might just need paying by Gongzhuang. She certainly won't be leaving the hospital before you. Just you wait and see.

Xiangsheng had also come back to see Xiaohong. He had a grim face on him, like he'd been on the wrong end of a kicking. He only smiled when he saw Xiaohong. Afterwards, Fanhua walked him out and asked how he was getting on with things. It was not looking good, he informed her. When she tried to get an explanation out of him, he just kept dragging on his cigarette without answering, spitting out gobs of phlegm all over the place until a passing doctor asked him to stop. He spat once more, pointedly loudly, as the doctor walked away. Fanhua asked him to tell her what was going on.

Xiangsheng tossed his cigarette end into a flowerbed. "Someone beat us to it," he said in a voice full of venom. "They got their work done well before us."

This was too ambiguous an answer for Fanhua. Who had got what work done?

"Felines have their feline ways, and canines have their canine ways. Men stand up and women squat. Everyone has their own ways. It would take too long to explain." Xiangsheng laughed a laugh so cold it brought Fanhua out in goosebumps. He placed another cigarette in his mouth but chucked it away after just a couple of drags. "Fuck it, I'm going back to my cold noodle business in Xiushui."

"But you only just got here," said Fanhua. "This job isn't finished yet. Wait until we get this done before you give up."

"Screw that. I've wasted enough time already. Nope, it's back to noodles for me."

Fanhua was angry now. "Oh, very nice, running off when Xiaohong's been wounded, and Qingshu's incapable of wiping his own arse by himself. What are we supposed to do next?"

Think you can up and vanish as easily as that? I haven't settled with you yet, Fanhua thought. There's a financial balance sheet, for one thing – the money you spent at the school – but we can put that aside for now. And then there's the destabilising situation with Scrawny Dog. That belongs to the political balance sheet. You were the one who told me it was a good idea to let Scrawny Dog dig up the tomb of Qinggang's mother, and look how that worked out. Could have ended up with a death on our hands.

But Fanhua didn't want to argue with Xiangsheng when there were so many other people around. "If you want to go, then go," said Fanhua. "But wait until tomorrow at least."

Xiangsheng agreed. Some more people from the village were arriving. Fanhua was about to leave when Xiangsheng spoke up again. To her great surprise, he brought up the subject of Scrawny

Dog unprompted: "I went to Xiushui Hospital. Fuck, if it was just the two of us, I'd have choked him to death right there." He demonstrated with a vigorously mimed throttling action, his facial expression and gesture indicating just how much he'd wanted to choke him.

THIRTY-TWO

F anhua went back to the village along with Xiangsheng in Qingshu's car. Qingshu had been over at Linshui Village, because Xue'e's grandmother's nephew was from Linshui, apparently, and then they'd stopped off at Wangzhai Hospital on the way back to check in on Xiaohong. Xueshi was along for the ride too, but he was too old to handle all this excitement and quickly fell asleep, snoring away with his clothes pulled up to cover his face. Qingshu recounted the day of the fight as they were driving along. Once battle had commenced, he said, it was inevitable that there'd be some casualties. Even a country as mighty as America couldn't prevent a few people from getting hurt when they went on a hostage rescue mission.

Fanhua had heard more than enough of his constant references to America. "Seriously though," she said, "why don't you explain exactly how the fight went down?"

Qingshu beat his hands against the steering wheel as he relived the memory. He'd been about to go out in his car, he said, when he heard people yelling about how the Gongzhuangers had come over here to steal our tree. He leapt out of his car and saw that people were heading in the direction of the hills behind the village. Being the public security commissioner for the village, he could hardly stand idle, so he grabbed his weapon and followed the crowds.

"This yelling you mentioned," Xiangsheng said, "who started it?"

"It was hard to tell," said Qingshu. "But there was definitely yelling."

"Fuck," said Xiangsheng, and he said it with real feeling. This was no ordinary habitual expletive. "You mean you couldn't even tell whose voice it was?"

Stunned, Qingshu found himself stamping on the brake, bringing the car to a very abrupt stop.

"Come on, who the hell was it?" Xiangsheng persisted.

"I honestly couldn't tell. Someone getting on in years, I think. Probably the kind of person who likes to stick their nose into other people's business."

Xiangsheng persisted in trying to get an answer from Xueshi: "Uncle, would that have been Qingmao?" But Xueshi continued to snore away, failing to respond in the slightest even when the question was repeated.

"But I heard the voice on the loudspeaker clearly enough," Qingshu volunteered.

"Oh?" said Fanhua. So a broadcast had gone out over the loudspeakers.

"It was Xiaohong," said Qingshu. "She kept saying something had happened up in the hills, something had happened up in the hills. She didn't say it was a tree being stolen. She just said something had happened."

Xiaohong was still young, Fanhua thought to herself, and when trouble appeared she'd acted impulsively. So I really am to blame. If I'd told her beforehand about what was going on – if I'd told her I'd given my consent to all this – she wouldn't have acted the way she did. But it was much too late for that now.

Xiangsheng started swearing again. His profanity of choice this time was "motherfucking cunt", and he put such force into his delivery that Fanhua felt his spittle hit her hand. It had suddenly become very tense inside the car. Fanhua knew how to remain self-composed. In moments such as this, she would sit calmly in her seat and gaze out the window as if they were off on an inspection. But the tension was getting to Qingshu.

"Shall we have some music?" he ventured.

No one answered. He put on a song anyway. It turned out to be from *Journey to the West*:

You carry a shoulder pole, I lead a horse,
Welcoming the sunrise, seeing off the dusk,
Our feet smooth the bumps along the way,
Struggling with hardships, we set off again,
We set off again.

This reminded Fanhua of Shortfur. But Qingshu got there before her: "I heard you were the one who got Shortfur to come back," he said to Xiangsheng.

Xiangsheng didn't reply.

"Weren't you the one who invited him to come here and put on a show?" Qingshu asked again. "Out of all the people we could have chosen, why did you have to go with Shortfur?"

Xiangsheng's breathing was getting heavier and heavier. Fanhua could sense he was ready to explode at any minute.

Qingshu whistled. "When's it going to be, the performance? Before the elections or after? Hmm?"

Still Xiangsheng said nothing.

"Both options have their appeal. It can be welcoming the sunrise before, or smoothing out the bumps in the way afterwards."

Not a peep from Xiangsheng. Instead of probing any further, Qingshu put on another song:

You don't know,
You don't know,
I've waited so long, all the flowers have withered.
You don't know,
You don't know,
I've waited so long, all the flowers have withered.

"What do you think, Xiangsheng? Has your uncle picked a good tune?" asked Qingshu. Wait, so now Qingshu was acting like he was Xiangsheng's senior? This was a whole new level of insolence. Scrawny Dog was right, Fanhua thought. Qingshu's bluntness concealed a sharp edge. He was deliberately trying to get a reaction out of Xiangsheng. Come to mention it, what did he mean by that line "waiting so long, all the flowers have withered"? There was some kind of an insinuation there. These two may have once been paddling the same boat, but now it seemed like Qingshu was attempting to undermine Xiangsheng. They must have had a serious falling out.

Xiangsheng finally reacted: "I'm *your* uncle!"

"Well that's hardly reasonable," Qingshu retorted. "The hierarchy's existed for two millennia. An uncle is an uncle, a nephew is a nephew. How can you turn that upside down? I *am* your uncle, and I would still be your uncle even if we were in America."

Xiangsheng made no attempt to reason with Qingshu. "I'm your grandfather."

The car came crashing to a halt again. Qingshu acted swiftly, jumping out of the vehicle, opening the door and grabbing Xiangsheng's collar.

"You dare disrespect your elder! Say that again!"

Well, well, this really was the sun rising in the west. So Qingshu was bold enough to lay hands on Xiangsheng.

Xiangsheng's astonished eyes were almost popping out of his head. Clearly, he had never envisaged this outcome. Nevertheless, he retained the same calm demeanour as always. "Let go of me," he said, after clearing his throat.

Qingshu not only failed to let go, he proceeded to shake Xiangsheng about a bit.

Xiangsheng managed a laugh. "Let go of me, please."

"Fuck you, why the hell would I do that."

Qingshu's expletive seemed to deflate Xiangsheng slightly. He hunched his shoulders. "I'm going to count to three," he said, in a wormlike voice. "Let go."

Fanhua had to resist the urge to laugh. "It was just a joke," she said, "no need to take it so seriously. Qingshu, get back in the car."

But Xiangsheng had already started counting. It was an unusually lengthy, laborious process.

"One. Still not letting go? Then I'm going to have to count to two. Two. Now will you let go? If you don't, then three will be arriving soon. Is that really what you want? I don't want you to have any regrets if I do. I'll start from the beginning again, just to give the chance to save face. One. Two. Are you letting go? After two comes three."

At this point, Qingshu did finally let go, but not before shoving Xiangsheng back into his seat.

This was when Xueshi "woke up". He stretched, yawned and smacked his lips. "I was having a dream," he said. "I dreamt I was teaching my grandson to count. And when I got to three, I woke up."

They'd barely started moving again before Xiangsheng gestured for them to stop the car. He said he'd just remembered that they were doing hygiene checks in the restaurants in Xiushui today, and he needed to go back there and deal with those sons-of-bitches, and then treat them to a meal the next day. This, it seemed to Fanhua, was his way of announcing that he was withdrawing his candidacy.

"Is it as serious as that?" asked Fanhua. "Can't you just go tomorrow?"

"No, you don't know what it's like. They're a bunch of ungrateful bastards, those sons-of-bitches. They act one way when you're there with them, and another way behind your back. There's one of them in particular, ex-army, he's the worst of the lot. I'm going to sort him out one of these days."

Obviously, Fanhua realised that he was referring obliquely to one of the other occupants of the car, but she had no objections. She certainly had no desire to stand up for Qingshu.

"Well, what are we going to do then?" she said. "Will you drive there yourself, or...?"

"What are the rest of you going to do if I drive there myself?" Xiangsheng replied. "I'll take a taxi."

"Save the receipt," Fanhua immediately said. "I'll reimburse you later."

Xiangsheng got out and headed back the way they'd come from. His silhouette diminished against the width of the road, making him look like some wind-lashed twig. Suddenly Fanhua felt sad, genuinely sad. Her eyes grew damp. She swore to herself that she'd think of Xiangsheng the next time the village came across an opportunity for someone to make serious money. They'd been members of the same team for years – three lives in the same boat. That wasn't nothing.

THIRTY-THREE

B ut at the end of the day, Xiangsheng was no more than a caltrop stuck in the sole of her foot. Did it hurt? Not really, because the sole was too hardened with calluses for it to cause any real pain. Though you couldn't exactly say there was no pain, because the pressure of a heavy burden across your shoulders would drive the caltrop deeper into your foot. But that was all better now because Xiangsheng had stepped out of the race. The caltrop had been pulled from the sole, and Fanhua could walk with a spring in her step again.

And what about Qingshu? He was a pond loach, Fanhua thought, the kind of lurking fish that would never cause any big waves. She didn't have to worry about him too much, so long as she remembered to keep an eye on him to make sure he wasn't stirring up too much trouble.

Xiaohong was out of hospital now, but Fanhua hadn't assigned her any work yet. She'd had a section of hair shaved away on the back of her head and a piece of gauze placed over the wound. Fanhua joked that it looked like Xiaohong had put on a surgical mask back to front. She made a point of buying a muslin scarf for her to wear over her head.

Today was the day Fanhua was hosting the quiz, and, since it was a happy occasion, she'd brought Xiaohong up on stage alongside her. There was a dazzling selection of prizes, including Fine and Bright soap from Xiaohong's cousin, towels, bedsheets and several copies of *300 Sentences of Conversational English* (including an audio cassette). If you answered a single question correctly, you could claim a bar of soap and a towel. The easiest question was the one about Marx's birthday because it had featured in so many previous quizzes. When Fanhua read that one out, the only people whose hands didn't shoot up into the air were the wives who'd only recently married into Guanzhuang. Fanhua noticed the wife of the butcher Xiangning had her hand in the air. She may be a bit older, Fanhua thought, but she only arrived here recently – how does she know this one? Fanhua asked her to stand up.

"Clap your hands and stomp and cheer, capitalism starts to cry," she replied.

"But when, exactly, was he born?" Fanhua asked.

"Stomp and cheer... Eighteen-eighteen was the year."

"Is Xiangning's wife right?" Fanhua asked the rest of the audience. Half of them yelled "yes", and the other half yelled "no". "Very well," said Fanhua, "let's ask Teacher Shangyi for his verdict."

Shangyi picked up a bar of soap and a towel, took the microphone from Fanhua and stepped down off the stage.

"But tell us," he said to Xiangning's wife after he'd handed her the soap and towel. "What was the *date* on which Marx was born?"

"Capitalism starts to cry... it's the seventh of July, duh."

"Wrong, I'm afraid," said Shangyi. "I'm afraid we're going to have to deduct half of your prize." So saying, he took back the towel he'd just handed her, before proceeding to analyse the cause of her error: "Please note, the correct mnemonic is 'capitalism runs away' not 'capitalism starts to cry'. The correct answer is thus" – and here he switched to standard Mandarin pronunciation – "Marx was born in eighteen-eighteen on the fifth of May, and not the seventh of July."

Everyone laughed, including Xiangning's wife. Fanhua passed the microphone to Xiaohong and asked her to take over as MC.

"I'm going down there to see if I can win a prize for myself," she said, chuckling.

"Xiangning's wife was very brave to try to answer that question," said Xiaohong into the microphone. "Let's give her a cassette as a bonus prize. And everyone who raised their hands just now gets a bar of soap."

Fanhua had no intention of remaining in the audience. She had noticed that several people were missing. Qingmao's wife wasn't there, and she never normally missed any opportunity for a freebie. Pei Zhen wasn't there either, but that was understandable since they'd already given her a box of soap and half a box of towels as thanks to her husband for coming up with the quiz questions. Tiesuo wasn't there, because he was forbidden from attending. He had to stay at home and think long and hard about what he'd done. Fanhua had two reasons for leaving: first, because she wanted to see what these people were up to, and second because she was hoping to find a quiet place to stay a while and think about all the work she had lined up.

When she was approaching the gate of Qinglin's place, she noticed Pomegranate Zhang. Oh, so Pomegranate was another one who hadn't come to the quiz. She never came to village events of this kind, which she considered beneath her. Pomegranate may have been a Party member, thanks to Qingmao's introduction, but she wasn't really a Party member in any real ideological sense. No Party member spent their days strutting around the village in slippers like she did. Though she wasn't wearing slippers now – she was wearing tall boots and woollen leggings that clung tight to her buttocks. She was walking away from Fanhua, singing vocal exercises as she went along. "Ahh! Ohh! Ahh! Ohh!" Not unlike the kind of thing you might hear from a seagull. Or an adult movie. From her arse up to her vocal cords, she was a vamp right through. It even had an effect on the wolf. Fanhua could hear the pattering of his paws whenever Pomegranate hit an "ohh!" And right on cue, Qinglin appeared at his door, clapping his hands and chortling.

His money's gone to his head, Fanhua thought, if he thinks he's entitled to skip village events. But Qinglin didn't look like there was anything wrong with his head, the way he stood there rubbing his hands together – he looked the very picture of an entrepreneur, affable and carefree. He must have assumed from the sound that someone was bringing him one of their bitches. His demeanour changed entirely when he realised it was Pomegranate.

"Fuck me," he said, slapping his thighs, "I thought it was someone here to mate with Grey."

Pomegranate Zhang: the older sister of Crystal Zhang, and a relative of the county head, which meant she was effectively Xiushui royalty. In short, she was not a woman to be trifled with.

"Save it for your wife," she shot back at Qinglin.

"Seriously though, my wolf can't sleep when you're around."

"Screw you, motherfucker."

"It's true! Listen to that, he never normally stirs in the daytime, but now he's scurrying around all over the place."

This was the point at which Fanhua joined them. "Qinglin, cut the crap," she said. Pomegranate placed her hands on her hips and continued her stream of invective. She had a dainty way of putting her hands on her hips that was beyond the capabilities of an ordinary country woman like Xue'e. The back of her hands pressed against her body and the fingers jutted out, a bit like the orchid hand pose of an opera performer.

"You're a son-of-a-bitch, and you come from a whole damn family of sons-of-bitches," Pomegranate informed Qinglin.

What Qinglin did next looked like something a Shaolin monk might attempt. With one hand palming his bald head, he bent forwards and charged towards Pomegranate. Pomegranate sought refuge in Fanhua's arms. Fanhua turned sideways on and smacked Qinglin in the head with her black leather notebook.

"Behave. You're starting to act like a wolf yourself."

Qinglin retreated, rubbing his head, but still in a good mood.

Fanhua turned back to Pomegranate. "Come on now, Sister Zhang," she said. "He's an arsehole. Let's not stoop to his level."

Fanhua walked Pomegranate home. Seeing that her anger hadn't dissipated, Fanhua followed her lead and directed a few more curses at Qinglin before turning the topic towards Pomegranate's husband, Li Dongfang. Pomegranate said he was away with her sister's husband, working on a project to repair the Xiushui Town bridge.

Fanhua acted like she hadn't heard anything about this. "That's a worthy project to be involved with, resurfacing a bridge. It's a big job, right? What does your brother-in-law do?"

"Nothing special, just resurfacing roads and patching bridges.

Dongfang's just doing it to earn some pocket money. No more than ten thousand or so, barely enough to fill the gap between your teeth."

Fanhua took Pomegranate's hand, placed it on her knee and patted it.

"Pomegranate, you know how to be happy with what you've got. You're not one to let that gap between your teeth get too big. Dongfang's ancestors must have burned an awful lot of incense for him to be lucky enough to marry you." She sensed an opportunity to move the conversation on to Tiesuo. "Now take someone like Tiesuo. He repairs roads too, but all he's managed to earn in a year is a few pairs of stinky shoes. Everyone's fate is different." She sighed. "And Xue'e's never going to make much money looking after chickens. Plus she's pregnant, or so I've heard. There'll be a fine to pay, ten thousand or so. Tough times ahead."

"I heard. And I heard people say my sister's to blame."

"Your sister?" said Fanhua. "What does this have to do with her?"

"There are a lot of wagging tongues in this village. I hear things. And women bring me money, tell me to put in a word with my sister and encourage her to turn a blind eye next time they go in for a check-up."

"My dear," said Fanhua, "we're members of the Party. We can't allow that kind of thing to happen."

"You don't need to tell me that. I tell them I can't stand babies, what's the point of them? Pooing and weeing all over the place. Better off with a pet dog."

Though she knew Pomegranate couldn't conceive, Fanhua still felt compelled to say something. "I'm going to have to criticise you there. You ought to think about having a child. You need something to put all that money Dongfang's earning towards. But I commend you for sending these women packing." Fanhua suddenly asked another question: "I still don't understand what Xue'e getting pregnant has to do with your sister. Is she the one who does the check-ups at Wangzhai Hospital? Even if she is, how is it her fault? We can hardly blame someone if there was a problem with the machine."

"Exactly," said Pomegranate. "Besides, mistakes are inevitable. You might manage to get through ten check-ups without any errors, but if you're doing a hundred of the things then you're bound to get one wrong sooner or later."

Fanhua wanted to tell her that she could sympathise if such a mistake had occurred in some other village. It would have made her happy, in fact. But not in Guanzhuang. She stood up and kneaded her back. "Talking about this has given me a headache again. I tell you, all this business with Xue'e is ruining me. I'd better go and get back to work on her case. Whenever there's the slightest hint of news about Xue'e, I have to go running off with my tail between my legs. Need to take her in for another check-up, but I still don't know where she's hiding herself."

"Well, unless she's flown up to heaven, she must be lurking around here somewhere."

"So where do *you* think she might be lurking?" asked Fanhua.

"Well, they barely have two pennies to rub together," said Pomegranate, "so they can hardly afford a hotel. Which means someone must be delivering food to her, right?"

"If you hear anything about her, you be sure to tell me," said Fanhua. "In the name of the Party, I swear I'll keep my source secret."

"I hope you do find her soon, and then maybe they'll stop scapegoating my sister. There's the water pump house behind the village, the paper plant, the school storerooms. All worth checking out. But you didn't hear anything from me. I don't want a thick-headed woman like Xue'e bearing me a grudge."

THIRTY-FOUR

anhua had always assumed Pomegranate Zhang was the kind of nitwit who spouts the first thing that comes into her head, so she didn't pay her advice much heed at the time. But when Lingpei told her the next morning that he'd seen Xue'e at the paper plant, she suddenly remembered that this was one of the locations Pomegranate had mentioned. Lingpei had arrived just as Fanhua had dispatched Qingshu on a trip to visit some distant relatives of Tiesuo's.

"There's someone under the bridge," Lingpei said as soon as he came in.

Assuming he was talking about people stealing from the plant, Fanhua dismissed him with a wave of her hand. "A weekly report will be fine." But instead of leaving, Lingpei repeated what he'd said about someone under the bridge.

"Could you be more precise?" said Fanhua, losing patience. "A live person or a dead one?"

"They looked dead to me," said Lingpei.

Fanhua sprang to her feet. "Completely dead?" she asked urgently. Lingpei couldn't say for sure. Fuck, it couldn't be Xue'e, could it? Surely she wouldn't go so far as to jump into the river. She asked Lingpei whether it was a man or a woman, and he told her it was a woman.

"Well, quit standing there gawping," Fanhua said, slamming her hands against the table in exasperation. "Hurry up and pull her out."

"No need to pull her out," said Lingpei. "River washed her up on the bank."

Struggling for breath, Fanhua asked Lingpei whether he was completely sure: was it a man, or was it a woman?

"You really don't think much of me if you reckon I've made it this far in life without being able to tell a boy from a girl."

"Did you see if it was Xue'e?" Fanhua asked in a whisper.

"Xue'e? Li Tiesuo's wife, Xue'e? I saw her just yesterday. Definitely not her."

Fanhua had already rushed out the door before she registered what Lingpei had said. "What did you just say? You've seen Xue'e? Where?"

"At the paper plant. What of it?"

The possibly drowned person suddenly seemed a less pressing matter. Fanhua pushed open the door and stepped back into the office.

"You'd better not be joking," she said in a serious voice. "When did you see Xue'e?"

"Yesterday. So what?" Lingpei appeared to have no idea what she was getting at.

Fanhua came closer. "Can you *guarantee* it was her?" she asked in a quiet voice.

Clearly alarmed by Fanhua's expression, Lingpei took a few steps backwards. "She's an old woman," he stammered. "There are plenty of other bean flowers out there. I didn't bother her."

"Good," said Fanhua, "very good. Then just act like you didn't see anything. Don't mention this to anyone."

"I knew it," said Lingpei, "it was you who hid her there, right? I won't say a word, you can be sure of that. But there's Pei Zhen. She knows already."

Fanhua was stunned. "How does Pei Zhen know?"

"She brings her food."

Fanhua seemed to have something caught in her throat, and it was a while before she was able to breathe again. "Did Pei Zhen see you?" she asked at last.

"The fuck she did," said Lingpei. "How would I let her see me."

Fanhua could have kissed him. "Whatever you do, don't let her find out. A few days from now, your aunt's going to have quite the reward for you."

Fanhua realised she should probably go and check out this corpse by the river. Lingpei, meanwhile, was busy fishing for compliments. Shortfur was telling him he ought to join his troupe as a magician, he said, because anyone who'd been in Lingpei's line of work had all the key skills already and could learn to be a master conjuror in just a couple of weeks, but Lingpei had always turned him down because he still hadn't repaid his aunt's kindness.

"What's this?" said Fanhua. "You want to leave now?"

"I'm thinking about it."

"You could make just as much money working at home as you could out there. Wherever you can earn the most, that's where you should be."

"You're quite right, Aunt," said Lingpei.

Fanhua asked him exactly what the deal was with this corpse. Lingpei said he discovered someone hiding under the bridge last night. At the time he wondered who it could be. Maybe some thief who was too afraid to come out? Could it be that Xue'e had been stealing from the paper plant, and was waiting there so she could sneak home when it got dark? Lingpei decided to play the waiting game, which was a game he'd got much better at while he was in prison. He waited and waited until morning arrived, and he realised something was amiss. He went down to look and discovered it was a dead body. Fuck! He'd lost the waiting game.

They were not the only ones to know about this discovery by the time they got to the river. There were a bunch of kids hopping around like it was a holiday. The crowd parted to let Fanhua through, and when she went down to take a look, she could finally let out a sigh of relief. The corpse was not from Guanzhuang. It had clearly floated downriver when the waters were high, getting beached on the bank once the rain stopped and the waters went down.

By now Dr Xianyu had arrived, and the crowd parted again for him. He stared at the corpse like he was examining a patient, and for a long time said nothing. Then he picked up a stick and used it to pull back the hair, followed by the eyelids. To everyone's surprise, a crab crawled out of the corpse's mouth. The crowd took a silent step backwards.

Xianyu moved the crab off to one side and then used his stick to poke at the shoes. They were canvas shoes, with buckles, still attached to the feet of the woman. Then the stick moved up to the waist of the trousers. From behind Xianyu, his wife Cuixian coughed. He ignored her.

"Maybe we should tell the police first," said Fanhua.

But Xianyu carried on anyway. There was no real belt around the trousers, only a few scraps of cloth knotted together. Some of the onlookers were waiting for Xianyu to pull down the trousers, but he didn't go that far. Now all the attention was on him, and not the dead woman.

"The police aren't going to care," he said, slowly pulling off his gloves, "because she's not from round here."

"So where is she from?" asked Fanhua."

"Qinglin would know," said Xianyu, deliberately drawing out the tension, "and Xiangmin too. She's from Shanxi."

Qinglin happened to be present, and he squeezed through to the front when he heard this. But he couldn't see whatever telling clues Xianyu had noticed.

"Look at the belt, the buckle on the shoes, and the toenails, in particular. There are traces of coal dust under the toenails. No question, this was a Shanxi woman. Just like Qinglin's wife."

"Surely the police will still care," said Fanhua. "It's still a life we're talking about."

By this point, someone had already got through to the police. When they heard it was someone from Shanxi, they suggested covering up the body with earth so the wolves wouldn't run off with it. This message was passed on to Fanhua.

Qinglin was infuriated. "As if a wolf would eat a thing like that. They're very picky eaters, wolves."

Tiesuo had come over too, to see what all the fuss was about. He avoided making eye contact with Fanhua.

"So you've come to take a look too?" she said when she eventually came close to him. "Did you wet your pants at the sight of it?" Tiesuo said nothing. "We need to make a trip to Nanchengzi tomorrow," Fanhua continued. "You have a granduncle there on your father's mother's side, isn't that right?"

"Hurry up and find her," said Tiesuo. "I still don't have anyone to cook my meals."

Half an hour ago, Fanhua would have found this remark infuriating. Now, however, she felt no anger. In fact, she felt a pleasurable sensation, akin to knowing you have a turtle trapped in a barrel and you can scoop it out whenever you fancy, or like standing outside the theatre with ticket in hand, anticipating the show you'll soon be watching.

"Good," said Fanhua, suddenly turning very polite, "very good." She even patted Tiesuo on the shoulder. "You just sit back and wait for the show."

THIRTY-FIVE

T he air was glorious. The grassy smell of seedlings growing fresh and green after the rainfall was faintly sweet and bitter at the same time. It was light and it was cool and it soothed the heart. Fanhua was in a splendid mood. It was time for the evening meeting, and she saw beauty even in the animal decorations on the ridge of the stage roof. The moon was also glorious, a delicate crescent like the lips of a maiden parted in a gentle smile. Fanhua was smiling too, but only on the inside. At the beginning of the meeting, she had Xueshi and Qingshu make a report on their work. Xueshi had temporarily taken over Xiangsheng's position and was now overseeing the school. Xueshi reported that they'd already dug out the new school toilets, and they'd need to have tiles ready for the next stage, which was putting up the walls.

"You're in charge of this," said Fanhua. "Spend as much as you think necessary. We can't scrimp on education, no matter how poor we get."

Qingshu reported on the progress of his search. He announced he was stretched so thin he'd almost fallen asleep while he was driving, and also that Xiangsheng was planning to drive to Shanxi, which meant they wouldn't be able to use his car any more. "But he's a businessman. Just looking to increase his profits. Pay him a slightly higher rental fee and that'll shut him up."

"Fine," said Fanhua, "we'll pay him a bit more. And if you

wouldn't mind reporting on your findings, in addition to any expenses you might have run up in the process."

There was petrol money, Qingshu said, and toll road money, and food money, but he needed Xiangsheng's signature on these invoices, and since Xiangsheng had done a runner, he didn't know what to do with them.

"Good. Very good. Leave them with me, and I'll pay you everything in one go when we've finished dealing with all of this." She noticed Qingshu was smoking Marlboros. "Did you get a receipt for your cigarettes?" she asked.

"Never mind the cigarettes," said Qingshu.

"Official business is official business," said Fanhua. "You always have to hand out a few cigarettes wherever you go, it's just good manners. Get a receipt tomorrow."

Then she moved on to the work they had before them, which fell into two categories: category one was continuing the search for Xue'e, and category two was preparing for the elections, and the one could not be extricated from the other.

"Even if I don't get re-elected," Fanhua said, "I won't leave the Xue'e problem for my successor to deal with. I don't know which of the people in this room will be the next head of the village council, but it doesn't matter. Whoever it is, I owe them this responsibility." Fanhua's eyes were reddening, so moved was she by her own words.

"That's true passion," said Xueshi.

"No one's heart is made of stone," said Fanqi. "If there's anything else you want to say, just go ahead. We understand."

"If – just to take an example – let's say the next head of the village council were to be Qingshu..." Qingshu quickly stood up. Fanhua indicated for him to sit down again. "If it is Qingshu – and I am just using him as an example – then Xue'e will have had her baby before he's even had a chance to warm the chair. Then what? The guys upstairs get mad and he's out on his ear already. That can't be right, can it? He won't know the taste of power any better than Pigsy knew the taste of the ginseng fruit he gobbled down. And so of course he's going to wish I was dead." Qingshu stood up again. This time Fanhua physically pushed him back down into his chair. "Our current work means we keep driving that Xiali car and keep searching for that Xue'e. Personally, I think Qingshu should take sole responsibility for this work." Fanhua's hands were still resting on Qingshu's shoulders, meaning he couldn't have stood up even if he tried. But his mouth was attached to his face, not his arse, which meant he could still voice an objection from his seat.

"Fuck me," he said, "you want me to keep running around all over the place? How is that fair?"

"This is me playing to your strengths," said Fanhua. "First, this was your job from the outset. Second, you can drive. Third, you know how to catch someone and wrestle them down, thanks to your army experience. You'll have no problem pinning Xue'e down all by yourself."

Qingshu sat there fuming, but for now, he said nothing.

"The other work is the election," said Fanhua. "We've done the quiz, with excellent results. The next step is to produce the ballots, a very big job. Xueshi and I will take responsibility for this one. What do you say, Xueshi?"

"I do whatever the group tells me to do," said Xueshi.

"Xiaohong, you'll be in charge of publicity," said Fanhua. "Starting tomorrow, we'll have three announcements on the loud-speakers a day."

None of Fanhua's comrades had objections to any of this. "Then shall we put it to a vote?" she asked.

This was the moment when Qingshu leapt to his feet. Had the pond loach finally picked his moment to make a splash? A pond loach will never make waves, or so the old folk like to say, and a flea will never be able to hold up a bedsheet. But perhaps Qingshu hadn't realised he was a pond loach. Or a flea.

"We mustn't starve ourselves for fear of choking," said Qingshu. "We can leave the Xue'e business to one side for now, and concentrate all our energy on the election."

"Qingshu," said Fanhua, "if you can find me someone else who satisfies any one of those three conditions, then you don't have to go."

"You're setting me up," said Qingshu. "This is a trap."

"Very well," said Fanhua, "consider yourself free. We'll do it like this then. The village will pay to hire a driver, and I'll sit in the car every day driving around to look for Xue'e. And Qingshu will be in charge of the work back here in the village. Let's vote. We go with the

266

majority. Everyone who agrees with this plan, raise your hand." No one raised their hand. Not even Qingshu himself. But Fanhua told Xiaohong to count the number all the same and note it down in the minutes.

Just when Fanhua was about to dissolve the meeting, several figures appeared in the yard. An old lady and a girl were sitting on a donkey-drawn cart. Fanhua could tell at once from their accents that they were from Shanxi. It was Gawp who'd brought them here. She's our leader, he said, pointing at Fanhua. The man who'd been driving the donkey immediately collapsed at the knees and prostrated himself before her. Fanhua guessed that this was the family of the drowned woman, and her intuition proved correct. The man was her husband, and the old woman was her mother-in-law. Fanhua encouraged them to sit down and talk things through, but the man suddenly pointed at an empty instant noodles container in the rubbish bin.

"What's that?" he asked.

Fanhua realised that this was his indirect way of telling her that they were extremely hungry. She sent Qingshu out to get some food, and he obediently hurried off. Spotting the girl still standing by the door, Fanhua asked the man who she was. He told her she was his sister-in-law.

At this, the girl stomped inside. "Fuck you, who'd want to be any sister-in-law of yours?"

The man hurried to bow in her direction, but the girl dodged out of his way. Then he explained to Fanhua that he had three sprogs already, fillies one and all, and he dreamed of a little lad but then out came number four and it was yet another filly.

At this point, Qingshu came back in bearing instant noodles.

"Quick, get Tiesuo," Fanhua told him. "I want him to hear this."

Qingshu wasn't impressed. "I'm still gasping for breath here," he said, leaning against the door, "in case you hadn't noticed."

"Fine, wait until you've got your breath back, then go," said Fanhua.

"I could go instead if you like," said Xueshi.

"No, let Qingshu go," said Fanhua. "It's his job."

"Great. Wonderful. Fantastic," said an angry Qingshu before sloping off. "Looks like everyone round here's my grandad."

"Would you look at him," said Fanhua, "the man's been spoiled

267

rotten." Then she encouraged the man from Shanxi to finish eating before speaking any further. Noticing that the old woman was struggling to chew the instant noodles, she told Xueshi to give Qingshu a call and tell him to pick up some bread on his way back.

"I can go get some," said Xueshi.

"No," said Fanhua. "He said he wanted to shoulder a weightier load. Well, the weight of one loaf of bread is hardly going to crush him."

The man quickly finished eating and started talking again. Fanhua encouraged him to drink some more water. The girl seemed hungry too, but she was sitting facing the wall, slowly eating the noodles and crying at the same time.

It wasn't long before Tiesuo and Qingshu arrived. When Tiesuo came in, Fanhua gave him her chair. "This is our true leader," she said. "Start over from the beginning again for him."

Thinking she was being serious, the man bowed to Tiesuo, prostrating himself on the floor all over again, before he began his tale. Apparently, when this fourth sprog was born, and they discovered it was yet another filly, the mother had told the midwife to dunk it in the water jar. Now, sprogs do tend to bob back up when you push them down, but three dunkings is generally enough to finish them off. Not this one, though. She was fixed on living. She passed out but she didn't die, so they were going to have to dunk her again.

"Murderer!" the girl suddenly yelled.

The man gawped at her, then gave her a smile and continued telling Tiesuo his story. So the midwife had asked him whether he wanted the sprog drowned or not, and he'd said he would have to ask his wife.

"I asked your sister, and she didn't say nothing. If you don't say nothing, then that means you agree."

"Bullshit," the girl wailed, stamping her feet. "Lies and bullshit."

Fanhua walked over to her, took her hand and wiped away her tears. "Let's at least listen to the rest of his bullshit," she said quietly. "So the baby was drowned, just like that?" she said to the man.

"Took another two dunks before it drowned," the man said. "Tell me, what makes a sprog so fixed on living?"

Fanhua had already deduced that the woman had drowned herself in the river, unable to bear the strain. But she didn't want to ask the man about it herself – she wanted Tiesuo to do it. "Go on, Tiesuo," she said. "Ask him how the child's mother died. Go on!" Tiesuo turned his face away. "Please explain to our leader here how she died. Did she throw herself into the river?"

The man squatted down on the ground and started crying. He said his wife was supposed to be staying indoors for the month after the birth, but she snuck out when no one was paying attention. No one else in the village saw her. She went down to the river, looking for her dead sprog. And then later they followed the river and ended up here.

Fanhua addressed everyone present. "See this? What a striking case study. Tiesuo, even if you had a heart of stone, you could hardly fail to be touched."

At this point the man started bowing to Tiesuo again, saying he had a favour to beg of him. Alarmed, Tiesuo jumped to his feet and ducked behind Fanhua.

"Sit down," she said, pushing him back into the chair. "Listen to what our case study here has to say."

The man said he hoped this esteemed village would be so good as to grant him a plot of earth in which to bury his wife.

Tiesuo jumped up again and went to hide behind Xiaohong this time.

Fanhua was still trying to think of how to reply when Xiaohong answered him for her: "We'd be happy to help in any way we can, but we can't agree to that. In this village, we have to cremate the dead."

Xiaohong knew how to harden her heart, Fanhua reflected. She would have struggled to find a way to tell him this herself. But in any case, the man didn't agree to cremation. He said he would come back later to dig her up and return her to his ancestral tomb. At this point, the girl spoke up to say that she gave her consent to cremation.

"Burn a body and there's nothing left," he said to her, almost beating his breast and stamping his feet in anguish.

"What's wrong with cremation?" said the girl. "Zhou Enlai was cremated, and so was Deng Xiaoping." She said she wanted to take the ashes home and put them at the end of her bed so she and her sister could stay together forever. The man stubbornly refused to admit defeat, pointing out that he didn't have so much as a penny left to pay for any cremation. The girl calmly replied that they could bury her sister first, while she took on a job here until she'd made enough money for the cremation. But there was no way her sister was going to go into his family's ancestral tomb. She clearly stood by her convictions, and she wasn't stupid. Even remote mountains can produce magnificent birds. In terms of looks, she was maybe thirty per cent better looking than Xiaohong. She wouldn't be a bad match for Lingpei, Fanhua thought. Both of them alone in the world. A silver flower was a fine match for a gold flower, but a squash was a fine match for a pumpkin; neither would have any cause to resent the other. Fanhua arranged for the girl to spend the night in the office. And the man and his mother? Tch, she didn't have any energy left to waste worrying about them. Let them sleep on the stage.

Xiaohong had noticed the girl too. "She's not bad looking, that girl," she remarked to Fanhua as they left the yard.

"What would you think if I were to play matchmaker for Lingpei?" Fanhua asked her. She thought this notion would please Xiaohong, but she didn't seem to approve of the idea.

"Doesn't Lingpei have his tofu puddings already? I think you'd do better to introduce her to Li Hao. You two are old classmates, aren't you? What do you say?" Xiaohong had thought this through more thoroughly than she had, Fanhua thought. "If you don't mind," Xiaohong continued, "I'll go fetch some bedding, and have Li Hao bring it over." Of course, Fanhua gave her consent. Xiaohong sprinted off like she was racing against the clock, her braids bouncing away in the moonlight. But she soon turned round and came running back.

"I had something else to tell you about," she said to Fanhua, panting for breath. "But there were too many people around to bring it up back there."

"Tell me," said Fanhua. "I'll sort it out, whatever it is."

"When we had the elections three years ago, we got a country theatre troupe to come down here and put on a show. Why don't we do the same thing this year? Think of it as a way of promoting the elections."

"Ach, I'd have forgotten about that if you hadn't reminded me," said Fanhua. "What play do you think would be a good choice?"

"Any play will do," said Xiaohong, "as long it draws the crowds. I'm going into town tomorrow to pick up some herbal medicine for my father. The doctor gave him a prescription for the shock he suffered, but I haven't had a chance to go get it yet. Do you want me to see the theatre troupe while I'm there?"

"A modern play would be best," said Fanhua.

"But the old folk would prefer one of the classics," said Xiaohong. "Think how happy it'd make Beanie's grandparents. Don't worry, those theatre types are very responsive. Feed them willow twigs and they'll poo out a basket. So long as we give them a reminder, they'll be happy to make the announcements about the election and family planning over the top of a Shandong clapper beat. You won't be disappointed, I guarantee it."

"Isn't there one called *Dragon and Phoenix, Harbingers of Prosperity*? About the warlord Liu Bei taking a wife. My dad's a big fan of that one."

Xiaohong said her father liked that one too. Its Henan opera title was indeed *Dragon and Phoenix, Harbingers of Prosperity*, and in Beijing Opera, it was called *Ganlu Temple*, but they were the same story. Xiaohong was so knowledgeable.

"Well then, let's go with the *Dragon and the Phoenix*. Bring us some good luck."

"And Shortfur?" Xiaohong asked. "His troupe have put on a performance in Xiushui Town too. And I heard they have some kind of modelling show. The young people in the village might like that. Shall I ask them to take part too?"

"Shortfur will be Shortfur," said Fanhua. "Let him do as he pleases."

THIRTY-SIX

F anhua had been planning to check out the paper plant that evening, but in the end, she didn't go. She was beginning to feel like she was taking part in a play. Qingshu was one antagonist, and Xiangsheng was another. So, it seemed, was Teacher Shangyi. Thinking of him made her angry. Trying to pull something like that with me, she thought, after the way I've treated you. You're not running for office, so what are you after? Think you can pass a jenny off as a jackass, do you? Fanhua couldn't figure it out. There was only one possibility: when Xiangsheng was in charge of education he must have involved Shangyi in his corrupt dealings. Not that Shangyi could've got very much out of Xiangsheng, who was the kind of person who'd split a penny if he thought he had a chance of keeping half of it. Maybe we're talking a few thousand, something like that. Fanhua was in no rush, in any case. She was happy to wait until Shangyi was ready to come and confess to her.

But another day passed, and Fanhua found she couldn't wait any longer. There was a naughty little kitten in her belly, and she couldn't sit still with it clawing away inside of her. By the afternoon, it was too hard to bear. She asked Dianjun if he fancied going along with her. Dianjun was drafting the promises for her election manifesto, and he'd just reached the issue of the paper plant.

"What sort of animal suits the climate here?" he said. "We have to think big."

"Come down to the paper plant with me," Fanhua said. "There's going to be quite a show to enjoy. Might give you some inspiration."

"You mean you've changed your mind about using it as a breeding farm?"

"Of course not," said Fanhua. "The breeding's already begun. Xue'e's there getting ready to have a baby as we speak." Generally, Fanhua hated the sight of Dianjun peering through his telescope, but she made a point of reminding him to bring it along this time.

Fanhua saw Lingpei as they were crossing the bridge. He was leaning against the filthy white marble lion, chatting away with one of his tofu puddings. Fanhua had seen her before, on the day Shortfur came back to the village. She had been holding hands with some other guy at the time. Fanhua couldn't resist taking a closer look at her now. She looked a bit trendier than the Shanxi girl, but definitely more vulgar, too. Look at her there, in her leather skirt, eyes all rimmed in black like a panda, hair done up like a spider plant. She was a vixen.

Fanhua called Lingpei over. "I thought you were supposed to be keeping an eye on Xue'e. What are you doing here?"

"I got someone else to watch her for me," Lingpei explained. He had thought everything through. He'd assigned a couple of his cronies to watch Xue'e, because she wouldn't suspect anything if she spotted them, not knowing who they were. Lingpei glanced up at the sky and said it was too early. Fanhua asked him what he meant – it'd be dark soon, very soon in fact, because black clouds were gathering. Clouds swirling like they were putting on a show, an opera of singing black masks, and tossed sleeves, and flying cudgels, and figures somersaulting hither and thither. It looked like rain.

The tofu pudding walked in front, and Fanhua and Linpei walked behind.

"She's quite the catch, this girl of yours," Fanhua said to him. "If things are going well with her then, why don't you marry and have done with it?"

"Haven't you noticed the way she walks?" Lingpei whispered from behind a raised palm. "The way she parts her legs." His tone of voice was very mysterious.

"How's she supposed to walk without parting her legs?"

"Xiaohong doesn't part her legs like that. When she walks she

273

keeps them tight together. If a woman parts her legs like that, it means she's had an abortion."

What disgusting nonsense was this? Lingpei dodged out of the way as she tried to hit him but quickly returned to her side. "I've been getting cosy with this girl just to annoy Xiaohong. I want to make her jealous."

"Get real," said Fanhua, "there's no way Xiaohong's going to fall for that."

By now they'd reached the west side of the paper plant.

"It's already working," said Lingpei proudly, after glancing around to make sure there was no one else nearby. "She came to talk to me and gave me two bars of soap. It's the thought behind the gift that counts – even a goose feather is heavy when it's travelled a thousand *li*."

Lingpei was dreaming, Fanhua thought to herself. "Xiaohong gave two bars of soap to Li Hao too. Proves nothing."

Lingpei made an indignant noise. "It's not the same. The soap she gave *me* was Fine and Bright brand. Now there's a deep message. That's her telling me she wants me to look to the future. *And* the two of us had a heart-to-heart, and she told me she wanted me to do a performance." Now *that* was odd. What sort of performance was Lingpei capable of doing?

Lingpei bent down to chuck away a branch that was blocking Fanhua's path. "She wants me to liven up the elections by showing how I pick a ping-pong ball from lard. I haven't given her my reply yet."

How was it possible that a perfectly intelligent person could so quickly become an utter halfwit? Lingpei was clearly so besotted he'd taken a sarcastic remark for genuine praise. Fanhua stood where she was, waiting for Dianjun to arrive. She said nothing while Lingpei continued to prattle on.

"I didn't agree to Honghong's proposal at first," he said. So he'd started calling Xiaohong "Honghong" now. "You shouldn't beat a man in the face, and you shouldn't draw attention to his shortcomings. Well, it felt like she was hitting me right in the face, bringing up my pickpocketing past like that. But after Honghong did some ideological work on me, I started to understand. She told me if I just took this one step then it would prove I'd made a fresh start, that I could dedicate all the talents I had to the service of the people. She was using very long words, was Honghong, long enough to leave you out of breath. I couldn't quite keep up with her, but I was very moved."

Fanhua just about managed to avoid laughing.

"And Honghong said Charter would be there alongside to accompany me."

Charter? Charter the blind man? Fanhua was stunned. Wasn't he supposed to be playing the fiddle and telling fortunes outside a Beijing subway station? Fanhua remembered people saying Charter had the looks of an artist, with his long hair, sitting with a teacup in front of him to catch the coins passers-by tossed in his direction. And now he was back in town too?

"Have you seen him?" Fanhua asked.

"Of course. And he's brought his wife with him."

Fanhua laughed. "His wife? Charter has a wife? Are you sure you've got that right? The man's nearly eighty years old."

"Not quite," said Lingpei. "I asked. He's seventy-seven. Charter, Charter, seventy-seven – gets hitched, seventy plus eleven. Ninety-nine, has a kid, and then – becomes a granddad at a hundred and ten."

"There you go again. That's quite enough of that sort of thing."

"He said that himself. It's what he's going to sing when we put on the performance. And I'm going to grab a hundred and ten ping-pong balls."

"Wonderful," said Fanhua. "You'll grab the ping-pong balls, and Charter will provide the musical accompaniment. Excellent. Your Honghong has really thought this through." Then Fanhua lectured him about how he really oughtn't to be hanging around with tofu puddings if Xiaohong was paying him so much attention.

Lingpei immediately assumed a very mysterious expression. "Love is like a pot of water. The water that is Honghong has not yet reached boiling point. This tofu pudding is the flame to heat her up."

There had once been an apricot tree grove on the west side of the paper plant, but they'd all been chopped down back in the days of Learning From Dazhai. Now it was scrubland, covered with weeds, thorns and wild jujube shrubs. There were a few scattered apricot trees that had grown out of the remaining stumps. But trees need attention, just like people. Without attention, these trees had grown wild, so stunted they barely looked like trees at all.

"We should mention this scrubland too. Plant a few trees, or just use it for grazing livestock. You can polish that and work it up into something."

"This would be a good place for camels. They're low maintenance, camels. Good at dealing with a drought, and they're lovely-tempered creatures. Every part of their body is a treasure. I've thought it all through. Shoes made from camel pelt – no one's doing that. If we get it to work, we could apply for a national patent."

Dianjun was still dreaming. How could they keep camels in a place like this? Camels were creatures of the sand. When all this was over, Fanhua decided, she'd make sure to take Dianjun to the hospital. Get his brain checked out. Camels this, camels that, there was no end to it. If that wasn't a mental problem, then she didn't know what was.

They discovered a hole in the wall, slightly larger than the hole in the school wall.

"Could a motorbike fit through a hole this size?" Fanhua asked.

"A camel could," Dianjun replied.

Fanhua gave him a look, and he went quiet. This hole had been covered up with apricot tree branches and wild jujube shrubs. Lingpei examined the arrangement of the branches, looked at the footprints on the ground and clicked his fingers.

"No one else has been in here," he said.

"What about your friends?" Fanhua asked.

"Inside." Lingpei pulled a crack in the covering, and sure enough, there were two young people on the other side. One boy, one girl. They were playing badminton, and from this distance, they looked like figures in a shadow puppet show.

"Have they run away to get married?" Fanhua asked.

"Something like that," said Lingpei.

Fanhua poked Lingpei in the side of his forehead. "When are you going to stop causing grief to me and your Honghong?" she said.

The young couple had also spread out a tarpaulin on the ground, the kind that was used to protect machinery from the rain, with some rice straw scattered on top.

"Huh, pretty romantic," said Dianjun. "Almost up there with Shenzhen."

"No way," said Lingpei. "Shenzhen is the tide of the future. The kids in Shenzhen can play golf. They have to settle for badminton here."

"Can you two try to concentrate, please?" said Fanhua.

Lingpei's face stiffened at once, and he began his work report. Except his "work report" comprised mostly questions and attempts to ratchet up the suspense. "You see that thing on top of the car tyre?" he said to Fanhua. "Guess what that is?"

He was referring to a little box that looked from a distance like it might be a funerary casket, covered with plastic sheeting. Fanhua used Dianjun's telescope to take a closer look, but she still couldn't see exactly what it was. She shot Lingpei a look that dispelled any thoughts he had of keeping her on tenterhooks. That is a television set, he said, and Xue'e came out last night to watch it.

"Pei Zhen too?"

Lingpei couldn't answer that one, he said, because the TV had only just arrived.

"Stolen?"

"It's mine," said Lingpei.

"So that means stolen then, yes? Don't think I don't know. You can't be doing that kind of thing in future."

Lingpei smiled. He said Xue'e was hiding in a house behind that billboard, pointing to a huge object that was not, in fact, a billboard, but a huge "Pollution Control Countdown" announcement board. Fanhua remembered back when the province's newspapers and TV reporters had all come along on the last day of the countdown. That evening, just after the countdown passed zero, Fanhua had led them to film a shot of the water channel where the plant discharged its waste. It was the finest hour of her political career.

Now, the countdown board was suddenly starting to wobble. The wind was picking up, a fierce gust of wind, followed by rain. It was a rare autumn storm. As the rain came down, the sky gradually began to brighten. The young couple had no intention of going indoors. They were leaping around like crickets in the rainfall that breaks a drought. Fanhua was quickly soaked right through. Dianjun took off his top and lifted it up above her head, but she told him she was fine. It's nice to get wet in the rain sometimes. Like grapes they were to her, these giant raindrops, when she was in such a good mood. But then, when Lingpei took off his top and offered it to her, she took it. She'd remembered how Tiesuo had deliberately allowed himself to be soaked in the rain, in an attempt to gain sympathy. Whereas Fanhua had no need to make Xue'e feel sorry for her. So she lifted Lingpei's top over her head and waited for the storm to pass.

Storms don't tend to last long, and this one disappeared as quickly as it had arrived. The skies cleared in the time it takes to finish a bowl of rice. The rain had washed the autumn leaves from the ground, and the yellowing weeds had turned a darker colour, almost black. The young couple, who had remained outside while it was raining, now disappeared inside once the storm was over.

A thought occurred to Fanhua as she was staring out at the vast, empty yard. Why not wait for Pei Zhen to show up and see how she reacted? She was even tempted to reveal to Xue'e that Pei Zhen was the one who'd informed against her. She wasn't going to, obviously. First, because that kind of behaviour would hardly be befitting of her official position, and second because she'd be making four enemies at once: Pei Zhen, Xue'e, Tiesuo and Shangyi. She shivered. It would be better to attack Pei Zhen right in her nest. Act like she didn't know anything, and see what kind of tricks Pei Zhen would try and pull on home turf.

And then Xue'e appeared. She walked around the yard, hands cradling her belly. There was something slightly girlish about the way she moved, dipping her toe into a puddle and then squealing. Xue'e was smiling. She picked up a badminton racket and swiped the air this way and that, laughing. It had never occurred to Fanhua that Xue'e's laughter could sound so pleasant. Like silver bells.

Fanhua laughed too, but without producing any sound. Her face turned red with the strain of holding it back, like a flower, no – not one flower, two flowers, three, more flowers than you could count. Every tendon was a flower, and they were running riot across her face. She had been standing there, nothing wrong, but now she suddenly stumbled and almost fell to her knees. When Lingpei went to help her up, Fanhua pushed him away and turned back the way she had come. She got faster and faster, almost jogging, her rain-soaked hair flying. She wanted to get to Pei Zhen's place as fast as she could and find out exactly what games Pei Zhen had been playing with her. Surely Pei Zhen couldn't be as happy as Xue'e? Lord above, she silently cried, surely I can't be the only person in the world who's wasting away with worries over other people's business?

THIRTY-SEVEN

It was dark already, and all the animals had returned to the village. The streets were a mess, covered with excrement: duck crap, goose crap, sheep crap, cow crap. All foul smelling. Qingshe, the cow trader, was driving two of his animals back home again, one a female with a swollen belly. Qingshe had got his hands on another calf, by the looks of it. He'd be running a whole cattle ranch before too long. As Fanhua passed between the two cows, her speed startled the male, who suddenly ran away, his tail hitting her in the face.

Pei Zhen was singing as she prepared dinner. Was that bak choi she was cooking? Because she was singing a song called *Bak Choi*: "Little bak choi, yellow in the ground, three years old but you've no mother around." It was a sad song, but Pei Zhen was singing it cheerfully. From where she stood outside in the yard, Fanhua thought she could smell a sour note as the vegetables slopped out of the pan. Vinegar-glazed bak choi, most likely.

Pei Zhen started singing again just as Fanhua was about to call out to her. This time it was pumpkins she was singing about:

Little hoe in my hand,
Planting pumpkins under Jinggangshan.
Dig a hole and sow some seeds,
Ladle out some water, because that's what the sprouts need.

The sun it shines and the rain it falls,
The shoots grow long, hey-ya-ya, hey-ya-ya,
Climbing up the frame, hey-ya-ya, hey-ya-ya,
A gold flower, like a trumpet, calls
Calls the pumpkin to grow.
Grow, pumpkin, grow!

You could tell Pei Zhen was a teacher all right, Fanhua thought. She had a fine singing voice, especially the "hey-ya-ya" part, which she sang in a childish kind of way that made her sound like a girl still yet to bloom. Fanhua felt a fire growing inside of her. Her body was trembling. She told herself to calm down. She was here to enjoy the show, wasn't she? What was there to get worked up about? She should be like a cat, a cat playing with the mouse it had caught before eating it. So Fanhua stretched out her back like a cat and stepped lightly into Pei Zhen's kitchen. Pei Zhen's little boy Squaddie was standing to one side, pulling at Pei Zhen for her to sing another song.

"When the children of Jinggangshan are your age, they already know how to plant pumpkins," said Pei Zhen. "Who do they learn that from?"

"From the teacher,"

"Fucksake," said Pei Zhen, "how many times have I told you? *Chairman Mao* is who they learn it from. Why can't you remember this?"

"Oh right, I remember now," said Squaddie. "And there's Commander-in-Chief Zhu. Does Commander Zhu have Trans-formers?"

Fanhua tapped on Squaddie's head. "Yes, he does, and guns besides."

Pei Zhen jumped. She spun around, but when she saw it was Fanhua she relaxed and smiled.

"Oh, Secretary, it's you."

Pei Zhen was wearing an old, oil-spattered military sweatshirt rather than a polo-neck jumper. It was very short, almost more vest than sweater, and the shirt underneath was clearly visible.

"What delicacies are you cooking up?" asked Fanhua. "You can smell it as soon as you step into the yard."

It was vinegar-glazed potato Pei Zhen was cooking, not bak choi.

281

But the bowl was indeed brimming with pumpkin. The sight of the potato reminded Fanhua of what Pei Zhen had told her before about how eating potatoes made you more likely to have a boy by raising the alkalinity in the womb. But Fanhua chose to discuss pumpkin, not potato.

"I do love a bit of pumpkin," she said. "Let me taste your handiwork."

Fanhua dipped her chopsticks down to the plate, acting intimate, as if she was one of the family. But when the chopsticks rose they were holding a piece of potato, not pumpkin. She screwed up her eyes like she was lost in a rapture of gastronomical pleasure. Then she picked out a piece of pumpkin. This time her eyes widened in her astonishment at just how delicious it was. "You could open a restaurant," she said. "Next time I have to host guests, I'll get you to come and wield your ladle. I won't have to pay you, because we're such close sisters, right?"

"Secretary, please, no need to tease me," said Pei Zhen.

"Seriously," said Fanhua. "Dianjun wants us to have some guests over, but I can't cook. So we actually need someone to cook for us."

"Shangyi always tells me the food I cook is fit only for the pigs."

"This pumpkin is so tasty," said Fanhua. "Did you put duck egg yolk in there?"

"Lingwen's duck eggs are too expensive," said Pei Zhen. "We can't afford them. I just used chicken egg yolk."

"It tastes just right to me, but it might be a little sour for Dianjun's taste. Did you add some vinegar?"

"Vinegar's good for you. It softens the blood vessels. Intellectuals have veins like straw, brittle and thin. They're spoiled."

Shangyi hadn't even been hired as a regular teacher, and here was Pei Zhen going on about how he was an "intellectual".

"Pregnant women love the vinegar. When I was pregnant with Beanie, I was always hitting the vinegar. A vinegar jar I was, sour right through. This might sound funny to an intellectual such as yourself, but I tell you, even my farts were vinegar-flavoured."

Fanhua pulled over a chair herself and sat down. It was a low chair, and it looked like it was made from jujube wood – except maybe, on closer examination, the grain was too narrow. The grain on jujube wood looks like it's been burned in with an iron, whereas this grain appeared to have been carved out with an embroidery needle. Could it be oak? The paper plant had ordered a batch of oak chairs that year. They'd sent someone to give Fanhua a few, but she'd refused to take them. Now, while Pei Zhen wasn't looking, Fanhua flipped over the chair and inspected the underside. There they were: the words "Wangzhai Paper Plant". A chair has legs but cannot move, while the sun has none but can travel round the world. This was clearly Shangyi's doing. Tch, Shangyi, taking his own chairs into school and then appropriating the chairs from the paper plant meeting room. That's what you call swapping a wildcat for a newborn prince. Fanhua replaced the chair and smiled at Pei Zhen. How come Shangyi wasn't back yet? He's always coming home late, Pei Zhen told her, now that they're focusing on student exam results. Running along behind like a dog he is, can't let up for a second.

At which point Squaddie piped up and said his daddy was out drinking, and he'd taken his handkerchief with him. Fanhua asked him why he'd want to take a handkerchief, and Squaddie explained that his daddy spat his drink out into his handkerchief rather than swallowing it. Squaddie was surely destined to end up in the secret service, were he to enlist in the forces.

"Now now," said Fanhua, "you mustn't talk nonsense."

"I know," said Squaddie, "I never do."

Maybe he didn't quite have the makings of a spy, after all. Never mind.

Pei Zhen laughed along. "Don't listen to his crap," she said. "His father'll be home soon."

"Well, in that case, I'll wait here for Shangyi," said Fanhua. "I have something to talk to him about."

Pei Zhen scooped out a bowl of rice for Fanhua, which Fanhua accepted after a perfunctory refusal. She asked Pei Zhen how things stood with Shangyi's prospects of securing a permanent teaching position.

"We don't have any connections to lean on, and we don't have any money for gifts. We can only wait and see what heaven wills."

Fanhua put down her rice. "That's no way to think about it. If there's even the slightest chance, then you need to go after it with everything you have."

Squaddie chose this moment to speak again: "Uncle Xiangsheng says he's going to make my daddy headmaster."

Pei Zhen's expression changed abruptly. She picked up a chair and made to hit Squaddie. "Idiot!" Squaddie started crying. "I'm not dead yet," Pei Zhen said, "so who are you crying for? Scram." Squaddie ran outside to cry. From the mouths of babes, Fanhua thought to herself. This meal certainly hadn't been a waste of time.

"Come on," she said to Pei Zhen, "he hasn't said anything wrong. Anyway, that was my idea in the first place. That Xiangsheng, you can't tell him anything. It's a steamed bun outside a kennel."

Fanhua started to feel chilly after they'd finished eating. It was that soaking from the rain. Possibly she had a cold on the way. But she had no intention of leaving just yet – she wanted to see how Pei Zhen was going to deliver Xue'e her dinner. But Pei Zhen was a cool customer, and she went right back to her knitting. Fanhua could tell, though, that she was a little flustered. Look how she let her ball of wool fall out of her lap, not once but twice.

"I heard Xue'e's gone away," said Pei Zhen nonchalantly, scratching at her head with a knitting needle. Not quite such a cool customer after all. "Would that be to visit relatives or to sell some eggs?"

"Let's not talk about her," said Fanhua. "Yes, she's run away, so people say. Let her run then. She'll be back eventually. The monk can run, but the temple isn't going anywhere."

"I've heard the gossip. Some people are saying it was me who reported her. Secretary, I didn't say anything to you, did I?"

"Say anything? To me? You? First I've heard of it."

"I'm serious. This is the kind of thing that leads to grudges that span generations."

"I'll be frank with you. I know where Xue'e's hidden. Someone said to me they'd seen you with her. I gave them a telling off, Pei Zhen, right there and then. How could Pei Zhen do a thing like that? I said to them. She's an intellectual, and intellectuals understand how things work. She'd never do something so stupid. If you saw Pei Zhen together with Xue'e, I said to them, then that means you saw Xue'e. So why don't you tell me where Xue'e's hidden?"

"That's right," said Pei Zhen, "you make them explain themselves, and if they can't explain themselves, then tear their stupid mouths to shreds."

Squaddie came in with the rice bowl he'd licked clean. Children have short memories, and he pulled on his mother's arm and asked if he could watch TV. Fanhua was hoping she'd let him sit inside and watch TV for a while, but a scowling Pei Zhen said no, and told him again to scram, and scram farther away this time. Squaddie ran outside in tears again.

Pei Zhen took his bowl into the kitchen. Fanhua was expecting she'd wash it before reappearing, but Pei Zhen came straight back out again.

"They did describe it very convincingly though," said Fanhua. "They said Pei Zhen brings food to Xue'e every day. So considerate of her, they said. She always puts a bit of vinegar in the dishes, and when Xue'e fancies pumpkin with fried egg, Pei Zhen makes pumpkin with fried egg. And that's not all – they say it's Tiesuo who brings the eggs."

Fanhua was just tossing this out there, expecting Pei Zhen to deny it. Her ball of wool had fallen to the floor again, and this time Fanhua picked it up for her.

"I mean, what next? They might as well be claiming Tiesuo laid those eggs himself," Fanhua said as she handed the wool back to Pei Zhen.

The one thing Fanhua truly hadn't been expecting was for Pei Zhen to confess. But the way she did, so sneaky, so utterly consummate, took Fanhua's breath away.

Pei Zhen took the ball of wool from Fanhua and blew off the dust. "I never did believe Xue'e would run away. Where would she run to? I knew she hadn't run away. She's staying at the paper plant."

"The paper plant?" Fanhua leant forwards and placed her hands on Pei Zhen's knees, grabbing her ball of wool. Pei Zhen had her hold it up to make it easier for her to unspool and rewind the wool.

"She's just been there for a couple of days," Pei Zhen continued, in a perfectly natural tone of voice, "waiting for Tiesuo to have a change of heart. Tiesuo's set on having a boy, but we can't always get what we want, now can we? If you gave birth to a panda, you could sell it for tens of thousands of *kuai*, but can you will yourself into producing a baby panda?"

"Enough with the panda talk. Can't give birth to a panda."

"Exactly. That's what Xue'e wants Tiesuo to understand."

"Tiesuo is as stubborn as a tree stump," said Fanhua.

"I was actually planning to wait until Tiesuo changed his mind and then bring Xue'e out and give her to him. But I guess now I'll have to give her to you."

"You've certainly thought things through, Pei Zhen."

But Pei Zhen was just getting started. All of that had really just been an attempt to allay Xue'e's suspicions. Fuck, Pei Zhen was on a whole other level, and she had another shock in store for Fanhua.

"But I *knew* you knew I was delivering food to Xue'e. Because you know everything Xiaohong knows, right? And it's Xiaohong's turn to deliver food today. She told me we couldn't let any more people know about Xue'e's pregnancy at such a crucial moment."

Xiaohong? Xiaohong knew about this? Xiaohong had been delivering food to Xue'e? There was a buzzing in Fanhua's brain, and in her ears, where it lingered, inert. She sat there without moving, still holding the ball of wool. It wasn't heavy, the wool, but Fanhua somehow felt like her arms were starting to ache, like it was a stump of iron, not wool, and the weight of it was hurting her back.

Now, Pei Zhen had turned the tables on Fanhua. "You're the one who started this. I knew what you were doing the moment you walked in here. But you couldn't bring yourself to just cut right to the chase, could you? I treat you like a sister. Maybe you ought to treat me like a sister too."

Fanhua could see Pei Zhen's mouth moving, but she didn't hear what she said next. There was a hint of foam in the corners of her mouth, like soap bubbles. Fanhua felt cold. It was becoming a struggle to keep her eyes open because her body was scalding, so hot you could use it as an iron. But her head was still clear, and she knew what she had to do.

"I can rest easy then," she said, "knowing Xue'e is being supplied with food and drink. Let's leave her there for a couple more days. Tiesuo may have an iron stump for a brain, but even an iron stump can melt."

Thirty-Eight

F anhua wasn't feeling quite right as she left Shangyi's house. At first, she felt top heavy, like her head had turned to stone and her feet were cotton wool, but then after a few steps it flipped, and it was her head that was feeling light and her legs that seemed to have stones tied around them. As she was passing Fanxin's house, she leant against the rails of the cowshed to recover. The cow was munching noisily away, like it was chewing gum. Qinglin's wolf was yowling again, but it was less a howl and more an intermittent, gasping sort of sound. Then it stopped and was superseded by the sound of a dog barking – no, not just one dog, a bunch of them. Clearly, the wolf was busy again with his conjugal duties. Qinglin had told her that all the dogs in the village barked every time his wolf did the deed. He provoked a reaction in all of them: with the males it was envy; the females, admiration. Amid all the barking was the pulse of a clapper beat. That must be Charter. Back in the day, he and his clapper beat had been a part of the Mao Zedong Art and Literature Thought propaganda team. And now he was chanting again. Impressive lung power. You'd hardly take him for an old man of seventy-seven. Maybe he could produce a child after all.

The cherries are ripe on the pomegranate tree,
The moon rises in the west and sets in the east.
Men and boys, listen carefully,

Women and girls, please do pay heed.
In Beijing, people are a surging tide,
Guanzhuang always held my heart,
No stars in the sky when you look up,
A pit in the road when you look down,
A pit they call a subway stop.
Spring onions grow in the subway stop,
On the spring onions there is ice,
On the walls there are some lights,
Behind the lightbulb is a nail,
Atop the nail there is a bow,
Atop the bow there lives an eagle,
The eagle soars back to Guanzhuang.
Back in the village, he meets a girl,
A fine-looking girl she surely is
But her facemask is back-to-front.
This girl's name is Meng Xiaohong.
She bravely jumped into a burial pit.
When Charter heard, he started to cry
At the deeds of this new Lei Feng.
This girl Xiaohong delivers food.
Guanzhuang water tastes the best,
Sweet-and-sour fish as big as a goose,
More fried tofu chunks than bones,
Chives in the river by the paper plant,
Catching river snails up in the hills.
Charter leads a wonderful life,
Disco dancing in his dreams,
Blowing the drum and beating the horn,
Carrying a barrow and dragging a sedan,
Upside-down, inside-out,
Pomegranate trees but cherries sprout.
The sun in the east shines down on the world,
Thieves steal kegs in the dark of night,
The deaf get busy when they hear the sound,
The mutes are forever shouting out loud.
Pull out a handful of a thief's hair
And you discover that he's a monk.

The monk says he's here to cast his vote
And fell through the window by mistake.
People snigger in the window.
Enough with the clapper beat, erhu solo,
A hen picks up a hungry vulture
And Charter is heading for the bridal chamber.
You won't Enjoy Coca-Cola
And Pepsi Refreshes Nothing.
Don't forget to vote please, everybody,
Charter will hand out wedding candy.

Was this old vulture Charter really headed for a bridal chamber? Seriously? How was it I didn't know anything about Charter coming back? How come he knows so much about everything, even that line about Xiaohong and her facemask, if he only just got here? Not stupid, not stupid at all. Liu Bei won acclaim by tossing his own infant son to the ground, and Xiaohong was doing much the same thing with her facemask. As she was thinking, Charter started playing his erhu. He was deploying all the talents he had at his disposal today. He may have never seen a TV before, but he knew the singer Song Zuying. It was her song *Today is a Good Day* that he started playing. A happy song that became a lament on the melancholy erhu. After that, he played *Zhuge Liang Pays His Respects*. Was this one for Li Hao? If Li Hao could sing *Records of an Empty City* then he could sing *Zhuge Liang Pays His Respects*. Sure enough, Fanhua soon heard Li Hao's voice:

Paying respects to a departed friend,
It pains me to remember your life.
To protect the Eastern Wu you gave your all.
One of Sun Quan's generals three,
Whom I was sent to recruit to our cause,
We'd hail each other as friends again,
Sat in a tent reliving glorious deeds,
The magnificent defeat of Cao Cao's troops.

It had a husky sound, like a broken gong. There was a fierceness to it, and a weight, as if he were wielding Zhang Fei's serpent spear or

Li Kui's battleaxe rather than Zhuge Liang's trademark feather fan. If Zhou Yu were alive, Fanhua thought, this recital of Li Hao's would be the death of him.

Before too long, Fanhua saw Shangyi on his way back home. He was tottering along, drunk, but he had someone at his side to help him along the way. It was Xiaohong. Intellectual that he was, Shangyi was a very polite drunk. He kept apologising to Xiaohong, saying he ought not to have thrown up in her presence.

"I've truly lost face, I ought to give myself a slapping. I'm not really drunk. Why would I want to be drunk on such a happy occasion? I could have a few glasses more, even, still wouldn't be drunk."

"That's right," said Xiaohong, "you're not drunk, you could keep drinking."

"When you go back, tell Xiangsheng. Tell him I said I'm not drunk."

"Right, you're not drunk," said Xiaohong. "He's the drunk one."

"All the students' parents listen to me, you know that? All these parents want their children to be mighty dragons when they grow up. Even a moron like Gawp. So they have no choice, you see. They have to listen to me."

"Absolutely, they have to listen to you. You're the awesomest."

The scent of alcohol lingered even after they'd passed by. Then another smell came to dominate: a hot, grassy smell, with a hint of animal pong. The noise of the cow's ruminations grew quieter as if it was sniffing the smell too. It kept reappearing, this smell, getting stronger each time, until eventually, Fanhua realised it was the odour of a freshly laid cowpat.

What was it people used to say? Fanhua was a flower stuck in a cowpat, that's what they said. And now that's literally what she was. Her head was still spinning when she finally emerged outside. What would people say a few days from now, when Xiaohong was elected head of the village council? She was the real flower, the one who was truly stuck out of a cowpat. Bright red, and easy on the eye.

THIRTY-NINE

The weather was starting to turn cold, but Fanhua's forehead seemed to be getting hotter by the day. Xueshi and Fanqi came to ask her advice on an upcoming county meeting that required the presence of a leading cadre from every village.

"It doesn't matter which of you goes," she said.

"I'm old," said Xueshi, "and my legs are going. Forget it."

"I'm older than Xueshi by a month and five days," said Fanqi. "If his legs aren't up to it, then neither are mine."

"My ears are going deaf," said Xueshi. "Are your ears going deaf?"

"They are, young whippersnapper, and my eyes are going blind too."

Fanhua wasn't interested in listening to them argue. "Let's just send Qingshu then," she said.

"Qingshu?" said Fanqi. "Aren't you worried that brainless idiot will end up causing you trouble?"

Fanhua knew what they were getting at. They were reluctant to mention her by name, but it was Xiaohong they wanted her to send. "Maybe Xiaohong's time has come," she said at last. "She's spent long enough serving the village. Perhaps it's time for her to take her servitude further afield."

But in the end, it was Qingshu who went, not Xiaohong. Xiaohong made him go. Qingshu made a phone call to the Guanzhuang

291

village council from the county meeting. He said they were praising Gongzhuang for successfully attracting foreign investment. Would you believe it? The investor, the American, was none other than Kong Qinggang himself. Kong Qinggang, who'd fled to Taiwan from the mainland, and then made his way from Taiwan to America. Word soon got out. Some of the villagers cursed his name. Are you Gongzhuang spawn? No, you're Guanzhuang spawn, obviously, so why did you go to Gongzhuang instead of coming back to Guanzhuang? Have you forgotten your roots completely? Xiaohong risked her life jumping into your mother's grave to try and protect it, and she was almost buried alive by the Gongzhuangers for her trouble, have you not heard? Hmm? And then there were others who said America must have ruined Qinggang. Americans were a rotten lot, that's what the news always said. Bullying this country today, that country tomorrow. A fistful of money to burn, dirty money, and all they know how to do is play the bully. Fuck, we thought they were all off on the other side of the world, but it turns out they were right here, ready to start bullying Guanzhuang in less time than it takes to shake a leg.

Dr Xianyu had a distinctive take on the matter, by looking at it from a physiological perspective. "It's because Americans have such good health that they tend to act so recklessly. They mess things around like there's no tomorrow and before you know it you've got yourself a matriarchal society that only recognises mothers and not fathers. Qinggang was in America so long he might have started turning into one of them. A bastard hybrid."

"I'm afraid I can't agree with you there, Charter," Lingwen replied. "Qinggang, a bastard? We all know how rumours stick to a lonely widow, but his mother wasn't a widow when she gave birth to him, was she? And anyway, even if he is a bastard, he's a Guanzhuang bastard. Say, Qingmao, which of our villagers got a leg over with his mother?"

Qingmao said that we belonged to a decorous nation, and nobody "got a leg over" with anyone in this village. Never. So, if Qinggang was a bastard then he couldn't be a Guanzhuang bastard. He could only be a Gongzhuang bastard. His mother must have been pregnant already when she married into the village. "But people were more feudalistic in those days," he continued, changing the subject slightly, "and that kind of thing wasn't likely. So, at the end of the day, we have to admit Qinggang is a true Guanzhuanger. But we all know he had his reasons for not investing in Guanzhuang. When all's said and done, we thought this duck was cooked, but it somehow still managed to fly away."

At this point, Xiangmin arrived in his car. He said he'd just come from Gongzhuang, where he'd seen the new tomb of Qinggang's mother. Scrawny Dog sure knew how to handle things. He'd done it up all extravagant, more extravagant even than the tomb of Confucius in Qufu. There were monks out front, and Christians too, and they were taking turns, one group reciting scripture while the other took a break. Xiangmin said he'd noticed one Christian in particular who truly had the gift of the gab. He was an ex-village head, according to Scrawny Dog. They must have picked him up at the church in Nanyuan and brought him over to Wangzhai, Xiangmin was sure of it.

People were cursing the name of Scrawny Dog before Xiangmin had even finished his narration. That good-for-nothing Scrawny Dog, if it weren't for the obstacles he put in our way, then that cooked duck would never have been able to fly away.

Lingwen had the final say in all matters concerning poultry, what with him keeping ducks and geese and all. "How can a cooked duck fly away?" he said. "It's never happened to me, and I cook ducks regularly. Must've left it half cooked."

"Doesn't matter how cooked it was, the point is it's ended up on someone else's plate," said Xiangmin. "Fuck, those Gongzhuangers have eaten our dinner."

All this talk eventually reached the ear of Fanhua. It had been years since Fanhua last cried, but she cried today. She was inconsolable. She cried and kept on crying until Fanqi came along and saw what she was doing.

"Fanhua," he said, "why are you acting like such a woman?"

This startled her into silence. Since when am I not a woman, she thought. I am a woman! And then she started crying again.

The county theatre troupe arrived the day before the election. As requested, they were here to perform *Dragon and Phoenix, Harbingers of Prosperity*. Shortfur was there too, but his show was to be in the school playground, not on the stage. Fanhua remained at home, attached to an IV drip. Her mother went to see the play, while her father took Beanie to see Shortfur. Dianjun was the only one to remain with her at home. He sat at the top of the bed, peeling an apple for Fanhua. He peeled away at it until he eventually ended up slicing the tip of his finger. He put down the apple and would have continued peeling the skin of his finger if Fanhua hadn't grabbed the knife off him. Now she was sure that something serious had happened to Dianjun while he was away. He needed to get to the hospital for a check-up, and fast. He was onto camels again, talking about how every part of their body was a treasure. She had always ignored him when he made this remark before, but now she went along with him.

"Oh yes," she said, "you can comb the fur of a camel and make it look lovely and pretty, and then people will want to take photographs with it, like a model."

Someone knocked at the door. Fanhua pulled back the corner of the curtain to see who it was. Xiaohong and Xianyu. Xiaohong was leading Beanie by the hand, and Beanie was holding a stick of candy floss. Xiaohong didn't seem at all self-conscious as she came in and sat down beside the bed. She pulled Fanhua's hand out from the covers and pressed it against her face.

"The fever's gone down a little," she said to Xianyu.

Fanhua stopped pretending to be asleep. "Oh," she said, seemingly astonished, as she opened her eyes. "When did you come in here? Look, I can't even sit myself up properly to talk to you."

Xiaohong raised a finger to her lips and shushed her quiet. "Don't say anything. Just rest and get better. You frightened me half to death. I was so worried. It's lucky you didn't get trampled by one of Fanxin's cows. You'd have had to slaughter the lot of them."

Well, wasn't that nice – not even elected yet and already telling me to keep my mouth shut. Dianjun, who was watching Xiaohong from off to one side, gave a creepy kind of laugh. He even reached out a hand to touch the wound on her head.

"Dianjun," said Fanhua, "why don't you go out and pour a glass of water for Xiaohong?" Dianjun went out, still chuckling to himself. Xianyu discreetly shook his head at the state of Fanhua's husband.

Xiaohong was smiling too, but her smile was directed at Fanhua, and it was a kindly smile. A graceful smile. She held Fanhua's hand in one hand and pressed the other against her wrist. "Shall we put it in the other hand this time?" she asked Xianyu.

"Might as well," he replied.

"Don't bother," said Fanhua. "It's not like it's going to kill me."

Holding the needle, Xianyu looked at Fanhua, and then at Xiaohong. He didn't know who to listen to. Fanhua pulled her arm out of Xiaohong's grasp and buried it beneath the covers, and had Xianyu insert the drip in the same place as before. Xiaohong frowned when she tried to ask her about Xue'e.

"Seventy per cent of recovery is treatment, but the other thirty per cent is rest. You should get some shut-eye."

"I was just wondering... how did Xue'e end up in a place like that?"

No frown this time. "She's a heartless one, is Xue'e," she said, concentrating on the IV bag as she reached out a hand to stop it swaying. "Hiding away like that, leaving behind her husband and two daughters."

Still not fessing up.

Dianjun was standing there now with a glass of water in his hand. "Xue'e," he said. "Big belly." Fanhua tried to get rid of him, but he continued to stand there. "Xue'e. Big belly."

"They planned it together, husband and wife," Xiaohong finally explained. "Those two piss in the same pot, let me tell you, and they come up with some nasty-smelling schemes."

Still not fessing up, and was that last remark meant as an implied criticism of Fanhua? If Xiaohong carried on like this, then things could get nasty.

Xianyu had finished inserting the drip. "I'll be off, then," he said before he'd even packed up his things. "I'll be back again before too long."

"You go and watch the show," said Fanhua. "Dianjun knows how to get out the drip."

"I know how to get it out too," said Beanie, who at some point had removed her jumper and trousers, and was now capering about alongside the bed in just a pair of knickers.

"Look at how clever Beanie is," said Xiaohong. "She knows how to walk the catwalk now she's seen Shortfur's show."

This made Beanie very proud of herself. She strutted along, wiggling her bottom and licking her candy floss. Fanhua knew, of course, that this was a treat Xiaohong had bought her.

"What are you doing, taking things from other people?" she yelled at Beanie. "What are you supposed to say?"

The shock of this rebuke made Beanie forget to retract her tongue back into her mouth.

"Say it. What did I teach you to say? Come on."

Beanie started bawling. "No thank you," she managed to say through her tears. "We have some at home already."

Xiaohong didn't make any attempt to argue with Fanhua or soothe Beanie. "You can take care of it, then," she said to Dianjun. "Look after Fanhua. You'll be doing the village a great service. If Fanhua should come down with pneumonia, or suffer a heart inflammation, or have some kind of unfortunate accident, we won't be able to forgive you."

Fanhua was finding this increasingly hard to take. Not because she was worried that Xiaohong was going to jinx her with a heart inflammation, but because of the way she was addressing her. Normally she never called Fanhua by her name, but now it was Fanhua this and Fanhua that. It was hard to get used to.

As soon as Xiaohong was out the door, Fanhua scooped Beanie up on the bed. Beanie stopped crying but started up all over again when Fanhua gave her a smack. Then Dianjun started crying too. His wails sounded like a pig getting slaughtered, while Beanie's sounded more like a dying lamb. Fanhua didn't know which of them she ought to try to console first. She didn't cry. But on the inside, she was a mess.

FORTY

Fanhua's fever had gone down by voting time the next day. She sat in the yard of her own home instead of going to the meeting hall. The village loudspeaker, which seemed to have been replaced with a new, higher-fidelity model, was playing *Ode to Beijing*, Qingshu's favourite song. It was a song that spoke of a magnificent new rosy dawn, of a giant forging ahead. Everyone else in the house had gone to vote – even Beanie, who went along with her grandparents. Fanhua was left alone in the house with the rabbits.

She recognised the sound of Township Head Bull chairing the meeting. On behalf of Wangzhai Township, the Bull thanked the departing village council members for the great service they had done Guanzhuang Village, with some special words of praise for Comrade Kong Fanhua. She had a special kind of drive, he said, a drive that meant she gave everything she had to the service of the people. This was the most precious legacy of the officials in Guanzhuang, and it must not be forsaken. Then it was time for the speeches. First up was Kong Xiaohong. Xiaohong usually spoke standard Mandarin when she was on the loudspeaker, but this time she was using the local dialect. Her main focus was the transformation of the paper plant. The paper plant was located in Guanzhuang, she said, and it was the pride of Guanzhuang, an emblem of the faith the township authorities had placed in Guanzhuang. She would work closely with the county authorities to seize manufacturing with one hand and reduce pollution with the other, and neither hand would waver. Her voice became quieter when she mentioned the death of her older brother. But she said he'd died from the pollution in the river water, which must have been a slip of the tongue. There was no one who loathed pollution more than her, she said, so everyone could rest assured that she was resolved to work with the paper plant to bring it under control. Then her voice grew louder again. The township had already given their consent to her plan of running the paper plant through a shareholding system. This would mean one million yuan of investment into Guanzhuang, and an opportunity for every household to purchase shares. Xiaohong made a point of mentioning that several villagers who had moved away for work had already agreed to buy shares. She produced a lengthy list of names, which included Pomegranate Zhang's husband, Li Dongfang, Li Xueshi's son Li Xiaoshuang, and Kong Fanhua's sister, Kong Fanrong. Wait, Fanrong was one of her investors? Fanhua couldn't believe her ears. The prime objective, Xiaohong continued, was to deal with the problem of Guanzhuang's labour surplus. The "idle hands" problem, as it might also be described. As a daughter of Guanzhuang, she wanted to treat the people of her village with the same filial respect she treated the elders of her own family.

After that, there was someone asking her a question. Fanhua recognised the voice of Li Shangyi. He was speaking in Mandarin, and his question concerned the issue of family planning. Fanhua remembered that Shangyi's family was a Model of Family Planning.

Xiaohong first offered Shangyi her thanks for his preemptive concern. Then she said that she was confident that everyone in the village – old men and young, aunts and wives and sisters – would support her, so long as she dealt with the issue in the appropriate manner. She gave the example of Xue'e, who'd behaved fairly and reasonably and agreed to cooperate with the authorities, even when it wasn't her fault that she had got pregnant after a mistake in the hospital check-up, in order to conscientiously resolve the problem. When it came to family planning, Xiaohong said, she would be sure to adopt a policy of "mutual respect". Under this policy, there would be no more retributive detentions or demolitions.

Fanhua felt a droning sound in her ears. Her head was thrumming.

Next, Xiangmin asked about the problem of cremation. If a villager died, they had to be cremated – so shouldn't the same policy apply to an outsider who died in Guanzhuang? And who was responsible for the cost if they did?

The family of the deceased should be responsible, naturally, Xiaohong answered.

Exactly, someone called out, villagers, outsiders, we're all the same, at the end of the day. We're all people, aren't we? Then came a sound of clamouring voices, until Township Head Bull was compelled to tell everyone to calm down.

The person who was swept downriver a few days ago had already been cremated, Xiaohong announced. The cremation costs had been paid. By whom, someone asked.

"In a few days' time, when we're all drinking wine at a wedding, you'll understand everything," said Xiaohong. "And it won't just be wine. There's going to be a whole roast lamb to enjoy too."

Obviously, it was Li Hao who'd paid for the cremation then. So old Iron Crutch is going to be sitting on the council too, Fanhua thought.

Xiaohong's turn at the microphone was over. Fanhua was waiting to hear what Qingshu had to say, but the music came on again instead. Huh, so it was time to vote already? Qingshu must have withdrawn from the race too. It was a different song now: the Liberation Army March. As she sat there picking grass to feed the rabbits, Fanhua found her feet starting to move in time to the music. They played the song on a loop, like a dog biting its own tail, until it finally came to an abrupt stop. Then Xiaohong made another speech, her inaugural address, of course. She switched back to Mandarin this time, and she spoke it well, almost as well as Ni Ping when she was stirring up the fervour of the audience during the annual Spring Festival TV gala. But there were so many firecrackers popping, just like it was the last night of the year, that Fanhua couldn't hear what Xiaohong was actually saying.

By evening, the village really was starting to feel like Spring Festival. Every streetlight was blazing, and the loudspeaker broadcast alternated between opera and comedic skits. Zhao Benshan made an appearance, selling crutches again. And then it was a live broadcast of Charter's performance. He truly brought the erhu to life, playing the instrument with such gusto that it almost didn't sound like an erhu at all. At the climax of his performance, Xiaohong's voice unexpectedly cut in to announce that from this day forth, the village's power supply would be paid for by the paper plant and that electricity would henceforth be distributed to each according to their need. Tomorrow, I'll change all our lights to hundred-watt bulbs, Fanhua thought to herself as she sat in the yard, Dianjun's jacket draped across her shoulders. A ball of wool bounced up and down on her knee; she was knitting a jumper for Beanie. Fanqi, who had retained his position as committee mediator, was sitting at her side, praising her knitting skills.

"It's nothing special," she said. "It's been so long since I picked up the needles that my fingers are as clumsy as my toes. I'll need to go and ask Pei Zhen how to do this bit around the armpit."

"I tell you what," Fanqi said to Fanhua's father. "This sister of mine would have no problem living off her knitting needles."

"Wasn't that Qingshu always talking about how he wanted to shoulder a weightier load?" Fanhua's father asked Fanqi. "How come he's still just doing the same womanly work?"

Fanqi clicked his tongue. "Wait until the next elections. Xiaohong said she's only going to serve one term, and then go work as an ordinary labourer in the paper plant."

"And you...?"

Fanqi was aware that the old man was referring to the fact that he had retained his position. "Sir, if someone wants to put me to use, well, what can I do? Yama the King of Hell isn't going to worry about his ghosts being too skinny." The "someone" he was referring to was Xiaohong, obviously. This was a sneakily ambiguous reply because it wasn't entirely clear whether he was praising Xiaohong or cursing her.

"But why did Xiaohong want to keep Xue'e hidden away in the first place?" asked Fanhua's mother. "That's the one thing I can't get my ageing brain around."

Fanqi rocked with laughter, his arms around his knees. "Xiaohong claimed Xue'e was there to keep an eye on the paper plant for her. She was going to have to start giving her a salary, she said." Then he lowered his voice to reveal some fresh information: "Xue'e's second daughter, Laddy? They've given her away. To Xiangning.

Changed her name to Lady. Xiangning's going to move away to live in Xiushui Town."

Oh, said Fanhua. How did I not think of that? Well, that solved the problem of Xue'e's pregnancy. Fingers crossed it's a boy, then.

"So Xiangning's going to give up on the meat trade?" she asked.

"Come now," said Fanhua, tucking his chin into his chest. "Pigs need killing wherever you go. The man can make better money as a butcher in Xiushui."

Fanqi's real reason for being here was to persuade Fanhua to buy shares in the paper plant. Everyone knew it was going to be highly profitable, so long as Guanzhuang didn't kick up a fuss. So why not invest? Fanrong has, why don't you?

Fanhua asked her father whether Fanrong had really purchased shares.

"She has. I signed up on her behalf. She called to say she was glad her big sister could finally produce a male heir for the Kong family."

So all this was good news, as far as Fanrong was concerned. Wasn't she always saying how Fanhua caused her husband trouble, and sooner or later she was sure to end up harming his prospects? Well, she wouldn't be causing them any trouble now.

"Is it true her husband's going to be a bureau chief before too long?" she said.

"Nothing's official yet. One of these days, I'll have to get Charter to do us a divination."

"See?" said Fanqi. "If even the wife of a bureau chief is investing, why don't you?"

Even if I wanted to, I couldn't, Fanhua thought. I need to raise money for Dianjun's treatment.

Fanqi handed Dianjun a cigar. "Nobody's heart is made of stone," he said. "I can't say I feel entirely comfortable that this is the way things have ended up. It's lucky for me that Fanhua hasn't taken it too much to heart, or else I'd be too ashamed to show my face around these parts. Am I right, Dianjun?"

Dianjun hadn't understood. "Bullshit," he said, in a fierce voice. "I want to keep camels. You can make shoes out of camel hide."

"Well that explains it!" said Fanqi. "You want to be your own boss. I understand. No wonder you don't have time for such a trifling investment."

Fanhua suddenly remembered the shoes she'd had Dianjun repair for Xue'e. She told Fanqi to take them to her. No charge for the man hours, but they'd added several new leather patches and replaced the heels. Three *kuai* per patch, five *kuai* for each heel. But if Xue'e was strapped for cash, then tell her never mind.

From outside came the sound of a confusion of footsteps. Looking through the window, Fanhua saw Xiaohong, Qingshu and Li Hao. Li Hao was carrying a glass tablet. This, Fanhua knew, was for her. The piece of glass wobbled, glinting like a mirror in the sunlight as Li Hao hobbled along. Unless Fanhua was much mistaken, the tablet would be engraved with the words "One Flower Across One World". As they approached the front door, Xiaohong took the tablet from Li Hao in order to carry it herself. Fanqi was already outside to greet them. Fanhua cast her gaze upwards. The light beyond the glow of the lamp was dim and boundless, and as the sound of footsteps drew nearer, it seemed to be coming down, down, down from the skies.

Translator's Note

Translating from Chinese to English, there are three options when it comes to the name of our protagonist, 繁花:

- Naturalise: find an English name that has some degree of overlap with the original – "Florence", for example
- Translate: convey the literal meaning of the name – "Blooming Flowers", let's say
- Transliterate: render the name phonetically in pinyin – "Fanhua".

Choose "Florence", and the juxtaposition of English names against the Chinese setting soon becomes jarring. Unless, that is, you keep going and naturalise the place names, brand names and cultural references, and very quickly find you have strayed beyond the remit of translation. You also burden the reader with the task of detaching the character from all the irrelevant associations that the name will evoke for them – the remnants left in their subconscious by every other Florence they have ever encountered. And surely no reader would be able to put up with "Blooming Flowers" – grating, clunky and shot through with dehumanising Orientalism – for more than a page or two.

"Fanhua" is the least bad option, but transliteration results in a meaningful alteration to the reader's experience of the book, especially one with as many characters as *Cherries on a Pomegranate Tree*: the cognitive burden of keeping track of all the characters is significantly higher when their names are semantically empty shells. The meaning of the name 繁花 is not foregrounded in the same way the meaning of "Blooming Flowers" would be foregrounded in English, but the meaning is there, and it constitutes a hook upon which you can hang everything you need to remember about the character. Without the Chinese characters, the name "Fanhua" is just a collection of sounds. You only have so much attention you can give a book, and when a chunk of that attention is occupied by keeping track of names, you can't give so much to the plot, the themes or the symbolic significance of camels.

Not to mention the fact that there are so many characters in this book who have extremely similar-sounding names. These overlaps actually serve a very specific function: they remind the reader of the Confucian heritage that underpins the setting. Confucius, as Xiangsheng remarks, is "the ancestor of us Guanzhuang folk". The "Xiang" in his name indicates that he belongs to the seventy-fifth generation of Confucian descent, along with Xiangning and Xiangmin. The "Fan" in the names of Fanhua, Fanrong and Fanqi places them in the seventy-fourth generation, while the "Qing" of Qingshu, Qingmao and Qinggang denotes generation seventy-three.

In *Cherries on a Pomegranate Tree*, I transliterated the names of most characters, but slipped in a translation here and there (Quartz Zhang and Ace Liu, for example) where I thought I could get away with it, in an attempt to slightly reduce the strain on the reader's memory. There are also one or two character names that are translated rather than transliterated in order to unlock a specific pun at some point in the book (Township Head Bull, for example). The humour is one of the most striking and distinctive qualities of the original Chinese text, and I was very conscious of the challenges involved in conveying it in translation. The character-based humour, which is focused primarily around Fanhua's perception of the people around her, is manageable, but wordplay is considerably trickier. There is a recurring bit about how the local teacher Shangyi is forever trying to get the villagers to remember the date of Marx's birthday, but despite my best efforts, I never quite found a way to do justice to his strained mnemonics in English. But a serviceable replacement for a pun will occasionally present itself: Jimmy Carter (卡特), might be 卡住了 – "held back" – in Chinese, but he can be "carted off" in English.

The invocations of Jimmy Carter's name are not completely random incongruities. They allude to the Carter Center, which was invited to send a delegation to supervise China's local elections when they were first introduced. Since 1998, villages across China have been legally required to assign leadership positions through competitive elections, including a secret ballot, a public count and a fixed term of office. Hopes that this would start an incremental move towards the full democratisation of the nation, a process Deng Xiaoping suggested might take fifty years, may have faded, but village elections remain a fixture in rural China today. ("Village" is not a general descriptor of settlement size, but a specific indicator of position on the bureaucratic hierarchy. Xiushui, the county, is divided up into townships, such as Wangzhai, Nanyuan and Beiyuan; every township is divided up into villages like Guanzhuang and Gongzhuang. Each of these names can therefore refer to both an area of jurisdiction and the main settlement within that area.)

The imminent village elections ignite the plot of *Cherries on a Pomegranate Tree*, but the engine of the book is a different political policy: China's one-child policy. Within the novel, this is referred to by the broader and more euphemistic term "family planning" (计划生育). The one-child policy might be the most familiar term outside of China, but it was no longer technically accurate in the first decade of this century when this story takes place. In the late 1980s, when it had already become clear that the policy was causing a significant gender imbalance by incentivising the birth of boys, rural families were permitted to have a second child if the first was a girl. The couples in *Cherries* with more than two children, or more than one boy, would most likely have had to hide the pregnancy until it was too late, pay the fine and then weather whatever societal shame that might be orchestrated against them by Qingshu, the head of family planning.

But this is not an option for Fanhua. Giving in to her parents' desire for a male heir would provide ammunition to her political rivals and make her position as village head untenable. So she must resist any inclination to have a second child, even as this places her in tension – as you now know – with the connotations of florescence, fertility and new life that her name suggests.

ABOUT THE AUTHOR

Li Er (李洱) is the pen name of the author Li Rongfei (李荣飞). Born in 1966 in Jiyuan, Henan Province, he graduated from East China Normal University in Shanghai. He was the former deputy director of the National Museum of Modern Chinese Literature and is currently a professor at Peking University's Department of Chinese Language and Literature. A prolific author, his notable long-form works include *Coloratura* (translated into English by Jeremy Tiang), *Cherries on a Pomegranate Tree* and *Brother Yingwu*. In 2019, he won the prestigious Mao Dun Literature Award for *Brother Yingwu*. His books have been translated into many languages, including English, Korean, German and French. He lives in Beijing.

About the Translator

Dave Haysom has been translating, editing and writing about contemporary Chinese literature since 2012. Joint managing editor of *Pathlight* magazine from 2014 to 2018, he has recently translated novels by Feng Tang, Li Er and Xu Zechen, in addition to *My Tenantless Body*, a collection of poetry by Yu Yoyo (in collaboration with AK Blakemore). In 2015 he became editor-in-chief of the Read Paper Republic project, a year-long initiative to release a weekly translation online, and he has organised literary events with organisations including the Southbank Centre, the Free Word Centre, Leeds University Centre for New Chinese Writing, the Poetry Translation Centre and Beijing Literary Festival. His essays and reviews have appeared in *Granta*, *Words Without Borders*, *The Millions*, *China Channel* and *SUPChina*, and his full portfolio is online at *spittingdog.net*.